The Blockchain Alternative

Rethinking Macroeconomic Policy and Economic Theory

Kariappa Bheemaiah

Apress®

The Blockchain Alternative: Rethinking Macroeconomic Policy and Economic Theory

Kariappa Bheemaiah
Paris,
France

ISBN-13 (pbk): 978-1-4842-2673-5   ISBN-13 (electronic): 978-1-4842-2674-2
DOI 10.1007/978-1-4842-2674-2

Library of Congress Control Number: 2017934075

Managing Director: Welmoed Spahr
Editorial Director: Todd Green
Acquisitions Editor: Celestin Suresh John
Development Editor: James Markham
Technical Reviewer: Garrick Hileman
Coordinating Editor: Sanchita Mandal
Copy Editor: Larissa Shmailo
Compositor: SPi Global
Indexer: SPi Global
Artist: SPi Global
Cover image designed by Freepik

Distributed to the book trade worldwide by Springer Science+Business Media New York, 233 Spring Street, 6th Floor, New York, NY 10013. Phone 1-800-SPRINGER, fax (201) 348-4505, e-mail orders-ny@springer-sbm.com, or visit www.springeronline.com. Apress Media, LLC is a California LLC and the sole member (owner) is Springer Science + Business Media Finance Inc (SSBM Finance Inc). SSBM Finance Inc is a **Delaware** corporation.

For information on translations, please e-mail rights@apress.com, or visit www.apress.com/rights-permissions.

Apress titles may be purchased in bulk for academic, corporate, or promotional use. eBook versions and licenses are also available for most titles. For more information, reference our Print and eBook Bulk Sales web page at http://www.apress.com/bulk-sales.

Any source code or other supplementary material referenced by the author in this book is available to readers on GitHub via the book's product page, located at www.apress.com/9781484226735. For more detailed information, please visit http://www.apress.com/source-code/.

Printed on acid-free paper

In remembrance of Professor Nigel F.B. Allington.
A teacher, mentor and friend who taught me how to learn.

Contents at a Glance

Contents

About the Author

Kariappa Bheemaiah, or **Kary** to his friends and colleagues, is a researcher, visiting lecturer, and technology consultant based in Paris. His articles and interviews on the Blockchain and the effects of technological change on society have been published in *Harvard Business Review*, *WIRED* magazine and *Les Echos*, amongst others. He is also a public speaker and gave his first TEDx Talk, "The evolution of currency," in 2014. He will be giving his second TEDx Talk, "Rethinking Capitalism with the Blockchain," in May 2017.

Kary is currently the head of research at Uchange, a digital transformation consultancy, consultancy, a research associate with Cambridge Judge Business School, a visiting lecturer at ESCP Europe and GEM, and a mentor and blogger at StartupBootCamp. Prior to this, he worked as a market intelligence analyst and financial controller in a number of international companies and also as an economic researcher for an EU project.

In a previous life, he was a legionnaire in the French Foreign Legion who was awarded the cross of valor for his services in Afghanistan.

About the Technical Reviewer

Dr. Garrick Hileman is a senior research associate at the Cambridge Center for Alternative Finance and a researcher at the Center for Macroeconomics. He was recently ranked as one of the 100 most influential economists in the UK and Ireland and he is regularly asked to share his research and perspective with the *FT*, BBC, CNBC, *WSJ*, *Sky News*, and other media. Garrick has been invited to present his research on monetary and financial innovation to government organizations, including central banks and war colleges, as well as private firms such as Visa, Black Rock, and UBS. Garrick has 20 years' private sector experience with both startups and established companies such as Visa, Lloyd's of London, Bank of America, The Home Depot, and Allianz. Garrick's technology experience includes co-founding a San Francisco-based tech incubator, IT strategy consulting for multinationals, and founding MacroDigest <http://www.macrodigest.com/>, which employs a proprietary algorithm to cluster trending economic analysis and perspective. Visit Dr. Garrick Hileman's website <http://www.garrickhileman.com/>

Acknowledgments

The best way to learn how to write is to read. Many authors and thinkers have heavily influenced the ideas that have been expressed in the book. Although it would be impossible to thank them all, I would like to thank the most influential authors to whom I owe a great intellectual debt. These include Lord Adair Turner, W. Brain Arthur, Doyne Farmer, Andreas Antonopoulos, Satyajit Das, Joyce Appleby, Yanis Varoufakis, Patrick O'Sullivan, Nigel Allington, Mark Esposito, Sitabhra Sinha, Thomas Sowell, Niall Ferguson, Andy Stern, Alan Kirman, Neel Kashkari, Danny Dorling, David Graeber, Amir Sufi, Atif Mian, Vitalik Buterin, Andy Haldane, Gillian Tett, Martin Sandbu, Robert Reich, Kenneth Rogoff, Paul Beaudry, Michael Kumhof, Diane Coyle, Ben Dyson, Dirk Helbing, Guy Michaels, David Autor, Richard Gendal Brown, Tim Swanson, David Andolfatto, Paul Pfleiderer, Zoltan Pozsar, Frank Levy, Richard Murnane, César Hidalgo, and Robin Hanson, among others.

An equal measure of thanks also needs to be given to all the academics and researchers whom I had the chance to meet via the Institute of New Economic Thinking. Without the conversations I had with them, the final chapter of this book would have had a very different look. Some of them include Sanjay Reddy, Jacky Mallet, Dominik Hartmann, and Perry Mehrling.

Garrick Hileman's contribution needs to be specially mentioned as, had it not been for his timely intervention and thorough review, a number of mistakes would have gone unseen. By ensuring that my writing was up to scratch, Garrick was able to lift this work to a new intellectual and academic standard.

This book would never have been completed without the indulgence of my employers at Uchange, Guillaume Buffet and Denis Dubois, who gave me tremendous amounts of leeway to pursue this project even when I was at work. Always willing to encourage their employees to pursue their dreams, Guillaume and Denis are the kind of bosses everyone dreams to have.

Lastly, I'd like to thank all my teachers and mentors from Grenoble École de Management, with whom I had random conversations over the previous four years when the idea for this book first began to emerge. Special mention goes out to Nick Sanders, who was the first person to take the risk of giving me a chance to study and then work in GEM when all I had was bold ideas and burning ambition.

Introduction

Infiltration was the name of the game in 2015. Indeed, both emotionally and economically, it was an extraordinary year. While the world horrifically responded to the spate of terrorist attacks within their own borders, such as in Paris and other parts of the globe, the world of finance bore witness to a new kind of infiltration within its own borders. The Blockchain, which up until then was a technology only being discussed on the fringes of the financial world, was suddenly on the tips of the tongues of investors, VCs, bankers, and governments.

From its relatively modest beginnings seven years ago in an obscure white paper, the technology was now in full bloom and one could hardly pick up a newspaper or a magazine without some mention of it. As questions began to be asked, a slew of blogs and amateur documentaries became available online, with even the BBC joining the ranks.[1] But if 2014 was the year of bitcoin documentaries, 2015 was the year of Blockchain conferences. Talks, round tables, and seminars abounded all over the world, with keynotes being given by bankers, politicians, academics, investors, coders, and technologists. As 2016 rolls out, it is definitely becoming the year of books on the Blockchain, with over 15 books and counting having been published on the subject this year alone.[2] It would be safe to say that the technology is becoming mainstream, which is a pleasure for people like me who have been following the subject for a few years.

So why another book on the subject? The answer to this question lies in scope, scale, and objective. While most of the brilliant works which have been published in the past year address a number of key issues, the conversation still does not allow most of us to gauge the gamut of this technology's impact. Previous and more recent works regarding the Blockchain have looked at the applications of this technology in terms of sectorial transitions. However, there seems to be a lack of insight geared towards the implications of this technology.

To be able to ascertain what the future implications could be requires that we not only understand the Blockchain, but also the other technologies and theories that are currently changing the way finance and economics is defined. Hence, this book is not just about the Blockchain. It is a review of the past and current ideas, policies, and technologies that are challenging and changing the functionality of the complex dynamical system of modern-day capitalism.

---

[1] The documentary was made available on BBC's iPlayer on 5 Dec 2015.

[2] This list consists of books with the word "Blockchain" in the title, made available on Amazon in 2016.

Naturally, as changes occur, it leads to a number of questions. But with the blockchain, the questions are intimately profound in nature, for as the technology begins to be adopted by commercial banks and financial institutions, the questions that need to be asked are with respect to, what does this mean to the rest of society? Will this technology provide us with greater transparency, democracy, and savings? Can it be used to create a better version of capitalism? And if so, then how?

The primary aim of this book is not just an attempt to provide answers to some of these questions, but also to rotate the direction of the current conversation being had in various circles in order to encourage a deeper level of thinking with respect to the technology and its uses. To do so necessitates a return to the fundamental beginnings of currency and the concept of money. Hence, the first part of the book deals not with the Blockchain, but with the mechanics of how money and debt is created. We begin by understanding how fractional banking, the current system used in the production of money, works and thus gain some insights into the operating system of monetary economics. This gives the reader a clear view of how debt and the financialization of assets are leveraged by the financial system to create the bedrock of modern capitalism. Without a sufficient understanding of these topics, there is no context for the conversation.

The second part of this book delves into the blockchain from the perspective of its transitionary role in finance. Following the financial crisis of 2008, the financial sector has been in a state of flux. On one side, governments and regulators now demand a greater level of transparency with respect to financial innovation, taxation, and cross-border transactions. On the other hand, technological progress is defragmenting the financial sector, causing incumbents to be challenged by tech firms. While the current dialogue looks at the blockchain as an independent technology, this section of the book attempts to clarify its amalgamator function when juxtaposed with other technologies that are currently fragmenting the sector of finance. By looking at the Blockchain as a tool that can leverage the advances being made in other disciplines of finance, now popularly cited as Fintech, it allows us to gain a more holistic viewpoint of the role of this technology.

Having gained an understanding of how finance is being fragmented in the context of technology, debt and money creation, the third part of this book attempts to determine what the implications of these paradigmatic shifts mean to societal monetary systems. While the reasons for the changes being seen in the sector of finance are often looked upon as independent fluctuations, they are in fact interrelated, and the precipitate of this interaction begets a need for a new definition of economics. This section attempts to articulate that definition by offering the reader an understanding of how different technologies, including the Blockchain, are transforming the sector of finance and creating a new paradigm of capitalism.

The third and fourth parts of the book look at the impact of this technology from a more macroeconomic level. After a brief discussion on monetary and fiscal policy, a review of the possible implications to central banking is made. We will also analyze what the consequences of multiple currencies, decentralized ledgers, and cryptographic control systems means to central banking. This sets the stage for what measures, tools, and theories need to be understood in order to create a new framework of monetary economics. It is here that the reader will also be introduced to the concept and the emergence of a cashless economy. Apart from describing the implications of a cashless system in terms of controlling excessive debt and economic pollution, the reader is also introduced to what new branches of science will help us gauge and govern this system.

While the subject of economics is old, the methods being used to understand these multifaceted ecosystems do not pay homage to the intricacy that results from its intertwined lattice structure. What is required in today's data-rich environment is an approach that allows us to have greater mathematical exactitude and a higher probability of identifying systemic risk than current economic models. As the world increasingly becomes digital in nature, there is a burgeoning need for a new way of observing and measuring economic systems. Not only are our techniques outdated, but so are the theories on which they are based.

Hence, the final section begins with an assessment on how current theories and techniques lack in addressing these conditions and offers the reader an introduction to the new principles being discovered, debated and tested. Reference to topics such as econophysics, adaptive markets hypothesis, complexity economics and super forecasting[3] will be made and the reader can expect to find reasoning statements that make the case for adopting these new theories and tools.

Having described the past and present interpretation of events, the section ends by attempting to connect the dots in order to show how the technologically powered defragmentation of the financial sector can lead to the creation of a new and less indebted system of fractional banking. It also investigates if these changes could offer sovereign states a new way to produce money and looks at alternatives other than inflation and interest rates to govern monetary policy. Finally, it reviews different scenarios of how this new structure can be used to implement innovative policies, such as overt money finance and universal basic income, which could help address issues such as income inequality and technological unemployment that currently threaten most economies.

While the purpose of the book it to shed more light on the implications of the widespread use of Blockchain technology, the growing diversity within the currency space cannot be fully excluded from the discussion. As the blockchain gains more traction in formal financial circles, its first manifestation in the form of Bitcoin is increasingly being excluded from the dialogue. This seems to be contrary to the symbiotic link between the two. What is more surprising is the fact that this tendency to separate bitcoin from blockchain is a repeat of what happened when the Internet first came into existence. As banks try to harness the power of the blockchain by creating private blockchains, we find ourselves witnessing the same execution of events as when private companies tried to create intranets instead of simply using the Internet.

Whether you are a fan of the bitcoin or the blockchain or both, having a nuanced or biased view on the subject needs to be developed using the scientific method. This is a new technology that has been in existence for less than a decade. But what it represents is a change in our perception of trust along with a change in the organization of authority from traditional hierarchical systems to network-centric flat systems. It allows us to redefine how money and currency derive their actual value and forces us to think about the rebalancing of power on a global socioeconomic scale.

This book aims to address these issues to a certain extent, being limited only by the author's own knowledge and experience. It does not attempt, by any means, to settle the dispute between bitcoin and the blockchain and the ongoing rift that is being created between the two. That, by itself, is a subject for another book. But by looking at

---

[3]A term borrowed from Philip Tetlock and Dan Gardner's new book of the same title.

the macroeconomic uses and potential impacts of this technology, it is the objective of this book to initiate a much-needed conversation on how this technology can be utilized to create a more sustainable and sensible economic system that can be deployed in the current socioeconomic ambience at a rate at which it can be absorbed.

As a growing number of academics from various disciplines begin to ponder similar issues, it is also the purpose of this book to give the reader a synopsis of the advances being made in this field of study. Anyone who attempts to cover a project of merging all these subjects and developments could only do so by conducting extensive research on the works of a plethora of researchers, academics, and policy makers who are rethinking these subjects in a variety of disciplines. Thus, although the author aims to provide the reader with a fresh perspective, this new portrayal of capitalism is the result of those minds who are currently battling with the existing state of affairs, and without whose efforts, this book would not exist. In this respect, the book might seem like an extended academic report from time to time, as it incorporates the works of a number of extraordinary new thinkers. Any inescapable criticisms faced by the author's mapmaking efforts are his own responsibility.

Prior to engaging with this book, it must be remembered that the Blockchain is not meant to be looked at as an answer to all our economic woes. There are a number of other technologies which are also currently transforming the subject of finance and economics. But as technology has the tendency to feed off technology, the Blockchain's role as an infrastructure technology allows it to be united with other technologies and hence amplify their effects. Thus, a final objective of this book is to clear the haze created by the barrage of information in today's digital world in order to allow readers to connect the dots themselves and witness the convergence of technology. Most importantly, it attempts to determine how the Blockchain could be used to find an antidote to our debt-addicted monetary system.

What this technology offers us is a front-row seat to witnessing history in the making and a possible memory of the future. After all, history is not just the past, but also the way we change the present to affect the future.

CHAPTER 1

■ ■ ■

Debt-based Economy: The Intricate Dance of Money and Debt

The story of banking, economics, and finance has been a story of continuous evolution that has mirrored the different stages of human civilization. This was best documented in Niall Ferguson's book, *The Ascent of Money* (2009). In his book, which was later adapted to an Emmy wining television documentary for Channel 4 (UK) and PBS (US), Ferguson traced the origins of cash and literally showed how "money makes the world go round."

This concept of money being at the epicenter of society can be looked at as an existential reality. It is referred to as the utilitarian approach and leads to an oversimplistic interpretation of our complex world often characterized as "linear thinking." The utilitarian approach measures the value of everything in units of money. As a result, it leads to one-dimensional optimization, as business interests become increasingly influential in science and politics. The related lack of a multidimensional approach thus significantly contributes to the dysfunctionality of many societal institutions, and their ability to fix the problems society faces. By showcasing the interdependence of systems in a hyperconnected world, Ferguson highlighted the impotence of our understanding.

In spite of commendable works like this, it is interesting to note that the curriculum in most universities and colleges today seems to consecrate very little content, importance, and time to the way money is made. It would almost seem like an irrational statement, but pick up any undergraduate level economics textbook published in the last twenty years and browse the contents. How many chapters or book sections deal with the creation of money and credit? Better still, if you have attended, or are attending, a business school or taken any business, finance, or economic courses, think back to the classes that you attended. How many hours did you actually spend learning where money actually comes from? Who are the principal parties responsible for creating money? Is it the government, the central bank, or the market? Better still, when was the last time you asked yourself this question?

© Kariappa Bheemaiah 2017
K. Bheemaiah, *The Blockchain Alternative*, DOI 10.1007/978-1-4842-2674-2_1

An Obsession with Cash

For me, it was this very question that led to not just a perpetual answer-finding expedition, but also to a personal reinvention. In 2006, when I was in my early twenties, I left my country of origin and travelled to France with a very clear objective. Dissatisfied with a budding career as a marine engineer, I left everything behind to seek adventure and camaraderie in the French Foreign Legion.

Between 2006 and 2011, I served in the renowned 2nd REP,[1] and during this time, I was deployed on multiple occassion in Africa and Afghanistan. Apart from being an extremely formative period, these deployments also led to the development of an introspective streak which sparked and channelled an intellectual curiosity. I realized that every time I was in a country of conflict, I began to ask myself the same questions. Some of the questions are those which every soldier thinks about. When will this be over? When will I get home? What will I do after that?

But the most recurring question was with reference to the gargantuan sums of money being spent by the government (French or otherwise), every time they put boots on the ground. Not counting the loss of life, the economic cost of the war in Afghanistan cost the French government over €3.5 billion between 2011 and 2014 (Conesa, 2015). For other countries the figures are even higher. The Watson Institute of International and Public Affairs,[2] states that the United States federal government has spent or obligated $4.4 trillion on the wars in Afghanistan, Pakistan, and Iraq (Watson Institute, 2015). As of 2016, a Congressional Research Service (CRS) report states that the cost of keeping a single American soldier in Afghanistan is a wincing $3.9 million (Thompson, 2015).

Where does this money come from? Is it being paid just by taxes or is there another source? These were the questions that I continuously asked myself as I came to the end of my contract with the Legion. In an attempt to find these answers, I enrolled myself in a master's in business degree program at prominent business school in France on leaving the Legion. It was here that one realised that although we are taught how to account and invest money, we never looked into the mechanics of making money, which is the origination of the subject. Moreover, this is a phenomenon that is not just restricted to one institution. A large number of institutions currently practice this teaching methodology. Just ask around your own entourage and note down the results.

While the reason for this occurrence will be looked at in a later part of the book, for the time being we come back to the question of how money is made and where it is created. In today's complex and sophisticated societies, it is insufficient to only examine the economic attributes of money in order to grasp its true meaning.

To understand the way money is created and to gauge its pertinence, one must be prepared to study it in the context of a particular society. Money, after all, is a means of communication wherein individuals communicate on how they will transfer value. Currency in this case is the medium that is used to exchange value, and the medium of value exchange can take different forms. But the underlying architecture and the executed purpose has always been the same: to facilitate trustworthy interactions.

---

[1]The 2e Régiment étranger de parachutistes (the 2nd Foreign Parachute Regiment in English), is the only foreign airborne regiment of the French Foreign Legion and France. It is part of the 11th Parachute Brigade and part of the spearhead of the French rapid reaction force.
[2]Part of Brown University.

If a certain kind of money is to exist, then it needs perform three functions: it needs to be a store of value, a unit of account, and a means of transfer. These three attributes manifest themselves in the form of a currency which is a physical representation of trust within a society. You do not need to trust a person to accept his money or vice versa. What allows trade to function in a modern-day economy is the fact that we trust the medium of exchange, be it dollars, euros, or anything else.

Currencies in general have always been in a gradual state of evolution, with its format varying as economies evolve. Early money was more a commodity rather than a currency and had an intrinsic value in itself. Examples of early money include cattle, seeds, and even wood. In fact, Tally sticks made of polished hazel or willow wood, were used in England from 1100 AD and only abolished in 1834.[3] Hence the origin of the phrase "tally up."

Gold and silver were the generally accepted forms of exchange and measurement of wealth for a long period in the history of money.[4] The bimetallic system of money gave rise to the gold standard in early 1900s and during the Bretton Woods conference in 1946, it led to the creation of a fixed exchange rate. By this method, a country's sovereign currency was pegged to gold, giving each denomination of the currency a value that could technically be redeemed in gold.

As gold and silver were cumbersome to store, carry, and use, towards the eighteenth century, a new much more portable and convenient form of currency in the form of "commodity-backed" money started to be used. The difference between this form of money and previous forms was that the currency by itself had no intrinsic value. Unlike gold and silver, this form of money was based on an understanding that the currency held by a person could be redeemed for a commodity in exchange.

As the century rolled on it was this form of money that evolved into fiat money, which is currently used by modern economies. Fiat currencies came into use in 1971 following the decision of President Nixon to discontinue the use of the gold standard. The end of the gold standard helped sever the ties between world currencies and real commodities and gave rise to the floating exchange rate. A distinguishing feature between commodity-backed currencies and fiat currencies, however, is the fact that it is based on trust and not a tangible value per se. Fiat currency is backed by a central or governmental authority and functions in purpose as a legal tender that it will be accepted by other people in exchange for goods and services. It can be looked as a type of IOU, but one that is unique because everyone who uses it trusts it. The value of a currency is hence based on trust rather than an exchange for a certain commodity.

It is the concept of trust that is quintessential to the story of money as it is directly related to debt and the production of cash. We trust our banks to hold our money and our borrowers to repay their debts. We might hedge against the chance of a default by charging interest rates, but the basic concept is a trust-based one. These two incarnations of trust are the fundamentals of money creation.

There are three main types of money: currency, bank deposits, and central bank reserves. Each represents an IOU from one sector of the economy to another (McLeay et al., 2014). Today, in a functioning economy, most money takes the form of bank deposits,

---

[3]Information about Tally Sticks can be found on the UK's Parliament website under the Living Heritage section and in the history of the parliament estate.
[4]Coins made of Electrum (a naturally occurring alloy of silver and gold) were traced back to 650 BC. Source: http://rg.ancients.info/lion/article.html.

which are created by commercial banks themselves. The public holds money in the form of currency, whilst their banks hold money in the form of non-interest paying demand deposits and interest paying checkable accounts. Paper currency and bank deposits hold no value as commodities. It is the confidence that people have with respect to their ability to exchange money for assets, goods, and services that give value to the currency.

The transfer of confidence from an interpersonal relationship to a proxy of value is what makes money a special social institution (King, 2006). In any given society, anyone could make financial assets and liabilities by giving out personal IOU's every time they wanted to purchase something, and then tally up their credit and debit IOU's in a ledger. Indeed, in medieval times European merchants would trade with one another by issuing IOU's and settle their claims at fairs, thus cancelling out debts (Braudel, 1982). However, for such a system to flourish, it would require a great deal of confidence that the person who owes you something is trustworthy and will repay their debt. Worse still, even if a person is trustworthy, they might have dealings with persons who are untrustworthy and who may default, thus making the trustworthy person unable to repay your loan. But with money, we no longer had to deal with this issue of untrustworthiness as everyone trusts in a medium that allows for the exchange of goods and services.

It is this symbol of trust that gives a currency value and allows it to execute its three functions. Fiat currencies lack intrinsic value but still function as a medium of exchange. The value of a country's currency is set by the supply and demand for country's money and the supply and demand for other goods and services of its economy. This value is also directly connected to the currency's availability, the price to be paid to acquire it, and the scarcity of its supply.

As cash is withdrawn from accounts, the amount of money circulating in the public physical realm conversely increases. This allows a currency to derive economic significance based on the currency's trading position, its parent country's GDP, and whether the country imports more than it exports. When the country is a large importer, it can also find its currency being used as a peg by other dependent economies, as is with the case with the US dollar and the Euro.[5] As the value of a currency is based on supply and demand of the currency, a question that arises is with respect to the manner in which the main drivers of money creation are adjusted in a free market. In order to understand this concept, we need to refresh our understanding of fractional banking, inflation, and the role played by central and commercial banks.

Fractional reserve banking and debt-based money

To understand the concept of fractional banking it is important to first acknowledge that although central banks and governments belong to the same ilk and work in unison with respect to the issuance of sovereign coin, it is the central bank that actually influences how much money to create based on the inflation targets and the interest rate.

---

[5]As of February 2015, 13 nations have pegged their currencies to the US Dollar and 17 to the Euro. Source: http://www.investmentfrontier.com/2013/02/19/investors-list-countries-with-fixed-currency-exchange-rates/

The reason for highlighting this distinction is because the central banks of most countries are independent enterprises and their monetary policy decisions do not have to be approved by a president or anyone else in the executive or legislative branches of government[6] . The working model, which is identical for more advanced countries, is based on the model of the Bank of England, which was established in 1694 as a joint stock company to purchase government debt.[7] Under this model, when a government needs money for carrying out its functions, they exchange bonds with the central bank. The central bank then creates and issues the money in exchange for the government bonds (T-Bills included) and interest. In this way the central bank works in unanimity with the government but still retains a relatively independent status.

The second point to consider is the relationship between the quantity of the currency and the value it represents. While scarcity plays a foremost role in giving value to a currency, this value is directly proportional to the usefulness of the currency to be traded for goods and services. This usefulness is measured by the demand for the currency, while the scarcity is determined by the quantity of the currency supplied. The delicate balance between these two scales gives a currency its value and it is the goal of every currency-issuing country to stabilize either the supply or the quantity of its currency in circulation within its territories as well as outside.

As the value of a currency is only calculated by the amount of what it can buy, its value is inversely related to the general level of prices of goods and services in an economy. Hence if the supply of money increases more rapidly than the total amount of goods and services provided by the economy, then prices will rise. This phenomenon is called inflation. The opposite of this phenomenon is called deflation and results in a general lowering of prices.

Thus, most central banks construct monetary policies that allow them to uphold a low rate of inflation, which in turn provides stability to the value of their currency. This in turn provides sustainable growth and economic constancy. As money creation and control of its supply play such pivotal roles in an economy, it is no surprise that the central banks play a major role of control in this domain. However, the process of money creation also occurs in commercial banks. In fact, the *majority* of money in the modern economy is created by commercial banks by issuing debt.

Prior to delving into the mechanics of money production and the issuance of debt, we also need to define the types of money that slosh around our economies, namely, broad money and base money. Broad money refers to the money that consumers use for transactions. It includes currency (banknotes and coin), which are an IOU from central banks, and bank deposits, an IOU from commercial banks to consumers. In general, broad money measures the amount of money held by households and companies (Berry et al., 2007).

Base money, also known as central bank money, comprises of IOU's from the central bank. This includes currency (an IOU to consumers) but also central bank reserves, which are IOU's from the central bank to commercial banks. Base money is important because it is issued by central banks and thus allows them to implement monetary policy.

---

[6]Who owns the Federal Reserve?: https://www.federalreserve.gov/faqs/about_14986.htm
[7]History of the bank of England: http://www.bankofengland.co.uk/about/Pages/history/default.aspx. The first central bank was the Swedish National Bank, also known as the Riksbank, which was founded in 1668.

Although the production of broad and base money is closely linked, broad money, i.e., IOU's to customers from commercial banks, is in much greater circulation than in base money, i.e., IOU's from the central bank. The graph in Figure 1-1, taken from a 2014 report from the Bank of England, illustrates this:

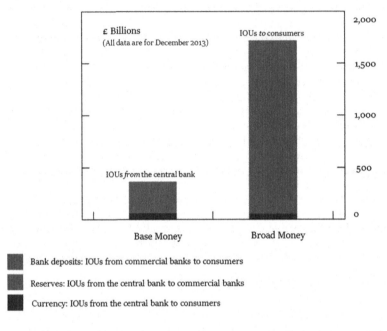

Source: 'Money in the modern economy: an introduction' (2014), published by the Bank of England.

Figure 1-1. *Different forms of money in circulation*

The reason for this large difference between broad and base money is because commercial banks have a greater capability to create money. If you were to pick up an undergraduate book on economics, this is something that is not lucidly stated. You might come across a description more along the lines of, "banks are financial institutions approved by law to receive deposits from individuals and savers, which they lend to businesses, thus allocating capital between various capital investment opportunities." But as seen from Figure 1-1, the role of commercial banks seems to go far beyond this simplistic definition.

The most important function of commercial banks is the creation of credit. Commercial banks do not simply act as intermediaries that hold savers' capital and lend out these deposits as loans. When a bank offers a loan, it is also simultaneously creating a matching deposit in the borrowers account. It is here that the intricate dance between central and commercial banks leads to the creation of debt-based money.

When a client makes a deposit of their money with a bank, they are simply exchanging a central bank IOU for a commercial bank IOU. The commercial bank does get an injection of capital, but it also credits the client's account for the sum deposited.

Once again, this operation works on trust. The client trusts the commercial bank to repay the sum deposited on demand. As a result, banks need to ensure they have sufficient amounts of money to be able to repay the IOU's. For this to occur, the bank deposits have to be easily convertible into currency, which is the case today.

As deposits can be converted into currency, the act of making new loans becomes crucial for creating money. When a bank makes a loan to one of its clients, it credits the borrower's account with a higher deposit balance. However, at the same time, it is also creating a new entry in the liabilities section of its ledger. Although this liability previously did not exist, and hence does not have any physical representation in the form of currency, it is in effect an entry in the bank's account. But as all these entries can be converted into currency, the instant it issues debt the commercial bank is creating new money. Hence, loans create deposits and not the other way around.

Th manner in which commercial banks create money by making loans or issuinig credit may be hard to digest if this is the first time you are reading about it, but it is how money is created today. When a commercial bank issues a loan to a client, for example to buy a house, it does not give this loan in cash. Instead, it credits their account with a deposit that amounts to the mortgage. As they make the loan to the borrower, they also credit their assets on their balance sheet. The house may belong to the client who has taken out the mortgage, but it is actually an asset of the bank till the loan is paid off. So even if the loan is payable at a later date, the money is available immediately for the small price of sacrificing ownership temporarily.

The owner of the mortgage now uses the loaned money to pay for the house. In doing so, they inject capital into another business, in this case a real estate agency, or a household if it was a private sale. Hence, via the issuance of debt, commercial banks create money, credit, and purchasing power. The vast majority of what we consider money is created in this manner. Of the two types of broad money, bank deposits make up between 97%–98% of the amount currently in circulation. Only 2%–3% is in the form of notes and liabilities of the government (McLeay et al., 2014).

How much debt commercial banks issue and how that debt is utilized are therefore topics of great importance. Rather than exchanging currency, most consumers use their bank deposits as a store of value and as the medium of exchange. Once a bank creates money by issuing debt, most people use that money to make and receive payments via their deposits rather than currency, especially as transactions today are mostly digital. That money is then swapped from account to account as consumers make payments via the interbank clearing system. As a result, once money is created, it is almost sure to rest in the banking system with very little being extracted to be used in the form of cash.

From the description above, it would seem that the amount of new money that was created by this method should equal the amount that is lent. But there are a number of other factors that change this equation. To understand how this works, we need to look at the subject of fractional banking from a quantitative perspective, as we ask ourselves how much new money can the commercial banks create in this way.

To respond to this question, we now turn our gaze from broad money to base money, which is created by the central bank. As mentioned above, since money creation and control of its supply play pivotal roles in an economy, central banks play a major role of control in this domain. As such, they are responsible for ensuring how much debt is issued by commercial banks, without which they would not be able to control the supply of money. This lever of control exists in the form of capital requirements.

Capital requirements play an important role in the production of debt-based money as they offer, among other things, a safeguard to a bank run. Since a bank creates money as it makes out loans, they are at risk of running out of physical currency in the case that a large number of the depositors decide to withdraw their deposits. To address this risk, commercial banks are obliged to hold some amount of currency to meet deposit withdrawals and other outflows, but using physical banknotes to carry out these large volume transactions would be extremely cumbersome. Hence, commercial banks are allowed to hold a type of IOU from the central bank in the form of central bank reserves, which is calculated as a ratio of the total capital held by a commercial bank. The central bank also guarantees that any amount of reserves can be swapped for currency should the commercial banks need it.

A modern commercial bank is required to hold legal reserves in the form of vault cash, as well as balances at their central banks which are equal to a percentage of its total deposits. This percentage figure is calculated to determine the minimal capital requirements which a bank requires to hold in order to minimize credit risk. The authority that sets out these international banking regulations is the Basel Committee on Bank Supervision, which is part of the Bank for International Settlements (BIS), an international financial institution owned by central banks.[8] The total capital that is held by a commercial bank is classified as Tier 1, Tier 2, and Tier 3 capital.[9]

As per the Basel III stipulations, the minimum amount of capital to be held by the central bank depends on the size of the commercial bank. Banks are grouped into two categories: Group 1 banks are those with Tier 1 capital in excess of €3 billion and are internationally active. All other banks are categorised as Group 2 banks (European Banking Authority, 2013). As of March 2016, under the implementation of the Basel III framework, the average capital ratio for Group 1 banks is 11.5%, with a Tier 1 capital ratio of 12.2% and total capital ratio of 13.9%. For Group 2 banks, the average capital ratio is at 12.8%, with a Tier 1 capital ratio of 13.2% and a total capital ratio of 14.5% (BIS, 2016).

In the context of creating money these capital requirements, in the form of tiered capital controls, allow central banks to control the issuance of debt, and hence money, by commercial banks. For the sake of simplicity, let's assume that the minimum amount of capital to be held by a commercial bank (Group 1 or Group 2) is rounded off to around 10% of its total capital. The capital percentage to be held at the central bank would then be calculated as:

$$\text{Capital Requirement} = \frac{\text{Tier 1 Capital} + \text{Tier 2 Capital}}{\text{Banks assets weighted according to Risk}} \geq 10\%$$

This 10% minimum requirement is the basis of fractional reserve banking. What it shows is that according to the rules stated by the BIS, a bank only needs to have a

---

[8]Established on May 17, 1930, the Bank for International Settlements (BIS) is the world's oldest international financial organization. The BIS has 60 member central banks, representing countries from around the world that together make up about 95% of world GDP. (Source: `http://www.bis.org/about/`)
[9]Tier 1 capital generally consists of common stock and disclosed retained earnings. Tier 2 capital generally consists of debt capital and undisclosed reserves. Tier 3 capital consists of subordinated debt that is used to meet market risks (BIS, 2011).

fraction of its money in reserve, in this case 10%, in order to make out loans. Based on this stipulation a commercial bank can expand the deposits held by them by keeping only 10% of a deposit in their reserves and lending out the remaining 90% at a fixed or variable interest rate. In other words, by only keeping a fraction of the initial deposit, the bank can perform lending activities on the totality of the deposit. It is for this reason that this practice is called *fractional* banking.

By the rules of fractional banking, if $10,000 is deposited at a commercial bank, then only $1,000 is to be held in the deposits, while the remaining $9,000 can be loaned or invested by the bank. The deposit figure in the depositor's account will read $10,000 even though only 10% of the account holder's original deposit actually exists in it. However, the loan is not made on the $9,000 now held by the bank. Instead the bank will make a loan and agree to *"accept promissory notes in exchange for the credits to the borrower's transaction accounts"* (Federal Reserve Bank of Chicago, 2011). Loans (assets) and deposits (liabilities) both rise by $9,000. Hence, the reserves are unchanged by this transaction, but the deposit credits in the borrower's account now adds new capital to the total deposits of the bank.

As a result, the initial deposit of $10,000 is divided into $1,000 in reserves and $9,000 ready to be loaned. The $9,000 to be loaned enters a borrower's credit account and continues to follow the same rule. Only $1,900 is to be kept in reserves and the remaining $8,100 dollars can be loaned. This cycle repeats itself, till the original deposit of $10,000 could theoretically lead to the creation of $100,000 in the bank's deposits.[10] It can thus be seen that savings of consumers are not the primary source of deposits that allow commercial banks to lend. In the modern economy, commercial banks are the creators of deposit money and rather than lending out deposits that are placed with them, the act of lending creates deposits—the opposite of what is typically described in most economic textbooks (McLeay et al., 2014).

The number of deposits that are created by commercial banks is significanlty influenced by the interest rate set by central banks (other factors include inflation rate, net interest margin, etc.). If the interest rate is high, it leads to an unprofitable lending opportunity, as the loans offered by a commercial bank are recorded as how much the bank owes it clients. Hence, deposit creation is lower at high interest rates and higher at low interest rates. If bank deposits are created by the issuance of loans, then the repayment of loans, in the form of currency or existing assets, leads to their destruction. Thus, a second factor that affects the number of deposits being made is the market. If the market sentiment is not friendly for investment, consumers could prefer to not take out loans or to pay existing loans back to stave off risk. This is further affected by competing banks, which might offer lower interest rates on the loans they offer consumers. As a bank's profitability depends on receiving a higher interest rate on the loans than the rate it pays out on its deposits, the limits to which it can create deposits and maintain market share are affected by the margins strategy executed by their competitors.

The central bank also sets the interest rate that is paid on central bank reserves held by the commercial banks. The interest rate that the commercial banks receive on the deposits they place at the central bank in the form of capital requirements thus naturally

---

[10]A theoretical summary of our example could extend to a factor of 10, thus creating $100,000 from a deposit of 10 $10,000. In reality, banks do not always use all their reserves this way and this factor will not be reached.

influences their willingness to lend money to consumers and to other banks (interbank lending). The central bank calculates this interest rate by enacting monetary policies which are aimed at meeting the inflation target set by the government. By keeping a stable consumer price inflation (generally around 2%), monetary policy tries to ensure a stable rate of credit and money creation. The interest rate is also not set by a chosen quantity of reserves. Rather, it is based on the price of credit, which is governed by supply and demand of credit. An increase in the demand for credit raises interest rates, while a decrease in the demand for credit decreases them.

Thus, the central bank controls the short-term interest rates based on the pricing of credit supply and the interest payments it needs to make on the reserves it holds in relation to the monetary policy objectives.[11] But as the supply for reserves to the central bank and currency (broad money) is determined by the loans given by commercial banks, the demand for base money is heavily influenced by the loans being made by commercial banks. Furthermore, the quantity of reserves already in the banking system does not directly constrain the creation of broad money by the issuance of debt. For example: The Bank of England has no formal reserve requirements. Commercial banks do hold a proportion of non-interest bearing cash ratio deposits with the Bank of England for a part of their liabilities. But the function of these cash ratio deposits is non-operational. Their sole purpose is to provide income to the Bank of England (McLeay et al., 2014). The real determinant behind credit extension by commercial banks is based on profitability.

Our Waltz with Debt

The profitability that is associated with the issuance of private credit is thus a subject of vital importance. It is through the issuance of credit to consumers and businesses that broad money is introduced into the economy. As the demand for private credit goes up, so does the money supply in the form of currency and deposits. This brings us back to the graph in Figure 1-1. Why is it that broad money is many multiples of base money? The answer is demand for credit. Remember that credit expansion is profitable for banks that are issuing loans, as it means more deposits. Hence, if the demand for credit goes up, commercial banks stand to gain. For over four decades this demand has been growing.

Between 1997 to 2007, private credit grew at 9% per annum in the US and 10% per annum in the UK[12]. At the same time, private sector leverage also saw a spectacular rise. In the UK, private sector leverage went from 50% in 1964 to 180% in 2007 (Turner, 2015), while in the US, household debt to income ratio went from less than 0.5 to 2.2 (Sufi and Mian, 2014). Figures similar to this were seen in most of the other developed economies

---

[11]The unemployment rate plays a significant role as well.

[12]The BIS has constructed a long series on credit to the private non-financial sector for 43 economies, both advanced and emerging. This series concerns credit provided by domestic banks, all other sectors of the economy, and non-residents. The "private non-financial sector" includes non-financial corporations (both private-owned and public-owned), households, and non-profit institutions serving households as defined in the System of National Accounts 2008. In terms of financial instruments, credit covers loans and debt securities. The entire data set can be found at: https://www.bis.org/statistics/totcredit.htm

and, more recently, this pattern has been repeated in many emerging economies as well. In most cases, private credit grew faster than the economy in terms of GDP.

By tracing and plotting these figures, we notice that the demand for debt has steadily grown over the past six decades. This increasing demand for debt was the result of actions and policies issued over this period that have defined the current highly leveraged economic climate. While it is beyond the scope of this book to analyze this subject in detail, a short note must be dedicated to it, as tracing the history of today's debt-ridden culture is as important as finding a solution to it. Sidebar 1-1 summarizes a series of events that offer some insight into how we got to where we are today.

SIDEBAR 1-1: JUNK BONDS AND REAGANOMICS

The trend in increasing indebtedness of households and companies can partly be traced to the energy crises of the '70s. As the oil embargo of 1973 tumbled with the outbreak of the Iran-Iraq war in 1980, it led to massive increases in the price of oil and caused economic and social chaos in the developed industrialized world. As a result, the newly elected governments in the US and the UK who came to power in the 1980s turned to radical new ways to create economic growth. This period is also referred to as the Reagan-Thatcher Era, and it led to the implementation of what is now colloquially referred to as Reaganomics (Hill, 2012).

When Ronald Regan came to office in 1981, he promised a regeneration of the US economy. But Reagan saw government as a hindrance in this effort. As he stated in his inaugural presidential speech, *"In this present crisis, government is not the solution to our problems. Government is the problem"* (Wisensale, 2001). His strategy was thus to take away economic decision-making powers from the government and hand it to the financial markets and Wall Street. Unsurprisingly, this became a moment of opportunity for most Wall Street bankers.

One of the bankers who leapt at this opportunity was Michael Milken, the future founder of the Milken Institute. Milken had invented a debt instrument called high-yield bonds (which the established banks called *junk bonds*) which he had used as a way to raise vast sums to build casinos in Las Vegas. Casinos were a business most banks avoided, as they were too risky. But Milken was able to show that as the risk involved with these investments was higher, it allowed investors to demand a very high rate of return. Even if some of the business did go bust, by investing across a large spread of these companies, on average, the investor stood to gain a fortune. It was like putting Harry Markowitz's modern portfolio theory on steroids.

While this itself was revolutionary in the eighties, the real transformation of these high yield bonds was that now outsiders from the financial system were given access to capital that was previously denied to them by traditional banks. Capital in the past was in the hands of the great American industrial families. But with high yield bonds, capital was democratized and no longer the property of a small group. An increasing number of new entrepreneurs who invested in junk bonds became wealthy, which brought in new investors who were eager to purchase these junk bonds. In essence it became a tool to challenge the established power on Wall Street as it began to be implemented in the form of takeovers.

One of the first policies passed by Reagan relaxed the rules that governed the takeover of companies. Milken realised that the passing of this policy could allow his high yield bonds to raise large sums of money, as although there was high amount of risk involved, hidden away in established corporations were assets that could be unlocked, sold off, and turned into fantastic profits for investors (Curtis and Hobley, 1999). Not only did this lead to hostile takeovers of the established incumbents, it also meant that the power of capital creation had now moved from the hands of a few to the markets. Executive decision making was now governed by stock markets and executives who maximised the profits of the stock holders.

As the power shifted to the markets, the free market economic mindset developed in the other developed countries as well. Bonds, and the debt they entailed, became a vital source of capital for entrepreneurs who were using debt to take over existing companies or parts of existing companies. Once acquired, the main strategy to increasing share prices was downsizing. As markets got increasingly bullish, unemployment soared along with corporate profits. Companies and households increasingly took on debt in order to adapt to the changes in capital markets. As the demand for debt went up, so did the interest rates that they were connected to.

The market-oriented policies enacted by these governments and the culminating steps that were taken by private industries seemed to work at first. Inflation was squeezed out of the economies and they began to stabilize. But there were also other consequences. As interest rates rose massively, this decimated the manufacturing industries of these countries. Highly paid skilled jobs were replaced by low-wage jobs in the service industries. These socioeconomic changes were best reported by English journalist and documentary filmmaker Adam Curtis in the documentary series *The Mayfair Set* and *Bitter Lake* (see Note below).

In the process of finding a solution, governments once again turned to the commercial banks and relaxed lending restrictions. If wages could not rise any more, then the banks could lend money. The result was a wave of borrowing that spread through these countries. Even if wages were static, people could borrow money and maintain a certain lifestyle. As a result, the ability to manage society and economics slid gently from the control of the state and the central banks to the commercial banks and financial markets. As regulations were relaxed, credit expansion grew and so did the profits for banks, as issuing loans meant more deposits.

The same process was repeated in 2001. After the shock of the attacks on Sep 11, the greatest fear was that the American economy might collapse as investor spending plummeted and markets froze. In response, politicians advised by their economic experts, cut interest rates to historically low levels in order to encourage spending. In response, cheap money began flooding through the system and the disaster was temporarily avoided, although the effectiveness of this buffer is a source of current debate. The aforementioned figures tracing the increase of private credit levels are representations of these transitions.

Note: *The Mayfair Set* (1999) looks at the birth of the global arms trade, the invention of asset stripping, and how British capitalists shaped the Thatcher years. It won the Best Factual Series or Strand at the BAFTA Awards in 2000. *Bitter Lake* (2015) traces the beginnings of Islamic terrorist groups and shows they have their origins in the longstanding economic alliance between the USA and Saudi Arabia. A good documentation of the US-Saudi alliance can also be seen in the 2005 PBS Frontline documentary, *House of Saud*.

The events described in this sidebar seem to portray debt as a necessary evil which was used unscrupulously under the guise of profit maximization. However, this was the result of economic pressures and the decisions of leaders of a new regime who were experimenting with new ideas. This is not to say that an increase in the demand for debt and the growth of the private credit industry was a completely manufactured process. Debt by itself is vital to growth, and any civilization that used some form of money has also used some form of debt instrument (Graeber, 2012). As individuals and businesses try to grow and achieve higher levels of prosperity, they often need debt in order to expand and scale. The question we need to ask ourselves is how much debt do we need in order to grow and achieve a certain threshold of prosperity at a societal level?

The reason we need to ask this question is because of the central role debt plays in our economies. As we have seen, the current monetary system is based on debt and debt-based money. In the words of Marriner Eccles, Governor of the Federal Reserve, *"If there were no debts in our money system, there wouldn't be any money."* Hence, to respond to the question of how much debt is needed, we need to understand our attachment to incurring debt. Could the same kind of prosperity not be achieved from equities instead? What is so enticing about debt and why is it omnipresent in all discussions?

The answer to these questions lies in security and ownership. With equities, the return to the investor is directly related to the success of the business project being funded. However, increased sales of equities come at the price of dividing the company's ownership pie. Even if the project is successful, the share of the profits now needs to be distributed among the other shareholders. A reaction to the reduced ownership has been seen witnessed in recent years in the form of bonuses. As business managers know far more about the business than the investors, they can siphon profits towards themselves and reduce dividends and returns to investors if they decided to. The increase in the size of salaries of business managers is representative of this practise.

In contrast, bonds are looked at as being more secure since they offer a fixed predetermined return and do not infringe on the owner's territoriality. Furthermore, there is more flexibility with debt as liquid bond markets offer investors the chance to invest in long-term assets which they can sell for liquidity in the short term. However, this sense of security with debt instruments comes with other complications. First, coupled with fractional banking, debt-based currency and debt finance can be used to fund even more debt. This can create a danger of excessive dependence on debt, as the repayment of outstanding debt also relies on the supply of debt. If a company needs capital to expand and uses bonds intensively to do so, then without the continued issuance of debt, these companies would be forced to stem investment and see the prices of their assets fall. This also makes them more vulnerable to falls in investor confidence and reductions in bank loans.

The effect of market conditions on the issuance of debt is hence a key issue, and recent research from a team of Bank of England economists has found that there is an interesting cyclical relationship between capital ratios and lending conditions. In a paper titled "In Good Times and in Bad: Bank Capital Ratios and Lending Rates," Osborne, Milne, and Fuertes found that in good times more bank capital was associated with more expensive credit, and in bad times it was the opposite. According to them, the reason has to do with changes in banks' risk appetite between boom and bust times. While the BoE research does not imply a causal effect from capital ratios to lending rates, to the extent that there is one, it gives pause to think about the vulnerability of debt-laden companies.

It is not just companies that are affected by this. As described in Sidebar 1-1 and in previous parts of this section, households as well have become increasingly leveraged over the past decades. Thus, market changes also affect their decisions as to where they employ their debt to generate prosperity. When the economic climate changed in the 1970s, to hedge against any future form of economic turbulence, households and businesses increasingly turned to the real estate sector, as for most consumers, land or home equity was and is their only source of wealth. As consumers turned their investments to the housing sector, the primary business of banks shifted from lending to develop companies to mortgage lending. In fact, the standard role of the financial sector to lend for investment in the business sector constitutes a minor part of banking (Jorda et al., 2016).

This relationship between debt and the real estate industry is particularly important, for when we analyse any developed or developing nation, we always see a pattern of economic disasters being preceded by large increases in household debt (Sufi & Mian, 2016). This phenomenon occurs because of the underlying inequality between borrowers and savers. Most savers have financial assets and little mortgage debt while most borrowers have a low net worth which is why they need to borrow to invest in housing. This is why the vast majority of lending for the purchase of real estate is highly skewed towards the acquisition of already existing assets instead of funding new commercial or housing real estate (Dorling, 2014). The banking and capital market system is thus lending borrowers capital to compete with one another for the ownership of already existing assets, which makes location pivotal given that land and location are immovable entities.

In good times, there is a high demand for credit (which pushes up the price of credit), and a number of households purchase leveraged assets. As competition for the same pieces of land increases, so do land prices and the credit needed to acquire it. But the claims on these assets belong to the savers who make the deposits that enable the loans. If market confidence were to dissipate (as it did in the roll-up to the sub-prime crisis), house prices fall as borrowers attempt to deleverage themselves. As this effect gains momentum, the losses are more concentrated on other borrowers who are the worst off to begin with (which is why they needed to borrow), as the value of their liquid assets begins to fall. The fact that almost 60% (as of 2014) of lending is siphoned to investment in real estate (Jordà et al., 2015) thus compounds the effect and accelerates the process in order to create a bust. Past and present remnants of events like these can be seen in the form of "ghost towns" that exist in various parts of Ireland, Japan, Spain, and, more recently, China.[13] Hence, a system that thrives on credit-financed consumption and directs large investments to the real estate industry, produces cycles of overinvestment, concentrates risk on the debtor, and is intimately linked to wealth inequality.

The cycles of overinvestment in real estate irrigated by the issuance of excessive credit thus creates a misallocation of real resources. But the problem is exasperated when the supply of credit is cut, as it occurs in the wake of bust or a crisis. What this leads to is a debt overhang effect. A debt overhang is a debt burden that is so large that a household or entity cannot take on additional debt to finance future projects, even if these projects are profitable enough to enable it to reduce its indebtedness over time (Campbell et al., 2010). Sufi and Mian describe this effect in their book, *House of Debt*, and so does Danny Dorling in his book, *All that is Solid*. What these researchers show is that during good times, house prices rise, which tempts debtors to borrow and acquire these assets of rising value. However, when the market turns, the higher the leverage the greater the fall, as the debtor falls in net worth with the fall of the asset price. If a household takes a 90% loan-to-value mortgage, then a 5% fall in house prices eliminates 50% of the household's equity in their house (Turner, 2015). As a result, the debtors find themselves in a situation in which the debt they owe becomes increasingly unrepayable. Without the ability to sell their asset for the price they bought it and without the ability to access another line of credit (as creditors become wary as well), their debt levels remain constant while wages remain unchanged. If the bursting of a housing bubble also leads to unemployment for the borrower, the situation is worsened as now there is no source of revenue to manage the debt. This series of events, or others similar to it, are one of the reasons recovery has been slow following the crisis (Jorda et al., 2016).

While crises can cause great harm, the debt overhang created by excessive debt issuance can have more long-lasting effects. As house prices fall, those households and companies which are highly leveraged attempt to reduce their debt levels by cutting expenditure and investment. At the same time, the lack of demand for credit causes creditors to also reduce their expenditures. The cumulative effect of these two changes results in choking investments, higher unemployment levels, and a reduced demand for goods and services. In the past, to overcome these effects and boost spending, monetary policies aimed at reducing interest rates and employed the use of nontraditional instruments, such as quantitative easing (QE), in order to boost the supply of credit. While the effects of QE and other recently employed tools will be discussed in a later part of this book, the key point to consider is that the use of such measures is limited, since borrowers who are already overleveraged do not wish to get into more debt. Hence, the demand side of credit availability becomes the more pressing issue (Koo, 2014), for even if credit is supplied at a low price, the debt overhang effect reduces the demand for credit.

When companies cut investment and households reduce spending, government deficits increase as tax revenues fall and social expenditures for the unemployed increase.

---

[13]Fuelled by strong incentives by local governments and a lack of investment options, capital investment over the past three decades has allowed China to build hundreds of new cities in anticipation of accommodating over 250 million rural inhabitants who were to move to urban zones by 2026. While some of these projects were very successful, some were spectacularly unsuccessful and, along with corruption and bad investment decisions of cash-rich states, it led to the creation of over 50 "ghost towns." Source: MIT Tech Review; https://www.technologyreview.com/s/543121/data-mining-reveals-the-extent-of-chinas-ghost-cities/

As a result, the debt that was issued in the private sector increasingly leads to rising public debt. Just as dancers move in gracious circles in a Viennese waltz, the interconnection of financial markets with a sovereign's economy further metastasizes the effect of the debt overhang and causes it to spread into other sectors of the economy and across other economies.

The figures show this effect: Between 2007 and 2014, global debt rose from 269% of GDP to 286% of GDP (Dobbs et al., 2015). Dissecting the branches of this increase in public leverage, however, leads to a dichotomous realization that is reflected across a variety of economies. For example: Between 2008 to 2015, the US household debt to GDP ratio fell from 99.03 to 79.95,[14] and private debt to GDP fell from 212.28% of GDP to 194.72 % of GDP.[15] At the same time, public debt to GDP went from 92.34% to 125.34%[16] for the same time period. Figure 1-2 illustrates this phenomenon.

In advanced economies, private-sector deleveraging has been accompanied by a rapid increase in public debt

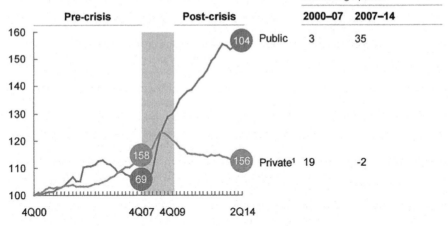

1 Includes household and non-financial corporate sector debt.
NOTE: Debt as percent of GDP is indexed to 100 in 2000; numbers here are not actual figures.

Figure 1-2. *Shifting of debt between private and public sectors Source: "Debt and (not much) deleveraging" (2015), McKinsey Global Institute*

---

[14]Data from Economic Research branch of the Federal Reserve Bank of St. Louis. Source: https://research.stlouisfed.org/fred2/series/HDTGPDUSQ163N
[15]Data from OECD Stats—Financial Indicators. Source : http://stats.oecd.org/index.aspx?queryid=34814
[16]Data from OECD Stats—Financial Indicators. Source : https://data.oecd.org/gga/general-government-debt.ht

Although the figure shows a general upward trend with regards to public debt growth, the same report goes on to show that evolution of debt and debt overhang is getting increasingly divergent and picking up pace. Moreover, in a few developed countries such as France, Sweden, and Belgium, private sector debt has actually grown since the crisis along with public sector debt. In emerging economies, the rising leverage levels in both private and public sectors since 2008 is also becoming a subject of concern.

This was to be expected after the crisis. As growth retracted in developed economies in the aftermath of the crisis, it led to a slowdown of the imports from emerging nations. As a consequence, these countries were forced to shift from export-led growth to domestically led growth, which was fuelled by an expansion in domestic credit. This was most noticeable in China but was not restricted to it. Also, as interest rates in advanced economies were reduced to ultra-low levels, investors seeking a higher yield on bonds began funding projects in emerging economies. As bonds offer a more secure option of investment, firms in emerging economies began to issue debt instead of equity to benefit from the change in market confidence and to attract this growing pool of foreign credit supply. As a result, in contrast to the early and mid-2000s phase, this new wave of FDI was primarily fed by the bond market and, as a result, the share of emerging-market bonds owned by foreign investors has doubled from $817 billion to $1.6 trillion between 2009 to 2013 (Dobbs et al., 2015) (Buttiglione et al., 2014). It would seem that the waltz of debt is the folk dance of GDP growth.

How much debt is too much debt?

The rising debt levels of countries forces us to revist the question we asked ourselves in the previous section, which is, how much debt do we need in order to grow and achieve a certain threshold of prosperity at a societal level? It would seem that debt and growth go hand in hand, as over the past few years, debt-type instruments have gained preference over equity-type instruments (in terms of stock market capitalization) (Buttiglione et al., 2014). As this trend grows in markets across the globe, it raises questions about why economies need growing amounts of debt to grow their economies. More importanlty, we need to determine if this debt-based growth model is sustainable.

The reason for this apprehension with regards to a debt-based growth model stems from a number of reasons. At the private level, the amount of debt affects investment and consumption decisions. At a public level, it affects spending and taxation as well as determines the resistance to crises and shocks, as considerable evidence shows that high quantities of debt stock increase vulnerability to financial crises (Jorda et al., 2011) (Catão and Milesi-Ferretti, 2013). However, the cause for the popularity of purchasing debt-based assets is because it is less likely to cause repayment problems and assumes that the debt will be repaid through future income streams. But this is where the issue arises. In light of economic stagnation and immobile wage rises, the capacity of repaying the debt is increasingly challenged. This is not reserved just to developed economies but also concerns the emerging economies and is most prominent today in China.

At the end of 2015, China recorded its weakest growth in a quarter of a century at 6.9%. In an effort to boost economic growth, in February, the Bejing government moved to inject cash into the banking system to provide low-cost credit to firms and consumers (Wildau, 2016). While this can be said to fund innovation, that argument loses some substance in light of other economic facts. Between 2008 to 2014, Chinese total debt increased by 72% of GDP, or 14% per year. This is almost double that experienced by the US and UK in the same period. As a result of this credit expansion, overall leverage of the Chinese economy is almost 220% of GDP, almost double the average of other emerging markets (Buttiglione et al., 2014). As a result, China is experiencing a growing credit expanion and slowing nominal GDP. While Figure 1-3 showcases this contradiction, the slowing down of China's productivity is indicative that servicing and repaying debt will be difficult in the future.

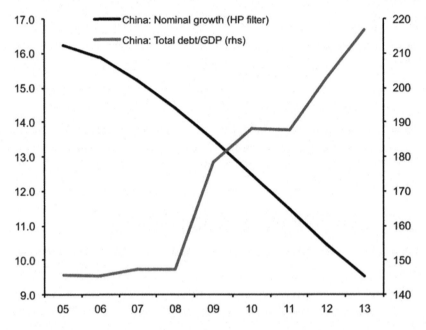

Figure 1-3. *Chinese leverage and underlying nominal GDP growth Source: "Deleveraging, What Deleveraging?", 16th Geneva Report on the World Economy*

As mentioned before, the ripple effects of debt are cyclic and excessive debt levels augment that effect. If households and businesses find themselves too constrained to pay off debts or take on more debt, then on the flipside, creditors become reluctant to extend new loans or renew standing commitments as they are uncertain if debtors are capable of servicing the debt. As a result, the cost of credit goes up, making debt unattractive and, in some cases, unsustainable. The interconnection of markets further spreads this effect, such that a credit crunch in one sector can induce a wave of foreclosures and threaten the banking sector, which in turn can produce a sovereign debt crisis if the banks need to be bailed out by their governments. This in turn adds fuel to the fire, as the expectation of bailouts could lead to lower repayment discipline among private-sector creditors, especially if debt problems are amply widespread in the economy to render punishment threats non-credible (Arellano and Kocherlakota, 2014). All in all, funding to innovation drops, entrepreneurial activity declines, unemployment rises, and a recession sets in.

The effect of rising debt levels is further affected by the fixation of investing in real estate and for the purchase of already existing assets. In the UK, for example, approximately 15% of total financial flows actually went into projects for new investments in 2013. The rest was used for the purchase of existing corporate assets, real estate, or unsecured personal finance to "facilitate lifecycle consumption smoothing" (Tett, 2013). Debt can be beneficial when it is used for generating economic activity. But as the evidence documented in this section shows, debt today is not used for the production of new businesses, and the increasing amounts of debt are reaching beyond repayment capacities. As debts are also deposits in banks, non-repayment of private debt affects banking and thus creates systemic risks.

Furthermore, debt problems of one country are not just a sovereign matter. As financial institutions are wedded together via a complex system of payments, the vulnerability of one state's debt levels can be contagious to other states. Large international banks and hedge funds typically borrow most of the money with which they purchase assets. If the prices of these assets were to fall due to pessimistic market conditions, the value of the firm's liabilities (i.e., debt) could exceed the value of its assets. In this case the value of the firm's equity drops as well. Hence, higher leverage levels create situations of insolvency. Ultimately, excessive debt resembles a Ponzi scheme (Das, 2016). Households, firms, and nations need to borrow increasing amounts of debt to repay existing loans and maintain economic growth. The fact that the credit system has been allowed to develop in this direction on an international scale with the aid of shadow banking is the final piece needed to understand this puzzle.

Shadow Banking and Systemic Risk

In 2005, Alan Greenspan gave a speech titled "Economic Flexibility" at the Federal Reserve Board in which he stated, *"These increasingly complex financial instruments have contributed to the development of a far more flexible, efficient, and hence resilient financial system than the one that existed just a quarter-century ago. After the bursting of the stock market bubble in 2000, unlike previous periods following large financial shocks, no major financial institution defaulted, and the economy held up far better than many had anticipated."*[17]

The financial instruments that he was referring to were the entities and instruments created by commercial banks,[18] to form complex credit intermediation chains involving multiple layers of securitization,[19] multiple leveraged parties, and an opaque distribution of risk (Dobbs et al, 2015). Two years after he gave the speech, the true effects of the financial complexity were seen with the sub-prime crisis.

---

[17]Remarks by Chairman Alan Greenspan, "Economic flexibility." Before the National Italian American Foundation, Washington, D.C. October 12, 2005. Source: www.federalreserve.gov/Boarddocs/speeches/2005/20051012

[18]This includes derivatives and other contract-based assets that derive their value from an underlying asset, index, or interest rate. They include, but are not restricted to, debt-based products such as collateralized debt obligations (CDO's), credit default swaps (CDS's) and other variants or by-products of these products.

[19]Securitization is the practice of combining various types of debt such as mortgages, auto loans or credit card debt obligations (or other non-debt assets which generate receivables), and selling their related cash flows to third party investors in the form of a financial instrument called a security. Different tiers of the instrument are then marketed to different investors and the process creates liquidity in the market as it enables smaller investors to purchase shares in a larger asset pool.

Understanding how this happened is a corollary to the growth of debt. As seen in Sidebar 1-1, following the Reagan-Thatcher era, the sector of finance and banking began to grow and progressed to become a bigger player in the economy. With growth in banking, asset management, insurance, venture capital, and private equity, innovation of financial products expanded and countries with financial hotspots like the UK, Switzerland, and the US gradually found the financial sector accounting for a greater share of employment (in the financial services industry) and GDP.

This growth of financial products was a by-product of the growing tendency to take on debt both by households and firms. As consumers demanded more debt, which was increasingly easily available, it gave the incentives to create these products and also led to the growth of the intra-financial system through which these products were traded. Increasingly, there was a strong accord that the activities which the intra-financial system were engaging in led to better price discovery, better allocation of capital, resources, and risk, and was making economies more stable and resilient to shocks. The statement made by Alan Greenspan was indicative of this consensus, although there is no evidence that economies have become more efficient since the increase in financial complexity since the 1970s (Turner, 2010). What had come out of this increased complexity was an addiction to debt-led growth and the development of the shadow banking system.

A 2012 paper by the Federal Reserve Bank of New York provides an understanding of shadow banking. It states, *"Shadow banks are financial intermediaries that conduct maturity, credit, and liquidity transformation without explicit access to central bank liquidity or public sector credit guarantees. Examples of shadow banks include finance companies, asset-backed commercial paper (ABCP) conduits, structured investment vehicles (SIVs), credit hedge funds, money market mutual funds, securities lenders, limited-purpose finance companies (LPFCs), and the government-sponsored enterprises (GSEs)"* (Pozsar et al., 2012). In essence, it is the practice of providing credit via non-bank channels.

Since 2008, as bank lending declined in most advanced economies, most of the credit for non-financial firms has come from non-bank channels in the form of corporate bonds, securitization, and lending from non-bank institutions. As these financial intermediaries offered credit intermediation outside the regular banking system, they lacked a formal safety net (IMF, 2014). In spite of being cognizant of this risk, prior to the crisis, financial institutions increased their financial engineering activities.

The reason banks participated in such high risk activities was the same reason they had issued credit easily prior to the crisis. It was profitable. As banks continued to grow, as they had for the previous forty years, they aimed to get bigger. The drive for growth and profitability thus encouraged them to take on more risk. This was first seen in the lowering of lending standards, which was the primary reason for the sub-prime crisis. As these mortgages got added to the assets section of the banks' balance sheet, they were channelled into speculative activities under the guise of securitization, and used for trades such as arbitrage, market-making, and position -taking, that had nothing to do with client needs and which added little to economic activity. The porosity of the inter-financial system with other banks, hedge funds, and asset managers ultimately resulted in the balance sheets of banks being filled increasingly with these shadow banking assets. Although it is broadly defined as credit intermediation outside the conventional banking system, shadow banking constitutes about one-fourth of total financial intermediation worldwide (IMF, 2014). The shadow banking system also trades in the OTC derivatives market, which had grown rapidly in the decade up to the 2008 financial crisis (BIS, 2008).

As of June 2015, after significant reductions and regulations, the OTC derivatives market was valued at $553 trillion (BIS, 2015). Global GDP amounted to $73.17 trillion[20] at the end of 2015.

As shadow banking grew so did its complexity. Intermediation was a long-standing practice in banking prior to the crisis. But as a result of the slicing and dicing of derivatives, simple forms of securitization became increasingly complex. In the case of debt-based derivatives, the maturity transformation risks of the underlying asset were further replicated in the securities, thus creating new forms of credit and multiplying counterparty risk. The opaqueness of information regarding these products were another factor that led to their spread. As there is a disproportionateness of information between the sellers, buyers, and regulators of these products, it is harder to regulate them. As a result, the financialization of securities weakens the market mechanisms in the long run, with contrived and volatile values (Das, 2016).

It would be tempting to say that the regulators were asleep at the wheel. But the reality of the situation is that regulators and macroeconomists had been following the rules to a large extent. Indeed, their models and policies were based on well-known economic theories, statistical analysis, and the understanding that increased complexity led to more efficient and just markets. So why did so many economists not see the crash coming?

The primary reason for the widespread belief that increased complexity of the financial market leads to better efficiency is because of the existing macroeconomic theories regarding the interconnection between financial markets and monetary policy. Over the past 30 to 40 years, the standard theories of economics have regarded and treated markets as a veil through which the monetary policy would permeate. The financial system was left to function as it was traditionally supposed to, holding deposits and issuing debt, and macroeconomists focused on controlling the economy via interest rates and inflation targets. This disconnection between macroeconomics and banking and financial markets have now gotten to the point that very little attention is actually paid to the way money and debt is created. This is representative even at the educational level, as most universities and business schools today do not focus a great deal of their curricula on banking and credit. Understanding the reason for this requires us to look at the way economics is looked at.

In spite of our technological evolution, macroeconomic theory is still firmly based on two well-known concepts: the efficient market hypothesis (EMH) and the rational expectations theory (RMT). As per these concepts, expectations of players in a market are formed on the basis of past experiences, typically as some kind of weighted average of past observations and the availability of new data. The players then make optimal use of this information in identifying opportunities and thus their expectations will be correct, considering any unavoidable errors. This is the crux of the rational expectations theory. As a result of these expectations, based on experience and new data, if there is a change in the way an event was supposed to occur (say a change in tax rates), then the players will immediately change their expectations regarding future values of this event even before seeing any actual changes. As all players have access to the same information, albeit at different levels of granularity, bad decisions made by one player are offset by good decisions

---

[20]Source : http://www.statista.com/statistics/268750/global-gross-domestic-product-gdp/

made by another. This makes beating the market impossible as the stock price of a share intrinsically incorporates all the relevant information. This is efficient markets hypothesis.

Although the EMH and RET might be a reasonable starting point for understanding economics and stock markets, it is not the whole story and is questionable in the present-day context. In today's complex economic climate, which is peppered with shadow banking, changing regulations, and cyber-attacks, real-world investors do not have access to "all relevant" available information. The theories have an explanation for this and state that expectations can fail to be rational in the strong-form sense[21] if investors fail to use all available relevant information, or if investors fail to make optimal use of all available relevant information. However, it fails to consider that even if investors have the same information, differences in psychological make-up can lead to systematic differences in expectations. It also assumes that stock prices are determined by "intrinsic value" and is thus static, as it ignores positive feedback loops.

Yet the models used by most central banks to gauge how economies function, called dynamic stochastic general equilibrium models,[22] are based on these theories. Even more surprising is that in these models the operations of banks are not taken into consideration, although they do look at microeconomic data pertaining to large companies and households in aggregate.

This approach to macroeconomic theory is a relatively recent phenomenon and coincidentally began being applied in the late 1970s. Prior to this period, work done by prominent economists such as John Maynard Keynes, Irving Fisher, and Henry Calvert Simons, focused profoundly on the way money was made. While the reasons for this divergence in academic disciplines is the subject for a book in economic history, this approach of using the EMH and the RET while subtracting the role of banking was the primary reason why a number of economists did not see the crisis coming. Although debt is so tied up with the monetary system, these theories and the economists who created models based on them, believed that increased complexity led to better price discovery, and thus considered debt to be vital to economic growth. Is it thus a surprise that we have not been paying attention to the creation of money?

Rethinking Debt-based Capitalism

One hopes that the arguments and facts provided in the previous parts of this chapter help clarify the reason we need to look at debt with a greater amount of introspection. Debt by itself is important and useful, but excessively high debt levels slow economic growth, push down wages, lower living standards and make it harder to borrow when hit by a crisis or an emergency. This is true for households as it is for nation states, and the net sum effect of bulging debt levels are periodic cycles of booms and crashes followed by recessions. Our tendency to invest in real estate, global imbalances, and the increasing

---

[21]Strong-form efficiency is the strongest design of market efficiency and states that all information in a market, whether public or private, is accounted for in a stock's price.
[22]Dynamic stochastic general equilibrium modelling (DSGE) is an applied branch of general equilibrium theory that attempts to explain aggregate economic phenomena, such as economic growth, business cycles, and the effects of monetary and fiscal policy.

inequality within societies are the fundamental reasons for a credit intensive cycle that has lasted for the past few decades.

Following the crisis of 2008, recent changes made by regulators are now turning back the wheel of time. During the Reagan-Thatcher era, financial markets were liberated from a large number of restrictions. This action was repeated in the nineties under the Clinton-Blair era. While the Blair government handed over the responsibility of setting interest rates from the Chancellor of the Exchequer to the independent Bank of England in 1997, the repeal of the Glass-Steagall act in 1999 effectively matched the same gesture in the US. The enactment of the Volker rule, which restricts US banks from making certain kinds of speculative investments that do not benefit their customers, is a return to the older form of banking regulations when deposits were not used to trade on the bank's own accounts.

While the net effect of these rulings, along with stricter regulations following the LIBOR[23] scandal, do apply new restrictions on the ability of commercial banks to participate in speculative activities, they have been coupled with extraordinary measures such as quantitative easing (QE) and quantitative and qualitative easing[24] (QQE). This is not to say that the regulators and central bankers were wrong in doing what they did. Following the events of the crisis of 2008, pumping money into the economy at ultra-low rates was better than not taking any action. But it replays the dance with debt all over again, as thanks to the current modus operandi, governments have to borrow and pay interest to central banks for the newly minted money they push into the economy. As a result, the payoff from conducting QE ends up as an income for the central bank and can be accounted as a profit.

The supply of cheap money has also exacerbated the inequality within societies as the public money that was used for bank bailout and stimulating the economy has fuelled a boom for those with financial assets. As QE stimulates the market by increasing money supply, and hence asset prices, it is those with the greatest amount of asserts that stand to gain. Apart from perpetuating the cycle of debt-based money, the benefits are skewed towards the rich due to the unequal ownership of assets. The increase in the prices of assets also means that those households willing to take loans to purchase them, now need to take on a higher level of debt than prior to QE. Public debt reductions are thus offset by private debt increases.

What is needed to break this cycle is a rethinking of capitalism from a fundamental level. Not only do we need to think of a less credit-based growth model, but we also need to relook at the theories and models that we use today, for they are blatantly out of date with respect to the complexity and diversity of today's financial markets. Furthermore, measures need to be taken to address both the underlying causes and disproportionate debt issuance and the ensuing instability fuelled by fractional banking and shadow

---

[23]The London inter-bank offered rate (LIBOR) is an average interest rate calculated through submissions of interest rates by major banks across the world. LIBOR is used to settle contracts on money market derivatives and is also used as a benchmark to set payments on about $800 trillion worth of financial instruments, ranging from complex interest-rate derivatives to simple mortgages. Source: The Economist: http://www.economist.com/node/21558281

[24]Qualitative easing means targeting certain assets to try to drive up their prices and drive down their yields, whereas quantitative easing is unspecific and intends to drive down interest rates across the whole spectrum of assets. Source: Bloomberg: http://www.bloomberg.com/news/articles/2014-10-31/what-the-heck-is-japans-qqe2

banking. While a number of measures have been taken to address some of these issues, these measures have been reactive rather than proactive. In light of increasing levels of automation and threats of robotization of jobs, this approach is akin to trying to stop a bleeding artery with a Band-Aid instead of a tourniquet.

In the meanwhile, the growing diaspora of FinTech and Blockchain-based solutions offers us a spectrum of possible solutions both at a technical as well as a managerial level. But the solutions provided by decentralized applications and tokenized pseudonymous identities also requires rethinking the regulations rule book. The following parts of this book illustrate how and why rethinking the rule book will be fruitful to society, and how these technologies could be employed to better measure and manage our financial systems and our economies, while offering solutions to the problems of the future.

CHAPTER 2

■ ■ ■

Fragmentation of Finance

Since the advent of the crisis, two stark realities were brought to the forefront of public discourse. First, banks were allowed to have such an impact on the economy due to their enormous size and influence. Second, they have diverged from the general definition of democracy owing to the concentration of power that comes from the centralization of information and the opaqueness of their operations.

Having seen how debt and money are created in the modern financial system, the question that needs to be answered is "How were banking and financial institutions allowed to grow to this scale and operate in such a manner?" What circumstances were responsible that led to finance being entrenched in every aspect of our lives? If money is an imaginary manifestation whose sole function is to aid in the exchange of value, why is it able to exert such influence and control in every aspect of society? A large part of the response to this question has cultural connotations, and to trace the roots of this cultural evolution we turn our gaze to the UK, one of the financial capitals in the world.

The Fuzziness of Financialization

In 1982, the *Financial Times* adopted a new corporate jingle: "No *FT*, no comment." The television advertisement related to this slogan showed a predatory fish trying, unsuccessfully, to catch a puffer fish. As the puffer fish gets away, the male voice-over states, *"You don't have to read the* FT *every day, but you can be sure you'll have to deal with people who have."* The advertisement was a great success: It went on not only to win 3rd place in the Advertising Slogan Hall of Fame,[1] but also entered popular culture when it was uttered by Francis Urquhart/Frank Underwood,[2] the central character in the popular television series *House of Cards*, as a response to every controversial question that was asked of him *("You might very well think that but I couldn't possibly comment")*.

---

[1]The Advertising Slogan Hall of Fame, sponsored by AdSlogans.com, recognizes excellence and best practice in advertising, identifying the best in branding.

[2]Ian Richardson played the character Francis Urquhart in the 1990's while Kevin Spacey, plays the character Frank Underwood today. The characters are based on the novel House of Cards, written by Michael Dobbs.

© Kariappa Bheemaiah 2017
K. Bheemaiah, *The Blockchain Alternative*, DOI 10.1007/978-1-4842-2674-2_2

Part of the slogan's popularity at that time was due to the fact that it reflected a cultural consensus. As the Reagan-Thatcher epoch unfolded, the privatization of state enterprises, coupled with the deregulation of markets and the dominance of junk bond capital, meant that finance was now entering all aspects of public and private life. As a primary source of financial information, "No *FT* no comment" embodied a reality where it would be judicious to check what the *FT* was saying about a subject or an investment, and thus educate oneself to be a player or a spectator in this new era. The popularity of the phrase represented a growing intellectual pattern that was immersing households and non-financial firms in the financial market.

Having become the *de facto* reference and provider of economic and financial information, the *FT* repeated this representation of societal mindset change again a quarter of a century later. In 2007, just before the crisis, the *FT* released its new advertisement campaign with three distinct images to signify globalization, mergers and acquisitions, and entrepreneurship. All three images carried their new slogan, "We live in *Financial Times*," almost alluding to the fact that irrespective of the sector or size of the industry, finance was omnipresent. A year later, as the crisis unrolled, their billboard advertisements showed a Saint Bernard carrying a copy of the newspaper in place of the lifesaving flask of brandy on its collar to promote its essential role during the economic downturn (Sweney, 2008).

These *FT* slogans represent the ascendency of finance into all aspects of our affairs. This phenomenon has been and continues to be referred to as "financialisation" and the Figures 2-1 and 2-2 show its ascent.

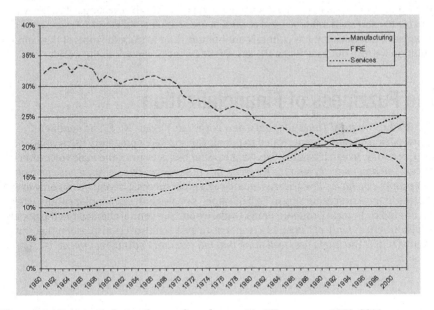

Figure 2-1. *Relative industry shares of employment in US economy, 1950–2001*

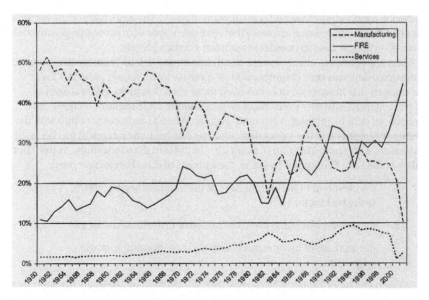

Figure 2-2. *Relative industry shares of corporate profits in US economy, 1950-2001 Image source: "The financialization of the American economy" (Greta R. Krippner, 2005)*

FIRE: Finance, Insurance, and **Real Estate**. Note the curve similarities of the Services and FIRE industries. *Image source: "The financialization of the American economy" (Greta R. Krippner, 2005).*

The definition of financialization differs from context to context. The Oxford dictionary defines it as, *"The process by which financial institutions, markets, etc., increase in size and influence."* But any process is based on a series of events. Hence, financialization needs to be looked as not as an existential realism, but more as a gradual build-up of events.

As the volume, diversity, and turnover of financial instruments has grown faster than the real economy, the financial sector has grown faster than the real economy (Smaghi, 2010). As a result, markets and institutions have exercised a growing influence on the conduct of managers of non-financial firms (Zorn, 2000), and households and non-financial firms have become progressively tangled in financial products and markets. Furthermore, as financialization continued its widespread infiltration, it was widely cited as a good thing under the guise of being a mechanism that allowed us to tame risk. As stated by Ben Bernanke in a speech to the Eastern Economic Association in 2004,

"One of the most striking features of the economic landscape over the past twenty years or so has been a substantial decline in macroeconomic volatility..."

Along with this cultural transition was the talismanic standing rendered to the importance of credit for economic growth. But, as seen in the previous chapter, the issuance of increased amounts of debt leads to debt overhang and the shifting of the debt burden from private to public sectors. In addition, sustainable, continuous growth in a consumerist society requires the constant purchase and consumption of goods. The availability of cheap credit meant that those with revenue increases that were out of sync with economic growth could be persuaded to borrow instead in order to maintain a certain lifestyle.

Thus, the collective effect of these trends has meant that an increase in economic performance depends on a disproportionate increase in consumer debt. It is for these reasons that household debt has risen faster than that of the general level of economic activity, and why every successive economic cycle requires a bigger dose of household debt to stimulate economic activity. When seen in conjunction with the previous statements and the topics described in Chapter 1, the net result has been the omnipresence of financialization in every fiber of industrialized societies. As per Thomas I. Palley of the Levy Economics Institute, the impacts of this change have been:

1. the elevation of the significance of the financial sector relative to the real sector[3];

2. the transfer of income from the real sector to the financial sector;

3. the increase of income inequality and contribution to wage stagnation.

While it can be extrapolated that these behaviors could increasingly threaten social cohesion, it must be remembered that the cultural infringement of finance is only part of the reason behind the growth of financialization. Finance, after all, is to be looked at as a catalyst that allows for the efficient production and distribution of goods and services. This function is executed by the provision of credit and the allocation of risk between economic agents who are best suited for these roles, thus resulting in the appropriate allocation of resources within the economy.

However, as it has been discussed, since macroeconomic theory only considers the production and exchange of goods and services involving "real" variables, money and credit have been considered to occur in a separate analytical sector. As a result, finance has been treated as a fuzzy veil behind which was the "real" exchange of "tangible" and societally impactful products. It is for this reason that macroeconomists have generally paid little attention to the workings of financial markets. The amalgamation of cultural transitions and the suprising disregard of formal macroeconomic academic investigation have in part led to the growth of financialization.

Financialization and the Innovation of Risk

No discussion about financialization can be considered complete without a conversation of its principal component, risk. The aspect of risk is at the heart of financialization. One of the functions of financial institutions is to act as an intermediary between economic agents who have unequal or unaligned objectives or who wish to hedge themselves from risks such as credit or interest rate fluctuations. By acting as a counterparty to these agents, financial institutions take risk on

---

[3]The "real" economy is defined as the part of the economy that is concerned with actually producing goods and services, as opposed to the part of the economy that is concerned with buying and selling on the financial markets (FT Lexicon)

their shoulders and, in doing so, provide a service by which they earn a revenue in response. But the growth of financialization has had a curious effect on the redistribution of risk. Rather than simply being redistributed, risk has undergone a transformative process and become a product in and of itself which can now be traded and sold as an actual good.

From the 1980s onwards, as non-financial firms increasingly became involved in financial markets, the incentive attached to those participants willing to take on the responsibility of risk gave rise to a set of esoteric and increasingly complex derivative products (Partnoy, 2009). The cumulative effect of this development meant that non-financial firms now began diverting from their core activities, such as the manufacturing of goods, to financial activities, such as the provision of credit for acquiring those goods, which was the territory of traditional financial institutions.

However, the transference of roles was not all bad news for financial institutions. As an increasing number of consumers took on debt to purchase products, it meant that the growth of the non-financial institutions had to be leveraged by taking on more debt. As the spiral of debt continued, the risk attached to loans grew in volume, to the point that it was now necessary to address the situation. It is here that financial innovation came to the rescue. As the power of banks decreased due to the issuance of debt by non-financial institutions, the banks installed a new risk management practise via their activities in exchanging securities and specifically through CDOs (Collateralised Debt Obligations), Collateralized Loan Obligations (CLOs) and CDSs (Credit Default Swaps).

Previously, banks controlled the amount of risk in the economy by providing or withholding credit. This was referred to the as the "originate-to-hold" model (Santos, 2012) of risk management. However, with the birth of CDOs, CLOs and CDSs, new possibilities were discovered. Under the originate-to-hold model, banks limited the distribution of risk to mortgages, credit card credits, and auto and student loans. However, with CLOs,[4] they were now provided with another venue for distributing the loans that they originated. As a result, the traditional originate-to-hold model grew into an "originate-to-distribute" model based on their corporate lending business. Further financial innovation in the form of CDOs and CDSs caused these models to evolve into a "originate, repackage and sell" model (Ansart & Monvoisin, 2015).

Financialization based on the production and exchange of risk has created transactions involving credit operations which are endogenous to the financial markets. As these transactions involve the transformation of risk into financial products, what has been observed is the slicing and dicing of risk products that multiplies the nominal value of the financial instruments in circulation (Davison, 2015). As a result, they manifest themselves in the form of increased financial turnover, bigger balance sheets, and growing revenues in financial markets. The exponential growth of the transformation of risk via increased financialization has led to a proliferation of financial claims and obligations, as a result of which a growing percentage of total wealth now exists not in the form of real assets but in the form of financial assets or claims by creditors. Its growth has also led to banks getting too big to fail.

---

[4] A CLO is debt-based security comprised of various corporate loans.

TBTF

The term Too Big to Fail (TBTF) has captured the headlines since the crisis. But the growing popularity of this term should not come as a surprise. In the same way that financialization can be considered as a process of events, TBTF was a looming event being built to fruition well before the crisis. Indeed, a number of noted economists, including Raghuram Rajan,[5] Dean Baker,[6] Steve Keen,[7] Ann Pettifor,[8] and Nouriel Roubini[9] (Cooper, 2015), had predicted the inefficiencies of financial markets, warned us about increasing private debt levels and wrote about the impending crash that was coming our way. All these economists also warned us about the increasing financialization of the economy, the deregulation of the market, the rising debt levels of households, and the risk of a recession. They were systematically and categorically ignored.

The reason for this dismissive behavior was first based on the exclusion of financial markets from macroeconomic models (See Blanchard et al., 2010). Second, there was also a cognitive dissonance and logical fallacy associated with financialization. As finance was omnipresent in every part of our society, it had achieved a sense of trust. If you could not believe in free markets and the appropriate allocation of risk when everyone else was, then what could you believe in?

This ideological kidnapping of economic theory, market policies, and societal mindsets occurred due to a monetary thought experiment now referred to as the Washington Consensus. Under this ideology, market discipline and self-regulation would be sufficient to ward off any serious problems in financial institutions, and if left to itself, the financial system would not only allocate resources more efficiently, but also redistribute risks better. Not only was this belief widespread, it was also contagious—the IMF, the World Bank, the Federal Reserve, the ECB, and the Bank of England were all infected by the same

---

[5]Governor of the Reserve Bank of India (till September 2016)—Rajan questioned the "worrisome" actions of the banks when he served as an economic counsellor at the International Monetary Fund (IMF) in 2005. In a 2014 article in *Time* magazine, he stated that he now fears long-term low interest rates and unorthodox programs to stimulate economies, such as quantitative easing, may lead to more turmoil in financial markets.

[6]Co-director of the Centre for Economic and Policy Research—In 2004, in an article in *The Nation* titled "Bush's House of Cards", he wrote: "The crash of the housing market will not be pretty….". In his 2010 book, *False Profits: Recovering from the Bubble Economy*, he states that the US needs to "rein in a financial sector that has grown out of control."

[7]Head of the School of Economics, History, and Politics, Kingston University—Keen is widely regarded as one of the first economists to have foreseen the crisis. In 2005, he set up the website debtdeflation.com as a platform to discuss the "global debt bubble." Commenting in *BRW* magazine, he argued: "This is how bubbles grow and burst and ignoring debt in this way is one of the great fallacies of modern economics."

[8]Director of Policy Research in Macroeconomics (PRIME)—In 2006, Pettifor published the book, *The Coming First World Debt Crisis*. In the book, Pettifor blamed the US Federal Reserve, politicians, and mainstream economists for endorsing a framework to support unsustainably high levels of borrowing and consumption under the guise of propping up the economy. The book was widely ignored on publication.

[9]Chairman of Roubini Global Economics—In 2006, in an address to the International Monetary Fund, Roubini warned of the risk of a deep recession that would reverberate around the world.

belief system (Ülgen, 2015). Hence, Lehman Brothers and AIG became TBTF because it was inconceivable that they could fail (Admati and Hellwig, 2013).

As it can be inferred from the term, the Washington Consensus, the growth of TBTF finds its roots in the annals of an American financial history story. Owing to the popularity and acceptance of financialization, over the past 40 years, the notion that oversight of the financial industry was unnecessary was entrenched in society. In 1998, Alan Greenspan stated that, *"participants in financial markets are predominantly professionals that simply do not require the customer protections that may be needed by the general public."* A year later, the American Congress almost unanimously voted in favor of the Gramm-Leach-Bliley Financial Modernization Act that removed the specialization of banks by repealing the Glass-Steagall Act and ending the prohibitions against the intermingling of commercial and investment banking activities. As stated by the Republican Senator Phil Gramm (who spearheaded the Gramm- Leach-Bliley Act in 1999*), "We have learned that government is not the answer. We have learned that freedom and competition is the answer"* (Myers-Lipton, 2009). It was erringly similar to what Reagan had said in his inaugural presidential speech almost 15 years ago (see Sidebar 1-1 in Chapter 1).

As the banks were given freer rein to grow within the economy, this also aided them in expanding across geographies. For most of the 20th century, they had been constrained in terms of geographies of growth because the McFadden Act of 1927 prohibited nationally chartered lenders from establishing branches outside of their states of incorporation. At the same time, the 1933 Glass-Steagall Act separated commercial from investment banking while the Bank Holding Company Act of 1956 extended the same prohibitions to bank holding companies, which had been developed to circumvent the restrictions against interstate banking (Maxfield, 2013).

Beginning in 1994, the US government began to relax the regulations with the Riegle-Neal Interstate Banking and Branching Efficiency Act which ended the geographical limits on banking activity and thus the McFadden Act (Ansart & Monvoisin, 2015). What started as a decision to allow interstate banking quickly gained momentum with the development of regional banking mergers. The aforementioned Riegle-Neal Interstate Banking and Branching Act of 1994 removed federal impediments to interstate banking and, in the process, ignited a series of mergers of like-sized banks. Coupled with the 1999 Gramm-Leach-Bliley Financial Modernization Act, it led to the rise of JP Morgan Chase, Citigroup, Bank of America, and Wells Fargo, among others (Maxfield, 2013).

As a result of the structural changes over the past 40 years and the accompanying financialization of business and society, today's markets are composed of large, complex, and highly leveraged companies, immersed in a sector where securities are financially engineered and linked to derivative instruments. This interconnected lattice is often touted to represent the adaptive and innovative nature of finance as it keeps pace with main street entrepreneurial innovations.

For instance, proponents of big banks state that large banks encourage the widespread adoption of new financial innovations, as they have a large customer base. Large institutions are thus better positioned to spread the costs of investment in a technology over more users, allowing them to offer new technological innovations at lower average costs than their new entrants. This in turn allows banks to offer economies of scale, as they offer clients a plethora of services under a single umbrella. It is for these reasons that banks undertake in mergers-and-acquisitions, as it allows them to harvest opportunities in providing customers with a range of transaction-related services, such as financing, risk management (in the form of derivative products), and foreign exchange, among others. It is hence more economically efficient for banks to provide numerous services in combination.

Although this is true to a certain extent, the stark fact is that banking innovations affect monetary and fiscal conditions on which the entire economy is girded, and thus changes in this sector affect the economic conditions to a greater degree. While large banks might offer greater efficiencies, their size also comes with more process, more red-tape, increased amounts of opaqueness, and larger mistakes.

Consider the case of the J.P. Morgan's "London Whale" episode in 2012. As the traders executed their hedging strategy by entering into a series of derivative transactions involving credit default swaps (CDS), one of the JP Morgan traders, Bruno Iksil, accumulated outsized CDS positions in the market and began distorting the market with massive bets. As other traders in the CDS market began to notice this activity, they moved in the opposite direction and began to take positions that were contrary to the J.P. Morgan positions. At the same time, they called foul and, following an investigation, at the end of which J.P. Morgan, the largest bank in the USA, suffered $6.2bn in trading losses (Scannell, 2016).

The inquiry of the incident further highlighted the inefficiency that is at the core of large institutions. When questioned about his actions, Iksil responded that not only were his actions in 2012 authorized, but that he was instructed repeatedly by the CIO and senior management to execute this trading strategy (*FT*, 2016). As per his interpretation, the investment office in London tried to sidestep capital regulation laws of risk management by fulfilling the bare minimums of regulatory requirements. Traders were thus given the incentive to score big, and therefore, instead of focusing on simplicities, the traders focused on the complexities of derivative markets and ignored the danger signals provided by the stress tests (Forelle, 2012).

The London whale incident is just one of the many financial scandals that have involved the TBTF banks following the crisis. Since 2008, HSBC has been involved in the LIBOR scandal, Standard Chartered in money laundering transactions, and JP Morgan, Citigroup, Bank of America, RBS, Barclays, and UBS (also known as the "Bandits' Club") were all involved in rigging the Forex market (*Independent*, 2015). Between 2010 and 2015, Barclays, HSBC, the Lloyds Banking Group, and the Royal Bank of Scotland have together incurred costs of £55.8bn to cover conduct and litigation issues, after being penalized for rigging Libor and foreign exchange markets, and for the misselling payment protection insurance (PPI) incident (Treanor, 2016). When talking in terms of efficiency, it's surprising how often advocates of big banks seem to leave these incidents out of their sermons.

What these incidents show us is that large banks are capable of making large mistakes. While there are benefits of scope and scale, such institutions are also harder to manage and oversee. Hence, the size of the banks and their stronghold on the direction of monetary and fiscal policy is a topic worthy of public discussion owing to the influence and the implications of the actions of banks that are TBTF.

#Ending TBTF[10]

It could be argued that breaking up the banks would not yield better results. Advocates of big banks often ask questions along the following lines when engaging in this repertoire:

- Had the banks been broken into smaller pieces two decades ago, would it have stopped the crisis?

- Is there a success probability in terms of financial stability that is calculable by breaking up the banks?

- Even if we break up the banks, then to what extent do we break them up?

- And is this break to be done on the basis of activities or in terms of asset size?

- Who will decide how to break up a bank?

All of these questions are valid and necessitate responses. If we are to ask for a break-up of banks, then the criteria for the breakup needs to be anchored to a measure of the systemic risk generated by the bank. This in turn would help us understand what the threshold of organic growth of a bank needs to be before it poses systemic risk, and what needs to be done when it reaches this limit. If splitting institutions by specialty or business functions reduces their efficiency, then what are the quantitative arguments against it? As it stands, most responses to the questions posed by fans of big banks are based on subjective judgments. This is not to say that they are unusable, but it must be recognized that more quantitative proof needs to be gathered in order to avoid the implementation of unambiguous guidelines to breaking up an institution. We will explore these quantitative methods in later parts of the book.

From a more ideological outlook, it could also be argued that markets should be allowed to make mistakes as part of the innovative process. This is a seemingly logical rationale, especially when taking into consideration the way the innovation mantra is being chanted across every sector and industry today. Indeed, this has even happened in the past. In the 1980s during the savings and loans crisis (S&L crisis), 1,043 out of the 3,234 savings and loan associations (FDIC, 2000) failed and affected millions of everyday investors. In 2000, the bursting of the technology bubble did affect investors and technology in general. Yet none of these failures posed systemic risks and came at the cost of a financial meltdown. The plumbing of the financial system and its connection to other institutions ensure that large, complex financial organisations are systemically important financial institutions (SIFI[11]) that pose risks to the financial system and the economy.

---

[10]Term borrowed from the Minneapolis Federal Reserve bank's initiative will explore various bold and transformational solutions to address TBTF.

[11]SIFI: A SIFI is an institution, activity or market considered so important to the functioning of the economy that special rules and buffers are put in place to (1) reduce the probability of failure and (2) minimize spillovers in case of failure.

It is for these reasons that the conversation of ending TBTF has been reverberating and gaining momentum in public and private anterooms. But as it can be seen, it is two-sided, with differences in opinion in terms of the cost, scope, and the scale of TBTF and ending TBTF. As the conversation stagnates, the biggest banks are still TBTF and continue to pose risks to the global economy.

It must be remembered that TBTF was not the sole cause of the crisis. But the job losses, home foreclosures, lost savings, and the costs to taxpayers following the bailout of banks represent the financialization of our societies and showcase the presence of banks that are TBTF in the center of our financial system while highlighting their significant contribution to the magnitude of the crisis and the extensive damage that it perpetrated across the global economy.

This is not to say that nothing has been done in order to address the issue. Following changes in regulation, large banks and SIFIs are now required to hold greater amounts of capital and have larger sources of liquidity. As a result of the Dodd Frank Act, firms identified as SIFIs are subject to stricter oversight from the Federal Reserve, have to partake in stress tests, write a bankruptcy plan known as a living will, and meet stricter capital requirements. All of these measures and a number of other changes were the result of the Dodd-Frank Act which was passed to limit systemic risk, allow for the safe resolution of the largest intermediaries, submit risky nonbanks to greater scrutiny, and reform derivatives trading (Lopez and Saeidinezhad, 2016). Following the crisis, these measures have been enacted not only in the USA, but also across other markets. As per the Basel III accord, large banks in every country are required to have higher capital requirements, annual stress tests, additional capital mandates, and new liquidity and asset-liability matching requirements (Bipartisan Policy Center, 2014).

Thus, stress tests done by regulators today gauge whether the most centrally important institutions can withstand external and internal shocks to the economy. To ensure that banks can fail without requiring massive taxpayer bailouts, regulators have adopted the use of the "Living Will[12] Review" process, which makes banks essentially think about their demise, and forces the banks to describe their company, their risk exposures, as well as their strategy for reorganizing themselves in bankruptcy without causing financial instability or using taxpayer dollars. If the banks fail to persuade regulators that they have a realistic and safe plan for winding down, the government can use Dodd-Frank's Orderly Resolution Authority to resolve them outside the court system if they get into trouble. In other words, banks have enormous incentive to make sure their Living Wills are convincing.

All these measures are important and significant progress has been made. Table 2-1 provides a summary of some of the goals defined by the Dodd-Frank Act and the degree to which they have been implemented. But despite these efforts, banks can still run into trouble and questions arise as to whether these efforts are sufficient, with the urgency of implementation fading as the crisis fades from memory. There is also the question of cost, scope, and scale: While the Living Will does look at the threat posed by a bank, it fails to consider the massive asymmetrical risks to society from a bailout and the widespread

---

[12]The Dodd-Frank Act requires large financial institutions deemed systemically important to submit an orderly resolution plan each year. These plans, called "living wills," can run up to thousands of pages.

external effects of the failure of a large bank on the rest of the economy, which include lost jobs, lost income, and lost wealth. To complicate the issue, the Dodd-Frank Act does not include any objective thresholds or standards for living wills. For example, there is no consideration given to the conditions under which the bankruptcy plans must work: in the midst of an economic boom when the firm fails in isolation, or in the midst of a financial crisis when many firms fail collectively. These are two very different situations and require very different plans (McCloskey & Kupiec, 2014).

Table 2-1. *Goals and implementations made by the Dodd-Frank Act*

SIFIs			
Category	**Rules**	**Targeted Outcome**	**Implementation (as ofJune 2016)**
Milestones	Identification	Any financial intermediary that could pose a threat to U.S. financial stability, based on the size, interconnectedness, cross-jurisdictional activity, complexity and non-substitutability, or mix of its activities	Banks, insurance companies and FMU. Successful Metlife's challenge in 2014.
	Stress tests	Assess an institution capital plan and ability to continue providing financial services, without government assistance, following a specified shock	Only for banks
	Living wills	Plan on how a SIFI would resolve itself if it failed. Based on that knowledge and in case of failure, the government would use Orderly Liquidation Authority to dismantle the firm so its losses would not affect others	Only 1 bank
	Money market fund rules	Stress testing, disclosure, floating NAV, liquidity fee, and redemption gate	Conformance period ends on Oct. 14, 2016

(*continued*)

Table 2-1. (*continued*)

Derivatives Dealing/ Securitization Activities

Category	Rules	Targeted Outcome	Implementation (as ofJune 2016)
Milestones	Volker Rule	Prohibit entities holding customer deposits from engaging in speculative derivatives activity	Conformance period extended to July 21, 2017
	Derivatives Clearing Organization Rule	Standardized derivatives transactions must be centrally cleared	Effective in January 9, 2012. In July 7, 2012, two DCOs are denominated Systemically Important FMU
	Swaps-related rules for banks and nonbanks	Enhanced regulations and increased transparency of derivatives markets regarding trade reporting, capital, and margin requirements for non-centrally cleared derivatives, exchange of electronic platform, cross-border activities	Work in progress, with 1/3 remaining

Financial Stability and Systemic Risk monitoring

Category	Rules	Targeted Outcome	Implementation (as ofJune 2016)
Milestones	Enhanced Prudential Rules (liquidity, capital, leverage, concentration limits, risk management...)	Enhance the stability and resilience of SIFIs	Focus on banks, FMUs and money market funds
	Transparency and harmonization	Simplify the US financial regulatory system	FSOC, OFR

(*continued*)

Table 2-1. (*continued*)

Consumer and Investor Protection			
Category	**Rules**	**Targeted Outcome**	**Implementation (as of June 2016)**
Milestones	Investment Adviser Registration	To protect pensioners; requirement to make the data publicly available, even for exempt advisers, in order to increase transparency and access for prospective investors; created to promote clear information for consumers and protect them from unfair practices; promote fair, efficient, and innovative financial services for consumers; improve access to financial services.	Pension consultants now need to register with SEC
	Consumer Financial Protection Bureau		Home Mortgage Disclosure Act

Source: Dodd-Frank: Washington, "We Have a Problem," Lopez and Saeidinezhad (2016), Milken Institute

These shortcomings were discussed by Neel Kashkari, the new president of the Federal Reserve Bank of Minneapolis, in a recent speech (February 2016) at the Hutchings Center at the Brookings Institute. In the speech, Kashkari questioned the usefulness and effectiveness of the measures and tools currently at our disposal and enquired if they were sufficient to deal with a future crisis, especially since we have no idea about what form it could take. In this public discussion, he presented two scenarios:

Scenario One: Individual large bank runs into trouble while the rest of the economy is sound and strong.

Scenario Two: One or more banks run into trouble while there is broader weakness and risk in the global economy.

In Scenario One, as per Kashkari, the aforementioned measures would allow us to deal with the failure of an individual large bank without requiring a bailout, but we don't know that for certain as the work on these measures is far from complete (refer Table 2-1). For example: A review of the Living Wills show that they have significant shortcomings[13] and do not insure that the failure of a particular bank will not lead to massive fallout. Until this work is complete (which can be years from now), he states that we must acknowledge that the largest banks are TBTF, and expresses doubt regarding the efficacy of the measures, stating that we won't know how useful they are until we use them.

He further went on to state that the situation in case of the occurrence of Scenario Two was even more dire. As per the Dodd-Frank Act, regulators have inordinate control on the restructuring of companies if their Living Wills are deemed unfit, and can require

---

[13]On August 2014, the Federal Reserve and the Federal Deposit Insurance Corp. rejected the living wills of 11 of the biggest bank holding companies in the U.S.

an institution to restructure, raise capital, reduce leverage, divest, or downsize. Given the other external costs of the bailouts (job losses, lost income, and lost wealth), Kashkari states that no policy maker will advocate for large-scale firm restructuring, as this would adversely affect creditors and shareholders if these measures were deployed in a fragile and risky environment.

Based on his experience as a *"policy maker on the frontline responding to the financial crisis in 2008,"* Kashkari pushes for breaking up the large banks into smaller, less connected, less important entities. Based on the risks posed by TBTF, he states that large institutions ought to be treated with a legislation system that is akin to that of the rules that govern the operation of a nuclear power plant and pushes for treating large banks as public utilities by forcing them to hold so much capital that they virtually cannot fail. Lastly, he believes in taxing leverage throughout the financial system to reduce systemic risk.

Evidently, there are oppositions to these statements, as many regulators continue to sing the praises of the progress made in the last six years. Shortly after Kashkari's statements, Janet Yellen, the current chairman of the Federal Reserve, issued a statement that took a stance against the regional Federal bank president, stating, *"I certainly have not arrived at the conclusion that my colleague has…. I'm pleased with the way things are going"* (Heltman, 2016). Three months after Kashkari's speech, Ben Bernanke published a blog post titled "Ending 'too big to fail': What's the right approach?", in which the former two-term chairman of the Federal Reserve argued against major structural changes that forced the break-up of large firms, stating that large firms have cost advantages, greater diversification of risk, the ability to spread overhead costs over a variety of activities, and the capability to offer multiple interconnected products and services at a global scale. He went on to state, *"Even putting aside the short-term costs and disruptions that would likely be associated with breaking up the largest banks, in the long run a US financial industry without large firms would likely be less efficient, providing fewer services at higher cost. From a national perspective, this strategy could also involve ceding leadership in the industry, and the associated jobs and profits, to other countries"* (Bernanke, 2016). Kashkari riposted to these statements by questioning the cost-benefit trade-off and by asking if the benefits of scale of large banks outweigh the massive externalities of a widespread economic collapse.

All three central bankers cited above provide different levels of perspective on a singular issue. Nevertheless, they all agree that TBTF does pose systemic risks and has to be addressed. The point of divergence seems to be with regards to what is the optimal level of fragmentation that is needed for an economy to function efficiently while reducing systemic risk. Just as the last chapter raises the question of what is the optimal amount of debt that is acceptable to have, we are once again faced with a similar predicament with respect to what level of fragmentation is ideal for the spreading of risk in the economy?

It is important to underline the word "optimal" in the above statements. Judging an optimal level is a complex and complicated endeavor, given that markets are highly interconnected, densely opaque (shadow banking), and increasingly rarified. Often the blame is directed at regulators for not being able to determine what this optimal level is, even after almost a decade since the crisis. But given the challenges and limitations that befall regulators, maybe a different manner of looking at the subject is required in the search for answers.

Before we delve into the investigation of how to determine the optimal level, it is important for the reader to understand that there are reasons for taking a stance favoring the breaking of TBTF. However, this stance is not being taken in order to turn the readers' thinking towards a certain bias. It is being done in order to look at the conversation from a much-needed different point of view. This is because, first, we already have TBTF. So from an investigative perspective, it makes sense to explore the other extreme. Second, although Kashkari pushes for ending TBTF,[14] his arguments are grounded in legislation and are challenged by others who base their statements on past laurels. Hence, Kashkari's hypotheses need to be tested via the scientific method. Third, as it will be shown in the next sections of this chapter, the fragmentation is already underway, with and without the blessings of regulators.

With these tasks in hindsight, we can now go about the challenge of understanding the fragmenting of an industry. To help us understand whether there are structural benefits to the fragmentation, we will need to see if this has occurred in the past in other sectors, as this provides us with some frame of reference. To this purpose, Sidebar 2-1 summarizes a case-study done by the Deloitte University Press titled "From monopoly to competition," which showcases how fragmentation of the US telecommunications industry worked in increasing competition, quality, and efficiency of the market.

SIDEBAR 2-1: A CASE FOR FRAGMENTATION – ANALYSIS OF THE US TELECOM INDUSTRY

Source: "From monopoly to competition," Deloitte University Press, 2014

The US telecoms industry has largely existed as an oligopoly for the greater portion of its existence. For most of the first 100 years of its history, the industry was highly regulated and companies were required to submit capital plans for services or service extension to the regulatory bodies. The regulators generally chose the lowest investment option and then calculated appropriate phone prices to deliver the regulated return. As a result, investors were guaranteed a return, customers were guaranteed an affordable service, and the telecom employee was provided with fairly secure employment. Owing to this structure, investment decisions were influenced by what the regulator wanted and was not under the complete control of the provider. Thus, technological innovation stalled and new market entrants were few and far between.

However, in the mid-1980s, this began to change. In 1984, the Telecom giant, AT&T Corp., broke up and this opened up competition in the long-distance (IXC) market and the interstate and interexchange services. The IXCs moved from operating

---

[14]#EndingTBTF is an initiative propelled by Kashkari which, over the course of 2016, has invited researchers, academics, and policy makers to send their proposals on ending TBTF. Apart from accepting proposals all year round, the initiative also hosts quarterly symposiums, where selected submissions are presented and where experts debate the issue in roundtable conversations. The discussions and presentations are live-streamed and the research is accessible to all via the website https://www.minneapolisfed.org/publications/special- studies/endingtbtf. Kashkari intends to present the findings of this year-long event at the end of 2016.

in a complex and heavily regulated environment to market-based competition and pricing, although with extensive rules. As new technologies such as cable, satellite, data, and wireless entered the market, there was a growing need for specialization and expertise for each new wave of technology. As the industry now began looking at their market from the perspective of customer retention, the need to respond to demands led to increased competition. The passage of the 1996 Telecommunications Act was thus carried out in an attempt to slake this need.

The trifecta of new technological innovations, open competition, and a new way of looking at the market caused a change in the strategies of these players. While the past was strewn with the remains of price-cutting battles, the key innovators in this space realized that *cheaper before better* would not function as a long-term strategy. Hence, market innovators such as AT&T and Verizon began to pursue *better before cheaper* and *revenue before cost* strategies. In light of the spread of the Internet and the growing consumer demand for a feature-rich, multimedia TV, telephone, and Internet experience, this strategy paved the way for putting the customer first when developing a business plan. The dropping cost and the increased demands of consumers also led to the creation of new entrants who provided different services using a host of technologies.

Although AT&T and Verizon remain large market players, the telecommunications landscape no longer resembles what it was 30 years ago. Piggybacking on this growth model and the innovations of the Internet has created a vast and rich diaspora of companies that offer different services in different micro-segments and in different parts of the world. Think about Netflix, China Mobile, Airtel, Orange, T-Mobile, or Vodafone. All of these companies are less than 30 years old.

This is not to say that there is no concentration of power in this industry. Just as in TBTF, there are certain providers that have been in existence for a very long time and do extend a certain weight within the sector. However, with the entry of Google and Amazon (none of which are established as telecom firms), the telecommunications sector is again in a state of flux and the next mixture of *better before cheaper* and *revenue before cost* approaches will once again change the landscape of this dynamic industry.

The banking industry is certainly not the telecom industry, but it can be seen that their market structures certainly bear elemenets of commonality. In light of the above stated remarks and with a retrospective view of the lessons learned from the telecommunications sector, it is thus safe to say that the fragmentation of the financial markets is an objective worth pursuing. But owing to the breadth, depth, and extraordinary role that this sector plays in all aspects of business and the economy, it would be obtuse to believe that a "plug-and-play" approach would be satisfactory to breaking TBTF.

To come to a more logical conclusion about breaking TBTF, we first need to comprehend what forces are currently changing the makeup of the sector, and based on elements of commonality, what takeaways could be applied from the experiences other sectors. Second, we must determine why we are so fixated with a regulatory approach to changing the composition of the sector when most of the change today is occurring due to technology. Third, we need to ask ourselves that if we are going to undertake an endeavor which will have large-scale effects on society, should we follow the models of the past, or do we need to move our gaze from regulatory and historical analyses, to understanding the behavioral complexity of societal groups owing to the multiple spillover effects?

A New Way of Looking at Fragmentation

Is it not curious to note that the solutions being discussed with regards to TBTF are highly concentrated in the realm of regulations? Why is it that when we talk about the complexities of such socially intricate institutions that we do not use the research findings and lessons from group behaviors as seen in evolutionary biology or sociology? Would it not be prudent to take into consideration the lessons from the past with regards to how decisions are made in complex systems and then hunt for indications that the same conditions are being created in our ever-changing financial ecosystem? Is the realm of finance that different from other human intrinsic ecological systems?

The reason for this regulatory-centric approach to solving TBTF is certainly political in nature. But it also the result of how the centralization of banking structures has occurred over the past few centuries. From its infancy in the 17th century,[15] the banking system has been constructed around a central bank and second-range banks around it. As a result, the banking framework has grown as a structure of strong, hierarchical institutionalization, and the construction of these edifices has mobilized governments to create elaborate, regulated, banking frameworks. The irony of this structure is that while banks have fundamentally contributed to the development of democracies, they by themselves are least representative of this trait and the increasing liberty given to banks has resulted in them becoming more unequal (Ansart & Monvoisin, 2015), with only a handful of banks[16] being considered TBTF. As a result, any talk of fragmentation resonates with haunting tones of disestablishmentarianism.

But in light of the current inefficiencies, maybe what is truly required is a new way of looking at ending TBTF that is not regulatory in nature. As the arsenal of policy makers is increasingly tested, some recent studies now say that mainstream finance is acknowledging the existence of a world beyond equations and regulations and is moving towards behavioral finance (Davison, 2015). A recent comment by Andy Haldane, chief economist at the Bank of England, bolsters this statement: *"Truth be told, the workhorse model in economics and finance, God bless it, does come with some strong simplifying assumptions, some of which mean it's not often well-equipped to deal with situations of stress"* (Nordrum, 2016).

---

[15]The Swedish National Bank, or Riksbank, was created in 1668, followed by the creation of the Bank of England in 1694. This model has been replicated in most industrialized and developed nations since then.

[16]Of the 6,500 banks in the USA, only 25 have more than a $100 billion in assets (Better Markets, 2015).

Haldane made this statement in February 2016, shortly after the publication of an article (of which he is one of the co-authors) in the major scientific journal, *Science*. Having acknowledged the insufficiencies of current economic models, the authors, who are experts in finance, sociology, and physics, state that traditional economic theory could not explain, much less predict, the near-collapse of the financial system. The subjects of complexity economics and econophysics, (which will be analyzed in detail in the last chapter), offer regulators a host of insights. While terms and concepts such as tipping points, networks, contagion, feedback, and resilience have entered the financial and regulatory lexicon (Battiston et al., 2016), the learnings from these subjects are not being used when considering how to build a better model from an economic or regulatory standpoint.

For example, when talking about tipping points, the authors of the article state, *"Analyses of complex systems ranging from the climate to ecosystems reveal that, before a major transition, there is often a gradual and unnoticed loss of resilience. This makes the system brittle: A small disruption can trigger a domino effect that propagates through the system and propels it into a crisis state.... Markers include rising correlation between nodes in a network and rising temporal correlation, variance, and skewedness of fluctuation patterns. These indicators were first predicted mathematically and subsequently demonstrated experimentally in real complex systems, including living systems.*

A recent study of the Dutch interbank network showed that standard analysis using a homogeneous network model could only lead to late detection of the 2008 crisis, although a more realistic and heterogeneous network model could identify an early warning signal 3 years before the crisis. Ecologists have developed tools to quantify the stability, robustness, and resilience of food webs and have shown how these depend on the topology of the network and the strengths of interactions. Epidemiologists have tools to gauge the potential for events to propagate in systems of interacting entities, to identify superspreaders and core groups relevant to infection persistence, and to design strategies to prevent or limit the spread of contagion."

With this introductory analogy to natural ecosystems and the functioning of networks, the article goes into deeper detail to showcase how the current network topology of systemically important banks and the systemic risk tied to the interconnectedness between banks could lead to the collapse of the global financial network *even if* individual banks seem to appear safe.

This is because, first, the banking network consists of a number of banks that have relatively similar business and risk models and whose defaults tend to be highly correlated. Banks realize that in a situation of distress, they are underwritten and likely to be supported by the United States government and the governments of Europe (Freeman, 2011). As a result, they tend to structure themselves along similar lines and this causes a herd mentality that reduces the diversity of behavior, notably when dealing with risk.

Second, there is information asymmetry within the banking networks as banks do not share their information with each other. Thus the tools, such as the aforementioned stress tests and Living Wills, being developed to reconstruct the network and estimate systemic risk, are done using partial amounts of publicly available information. These tests would be greatly improved if the banks publicly reported more data and informed us of their connections with other banks. But it is not the case today. As stated by hedge-fund manager Paul Singer, *"The opacity of financial institution financial statements has not been addressed or changed at all... Rumor and feeling is all you have. You don't know the financial condition of [Citigroup], JPMorgan, Bank of America, any of them... We have a very large analytical research effort here and we have not found anybody that can parse the sensitivity of big banks to changes in interest rates, asset prices, and the like. You can't do it"* (Freeman, 2011).

Coupled with these limitations is the fragility caused by individual nodes. The complexity article goes on the state that *"systemic repercussions of the failure of individual nodes...shows that the issue of too-central-to-fail may be more important than too-big-to-fail"* (Battiston et al., 2016).

Hence, although Kashkari and others who are pushing for the end of TBTF are right in generating scenarios, what needs to be done is to think about the concept of ending too big to fail from a more multidisciplinary perspective. Using the scientific methods cited in the aforementioned article would not only give the regulators the ability to simulate more scenarios, but would also help answer the questions of those critics who have defended the current structure of the financial system under the pretext of advantages offered by economies of scale.

The concept of fragmentation by itself is thus worthy of deep exploration, for if we are to legitimize the breaking up of banks, then it becomes mandatory to determine whether larger or smaller groups function better in an interconnected economy. Without this understanding, we have no logical ground to justify fragmenting an institution that is a societal functionary and even less chance of determining what is the optimal threshold of fragmentation.

To find a response to the optimal threshold of fragmentation, we first turn our attention to the pith and marrow of what the banking network is. When boiled down to its essence, the network is essentially a large group of individuals who are collaborating with each other for maximising individual benefit and curtailing risk. When looked at from this perspective, the question then becomes how group behaviors—such as collective actions or decision making—are done, based on experience and how these behaviors emerge and persevere in an evolving system.

Thankfully, research from the field of evolutionary biology offers us a response to these questions. In another recent paper published in *Nature* titled "*Small Groups and long memories promote cooperation,*" researchers show that wherever social interactions play a part, organisms behave differently depending on their social environment and their past experience. By developing a framework that looks at the evolution of multiple players exchanging "public goods," the researchers demonstrated that when groups were small, longer memory strategies made cooperation easier to evolve, as they allowed for an increase in the number of ways cooperation could be stabilized until a point of optimal stability was reached. By exploring the co-evolution of behavior and memory,[17] they found that that even when memory had a cost, longer-memory strategies often evolved, which in turn drove the evolution of cooperation, even when the benefits for cooperation were low (Stewart & Plotkin, 2016).

---

[17]It is the relationship between memory and cooperation that needs to be looked at as a focal point, since it is relevant to our thesis. Owing to the fanfare that has been given to Blockchain over the past few years, most of us are already aware of its immutability features. Once a transaction has been performed, there is no way to reverse it and the Blockchain stores every transaction that has been performed on it since its inception. The next section of this chapter will explain the technical underpinnings of this technology. For now, just keep this in mind and try to connect the dots as we attempt to form a train of thought that is truly multidisciplinary in essence.

The reason for citing the findings from evidently different disciplines of study is because they offer problem-solving approaches when we think about fragmentation. Moreover, the findings from the *Science* and *Nature* journals are industry- and technology-agnostic. For example, as we saw in Sidebar 2-1, the US telecommunications industry went through a series of transformations that changed the way the industry defined itself. All of these changes involved the entry of new players, old players redefining their business model, introduction of new technology, and the removal of monopolies. Over the past 30 years, as competition and openness increased, not only did the sector see a myriad of new entrants, but in terms of services offered, it cannot even be compared to what it was before. From the days of dial-up Internet access, the industry has grown to offer free encrypted texts (WhatsApp) and free calls (Skype). The change has not only resulted in creating metrics-saturated, hyper-efficient business models, but it has led to a change in the mindset of society. Ask a teenager to surrender their smartphone for a day and watch the symptoms of a panic attack set in.

Thus fragmentation does seem to be the antidote to the current economic malaise. It might be argued that based on the opinions of certain academics, business magnates, and policy makers, there is no certainty that breaking up the banks will save us. But much in the same way that technology feeds on technology to create new technology, the introduction of an unfamiliar concept is bound to raise doubts. Hence, it is important to recognize and acknowledge that some readers might find this intermixing of findings from other subjects unsubstantiated and divergent from the subject at hand. But this is exactly the point of this book. In light of the inefficiencies and ineptitude of regulatory filibusters, what is needed is a new way to look at the question of fragmenting TBTF.

If this by itself is not enough reason to support the fragmentation argument, then there is one final reason worth considering: With the advent of technological progress and increasing support for entrepreneurial initiatives, the fragmentation of the financial sector is already underway. You may have heard of this fragmentation is less sinister terms… In today's popular culture it is goes under the aliases of FinTech or Blockchain.

Sharding

In early 2015, at the World Economic Forum in Davos, the current governor of the Bank of England, Mark Carney, told a room full of the most influential voices in business and economics that we're now looking at "*an Uber-type situation*" for banking (Edwards, 2015).

Carney, who is Canadian in origin, is a person worth listening to not only because of his past achievements in the private sector,[18] but also because he is in a truly unique position today. As the 120th governor of the UK's Central Bank, he had to act quickly to stem the panic in the aftermath of Brexit, Britain's referendum vote to leave the European Union. The list of challenges he faces today is intimidating: he needs to preserve London's position as a global financial hub, prevent a downward spiral of lack of market confidence following Brexit, equalize the UK's economy, avoid making a recession a depression, and continue to fan the flames of entrepreneurship in the City, the financial district of

---

[18]Mark Carney started his career in Goldman Sacks.

London. In regular circumstances, a central bank governor would be content to take on one or two of these objectives. So to say that he has a full plate is an understatement.

A little over a year after his speech at Davos, Carney once again made some thought-provoking remarks at a speech given on the 16th of June, 2016 at the Lord Mayor's Banquet for Bankers and Merchants of the City of London.[19] In his speech, titled "Enabling the FinTech transformation: Revolution, Restoration, or Reformation?", Carney went on to state that FinTech and Blockchain could transform the global financial system and UK economy. Here below are a few extracts from his speech, which shed light on his vision of the future and which, coincidently, also touch upon a few topics discussed previously in this book:

- *"FinTech...will change the nature of money,[20] shake the foundations of central banking, and deliver nothing less than a democratic revolution for all who use financial services."*

- *"FinTech [has the] potential to deliver a great unbundling of banking into its core functions of settling payments, performing maturity transformation, sharing risk, and allocating capital. This would mean revolution, fundamentally reshaping the financial system."*

- *"...Some financial technologies could make incumbent banks more efficient and profitable, reinforcing existing economies of scale and scope in banking. This would mean a restoration, reinforcing incumbents' power."*

- *"The balance of these forces may yield a third alternative—a reformation—a more diverse, resilient, and effective system for consumers. One where large banks exist alongside new entrants who compete across the value chain."*

The speech goes on to describe five steps that will be put in place simultaneously over the course of the year to enable the FinTech transformation of banking. These steps include the testing of new proofs of concept, the use of a distributed ledger, and the launch of a FinTech accelerator which will help boost the partnership between the Bank and selected FinTech companies. The point of displaying excerpts of Carney's speech is not just to show his forward thinking mentality or his vision of the future of finance. It is to show that the fragmentation of banking is already underway in the more subtle and decorous guise of technological change.

FinTech is short form for Financial Technology. Over the greater part of the past decade, new technology firms have been able to leverage digital technology to develop financial services and banking products that are more customer-oriented, cost less to

---

[19]The speech was given at the Mansion House, London. A full copy of the speech can be found at: http://www.bankofengland.co.uk/publications/Documents/speeches/2016/speech914.pdf

[20]Said in reference to the balance between inside money (created by commercial banks) and outside money (created by central banks)

deliver, and which are native to digital networks. As these players are less fraught by stringent regulatory compliance, which banks are subject to, they have greater space to move in specific markets. Unburdened by complex and complicated legacy information systems, they have a greater degree of technological flexibility, which makes them more adaptable to changes in markets. Being small in size, they generally focus on a single product or service and place the emphasis on customer ease of use. Lastly, they are more in tune with the peer-to-peer (P2P) culture that has formatted the social media generation in the past decade. The result of their flexibility, low costs, and user-focused strategies have resulted in rapid popularity, staggering successes, and immense growth.

Globally, investment in FinTech ventures climbed to $22.3 billion in 2015, up from $1.8 billion in 2010 and $12.6 billion in 2014 (Accenture report, 2016). 2016 may hold greater promise, though, as Fintech investments in Q1 2016 surged 67% compared to the same period in 2015, to reach US$5.3 billion (Fintech Innovation report, 2016). The first quarter of 2016 saw thirteen rounds of VC funding to FinTech companies that crossed the $50 million mark, a slight rise from the ten rounds of similar amounts that were seen in the fourth quarter of 2015 (KPMG report, 2016). Moreover, the growth is global. While North America leads the way, Asia (notably China) and Europe are increasing VC funding into this space (see figures 2-3 and 2-4).

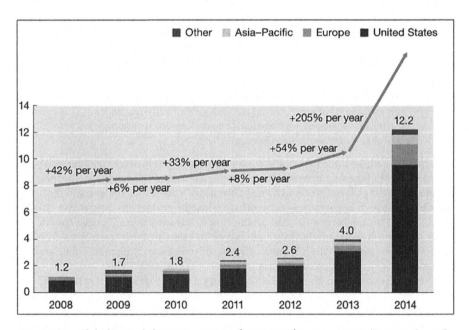

Figure 2-3. *Global Fintech financing activity (2008–2014) Image source: "Cutting through the noise around financial technology," McKinsey (2016). Data source: CB Insights*

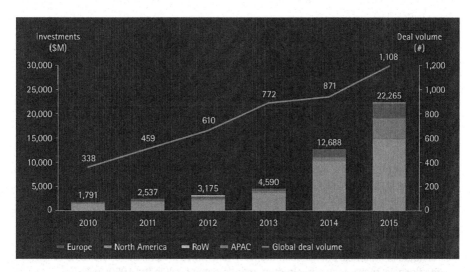

Figure 2-4. *Global Fintech financing activity (2010–2015) Image source: "Fintech and the evolving landscape: landing points for the industry," Accenture (2016). Data source: CB Insights*

The reason for this widespread investment is because of the widespread impacts in a variety of financial services. FinTech inventions are affecting services such as lending, payments, asset management, transactions, capital markets, trade finance and even insurance. The Blockchain can also be roped into this basket case as it is fundamentally a technology that is native to the exchange of value. But for the case of simplicity, we will consider it separately, owing to its uniqueness.

As it can be imagined, this level of investment has also generated curiosity at different levels of business and academia. My first piece work on the Blockchain was put online in 2014. Since that time, there have been over fifty books, just in the English language, published on FinTech and Blockchain. Try conducting a search on Amazon with the keywords "FinTech" or "Blockchain" and observe the results. It would be pointless to even try and count the number of blog posts on these subjects over this time period. Even on a single platform such as LinkedIn Pulse, the results are too many to count. Coupled with the innumerable conferences, speeches, and round-tables, it is almost impossible for a researcher with my qualifications to come up with an original text on the subject that mentions some technical point about these topics that has not been mentioned before.

It is for these reasons that it is not the primary goal of this book to explain these technologies in a granular level of detail. As most of the books published today focus on the applications of the technology, they explain the technical underpinnings in incredible detail and offer sharp business insights based on decades of specialist acumen. Thus, rewriting a text on these subjects would be repeating the same endeavor with negligible marginal utility. As we are more focused on the implications of this technology from a macroeconomic context, we shall stick to this objective.

Nevertheless, prior to understanding the implications, we ought to have a quick revision on the current usages of these technologies. Sidebars 2-2 and 2-3 provide brief notes on FinTech and Blockchain, respectively, and showcase the reason why they are bringing about a revolution in the industry. For those readers looking to gain more specific technical knowledge, a list of recommended books worth consideration is provided in the notes section at the end of this chapter.

SIDEBAR 2-2: FINTECH – A BRIEF YET EFFERVESCENT HISTORY

FinTech represents the merging of finance and technology to form advanced solutions in the financial services industry. This phenomenon is nothing new. Since the advent of the digital age, banks and entrepreneurs have systematically updated or created business models in order to adapt to the new behaviors and demands of their clients.

As noted in an article published in the *New York Times* in April, 2016, the roots of the financial technology infrastructure were created back in the 1950s with the introduction of the modern-day credit card (Zimmerman, 2016). As the sixties rolled in, ATMs were introduced by Barclays and the global telex network was established, which later went on to become the Clearing House Interbank Payments System (CHIPS). As banks and companies began to trade faster, the seventies saw the birth of NASDAQ. As the eighties rolled in, we bore witness to E-Trade, which allowed for electronic trading, and the introduction of online banking in Britain. In the 2000s, the Internet led to the creation of PayPal and eBay, with the latter part of the decade seeing the nascence of bitcoin and the entry of startups and non-financial companies, such as Google, into the world of finance.

Today, FinTech continues to affect a number of financial services, owing to advances in computing, automation, encryption and, most importantly, customer focus. Having being suffocated by the tyranny of a "one size fits all" approach, consumers today pine for personalised experiences which offer security, transparency, and interoperability. FinTech offers a refreshing buffet of options in this respect by mixing and matching technologies to client needs. As a result of this convergence of technology, gauging its effect necessitates the development of a certain sectorial taxonomy to define the assembly lines of technologies that are currently blazing these sectors.

1. Payments

Stance: Customer-facing

Main technologies: Big Data, Biometrics, Digital Wallets, Mobile Apps, NFC, Platforms

They key word to be kept in mind with regards to payments and FinTech is "cashless," which is a subject we discuss in Chapter 3. Over the past five years, mobile devices and connectivity have been leveraged to increase payment simplicity, while digital wallets and automated machine-to-machine payments offer more value to customers. As Near Field Communication (NFC) gains popularity, owing to its ease of use, credit cards are getting gradually obsolete. Google Wallet and Apple Pay offer digital wallets on platforms which allow users to connect multiple cards to them (eight for Apple Pay, unlimited for Google Wallet). Apps like Walla.by help clients make the right decision on which card to use, thus helping them save money by optimizing preferences.

Payment platforms also allow clients to make bank account-funded transactions instead of credit card-funded transactions. While this affects the transaction fees earned by card providers, it is cheaper for both clients and merchants, as there are higher service charges on credit card-funded transactions. The platforms also provide merchants with access to client data, which can be harnessed for customised offerings via big data analyses. Biometric identification is also providing clients with better security by allowing them to authenticate mobile payments by scanning their face with a smartphone, a.k.a. a selfie! (e.g., Alibaba's Smile to Pay). Remittances is an area where innovation is also being seen in terms of street-smartness. As per a 2015 World Bank report, around two billion adults are still unbanked. These individuals are hence obliged to use private remittances networks (e.g., Western Union) in order to send and receive payments from abroad, which can be extremely expensive. For example: When sending money to some countries, remittance fees can go up to 30% of the sum being sent. Astute solutions offered by M-Pesa and Transferwise are removing these barriers by offering very low fees, less forex risk, a high amount of transparency and ease of use, as users can send and receive money with a mobile app. This is adversely affecting the business models of the incumbents. We will come back to payments and remittances when discussing Blockchain.

Advantages: customized engagement, higher security, transparency, speed, and lower costs. Risks: unestablished standards, regulation, and data privacy

2. Lending

Stance: Customer-facing, B2B

Main technologies: P2P platforms, Big Data, Mobile Banks, Machine Learning, AI.

Since the crisis, owing to stricter regulations and changes in business models, retail banks have developed lower risk appetites and limited access to lending, especially for sub-prime borrowers. This has been counter-balanced by the growth of alternative lending platforms that are based on P2P models. By using automated processes, big data-based risk assessment methods, and real-time analyses, these new entrants are increasingly gaining market share in a sector that was previously the exclusive purview of commercial banks.

These online P2P (P2P) lending platforms have led to the rise of crowdfunding platforms which provide customers low-cost, fast, flexible, and more customer-oriented alternatives to mainstream retail banking. While they use similar advanced adjudication methods and streamlined processes, the business models of these alternative lenders varies as per the clientele. As a result, the diversity of business models distributes the risk of borrowing. This is contrary to what is seen in traditional bank lending, in which banks have relatively similar models. For example: Companies like Funding Circle and Lending Club create P2P online marketplaces which use client data to offer multiple value propositions and matching strategies, reducing the cost of funding in the process. Using multiple sources of data, Kabbage analyzes banking information along with the size, volume, and the reputation of a business (via social media transcripts) to calculate a risk score in real time. Using this methodology, they can offer SME's loans of up to $100,000 within six minutes of creating an account. Using lean, automated transparent processing and more accurate underwriting, they are challenging incumbents on the basis of speed and ease of access to capital. As a result, large banks are now partnering with these new entrants in order to regain market share in specific demographies (especially in the market of short- and medium-term loans).

Advantages: easier and faster access to funds, less red tape, transparency, reputation awareness, and appropriate matching of risk based on client segment diversity

Risks: reputational risks (right to be forgotten, unestablished standards, regulation, and data privacy

3. Investment Management

Stance: Customer-facing

Main technologies: Big Data, Machine Learning, Trading Algorithms, Social Media, Robo-Advisory, AI, Natural Language Processing (NLP), Cloud Computing.

One of the most adverse outcomes of the crisis was its impact on wealth management: banks suffered a loss of trust, while potential clients now required higher amounts of capital in order to invest. As wages stagnated and employment slowed, it became increasingly difficult for new investors to invest smaller sums of money. Since 2008, a growing number of automated wealth management services (also known as robo-advisory) have arisen to provide low-cost, erudite alternatives to traditional wealth management.

By using data models and trading algorithms that are trained on large amounts of stock and market data, companies such as Betterment and Wealthfront provide automated analysis and personalised portfolio management. For example: Wealthfront not only helps investors set up a portfolio with $5,000, but also sends notifications informing the users about changes in personal tax payments when the value of their portfolio changes (Johns, 2015). Along with these platforms, websites such as StockTwits and Covestor allow investors to share their opinions and gain market insights from experts and other investors. Websites like Quantopian and Algofast also allow users to effortlessly build, test, and execute trading algorithms even if they have no technical knowledge and infrastructure. They also allow seasoned investors to manage other investors' investments for a fee, thus leveraging the power of the crowd. By catering to customers who are less affluent than the clients traditionally sought by wealth managers, these new firms are providing accessibility and low cost bespoke services to a broader customer base.

Increasingly, these firms are also taking over core businesses of incumbent institutions. Using refined algorithms, they are automating the large-scale management of multiple portfolios even at the decision making level. For example: Companies like Ayasdi and Kensho use data to draw out correlations and outliers in markets. These results are then analysed by an AI and used to create hypotheses, develop trading strategies, and automatically model investment scenarios. As the operating processes of these companies are almost completely digital in nature, firms such as FundApps have arisen to provide regulatory information via a cloud-based managed service in machine readable language. This allows these firms to adapt faster to changing regulations in the sector. We will touch upon this topic again when discussing smart contracts.

Previously, portfolio management and scenario generation required the employment of senior-level executives. However, the automation of these tasks has encouraged incumbents to switch to these services, raising questions on the future landscape of the sector. As stated by Daniel Nadler, CEO of Kensho, at a Milken conference (2016), *"It's not just associates and VPs … [it's] also the thousands of software engineers [at banks] …. Those jobs are going to get decimated, literally."*

Advantages: greater inclusion, increased competition, data standardization

Risks: compliance costs, regulation blocks risk monitoring, and technological unemployment

4. Capital Markets

Stance: Business-facing

Main technologies: Trading Algorithms, Big Data, Neural Nets, Machine/Deep Learning, AI

If we were to increase the scale, speed, and volume of the transactions and services stated in the private wealth management industry, we would find ourselves in the high-frequency trading (HFT) world of capital markets, which encompasses the trade and management of private equity, commodities, and derivatives. HFT has been in place since the early 1990s. By building trading strategies that respond extremely fast to market events, high-frequency traders created faster price discovery and liquidity ratios in markets.

This is done because fast reaction to market events can alleviate risks inherent to fluctuations in the value of a trader's position (inventory risk), and reduce the risk of trading with better-informed investors (trading at "stale" quotes). This also allowed traders to take positions in anticipation of future price movements ("directional" strategy) and provided arbitrage opportunities between related assets. However, since the crisis, lower volatility, improved liquidity, rising costs of trading infrastructure, and regulatory scrutiny have declined the profitability of HFT, while dislocations such as the 2010 flash crash, the 2014 treasury flash crash, and the 2015 ETF flash crash have declined the popularity of HFT.

In light of these shortcomings, FinTech firms using algorithmic trading strategies with smarter and faster machines are changing the market structure in terms of volume, liquidity, volatility, and spread of risk. Companies such as Neuro Dimension conduct technical analysis with AI (using neural networks and genetic algorithms) to "learn" patterns from historical data. They then optimise the power of big data by combining search data with multiple macroeconomic factors and quantified news insights to calculate potential upside/downside scenarios. With the aid of machine learning algorithms and prescriptive analytics, these scenarios are then tested and self- corrected updates are used to continuously improve trading strategies with minimal human interaction. These companies are also capable of capturing buy and sell signals by datamining feeds from social media outlets like Twitter, although this has led to some complications in the past. In April 2013, a false report of explosions at the White House was posted on the hacked Twitter account of the Associated Press. As algorithmic traders' systems are linked to key Twitter feeds, it caused a selling spree that led to $136 billion being wiped out from the S&P 500 index within two minutes of the tweet's posting.

As seen in wealth management, the involvement of humans in the overall trading process is decreasing as machines automate a wide range of core activities from hypothesizing to decision making (WEF, 2015). As trading algorithms become more intelligent, the breadth and accuracy of their analyses will expand, and could result in a convergence toward a single view of the market. The increased infrastructure costs could also wedge a gap between trading institutions and individual investors as information barriers begin to be mounted.

As technology continues to trailblaze this sector of finance, the onus falls on the development of regulation that can target specific strategies that curtail risk and freak events, rather than fast trading in general. We will touch upon to this sector when we discuss the applications of smart contracts.

Advantages: more entrants via economies of scale, higher liquidity, increased data feeds, standardization of data, improved price discovery and price accuracy, transparency, speed, and lower costs

Risks: false signals, convergence of strategies, higher barriers of entry, more suffocating regulation, data integrity, technological unemployment

5. Insurance

Stance: Customer-facing

Main technologies: Biometrics, Big Data, IoT, Sensors, Machine Learning

One of the recent sectors to be engulfed by the FinTech wave is the gargantuan insurance sector (Global life insurance premiums: $2.7 trillion, Global non-life insurance premiums: $1.4 trillion, Source: CB Insights, 2016), which has led to the coining of the term "InsurTech." As autonomous cars become a reality, the data that can now be acquired from IoT sensors and telematics is changing the way insurance plans are made. Previously insureds had few options when it came to an insurance plan. But with the rise of granular levels of personal data provided from a whole range of sensors in houses, cars, FitBits, and other everyday objects, new entrants are proposing insurance plans that are customised to the lifestyle and risks of the client. Discovery, a South African insurance company, uses data that comes in from fitness monitors and constructs a business offer based on that. Clients are motivated to form healthy habits as they receive premium discounts as their fitness improves.

P2P and micro insurance are also scaling thanks to FinTech. P2P insurance has always existed to a certain extent in the form of mutuals, fraternal benefit societies, reciprocal inter-insurance exchanges, etc…. But new platforms bring a wider range of parties together online and tailor insurance products to meet individual needs. As insureds deal with other peers, the risk of false claims is reduced owing to the reputation in the entourage. This kind of model also allows for risk-pooling: Friendsurance allows people to insure one another for home contents, private liability, and legal expenses, while offering a cash-back bonus of up to 40% of premiums for participants who remain claimless. Another example is Guevara, which organizes like-minded auto insureds into P2P groups. These platforms also provide the ability to purchase episodic insurance which is valid for small units of time, e.g., while skydiving.

We will touch upon the insurance industry when we discuss the Blockchain and the applications being developed with smart contracts in unison with IoT.

Advantages: customized contracts, P2P models, micro-payment models and lower premiums

Risks: KYC, fraudulent claims, long-term risk pooling, complication of underwriting process, and new regulations

SIDEBAR 2-3: BLOCKCHAIN – A SKELETON KEY OF SORTS

So much has been published about the Blockchain that writing about it today has been reduced to syllable adjectives. What is the Blockchain? A ledger, a data repository, a value transfer mechanism, a decentralized network, or the setting stone of a new vision of capitalism? It is all of this, but it can be less or more depending on the context for, as we will see, context matters.

Blockchain is at the forefront of today's technological and financial innovation with pulpits prophesizing its creation being equivalent to the invention of the Internet. This is amusing to hear, as the history of the technology behind the Blockchain goes back well before the publication of Satoshi's paper in October 2008, and is intimately linked with the technology of the Internet.

In 1974 Vint Cerf and Robert Khan created the TCP/IP protocol as a way to time-share the use of the ARPANet hardware architecture. A protocol is like manners. When we say *"Thank you"* to someone, the normal response we expect to hear is *"You're welcome."* There is no rule that states that someone has to do this, but it remains a protocol of communication that is commonly followed. In the same vein, TCP/IP was developed as a way for any computer to connect and communicate with the ARPANet. More importantly, by using data packet-switching, Cerf and Khan had found a way to eliminate a single point of failure. As there were many computers attached to the network (the ARPANet), a message could be broken into pieces and sent via various channels. If one of the computers was not connected to the network, the message could still be sent via the other computers. This distributed task-management and communication system is the basis of today's decentralized ledgers.

Based on the fundamental principles of packet-switching and a protocol for decentralized communication, other protocols like HTTP, SMTP and VoIP were developed for specific communication purposes. As protocols evolved, they went on to create a digital, decentralized, and distributed environment that was fertile for innovation. Tim Berners-Lee's invention of the World Wide Web led to the creation of the Internet which changed the way we work and live.

As email (based on SMTP) became the preferred medium of communication, malicious agents created other inventions such as spam email and malware. Thankfully, Adam Back was there for the rescue. Malware and spam email are predicated on economies of scale. If sending spam email becomes too much of an investment, in terms of time or money, then it would not make any economic sense to do it. Using this commonsensical approach, Back created "proof of work," which was essentially a way of providing evidence to show that some computational effort was actually undertaken in order to send a particular email. Today, we see the use of Back's idea almost every day when we use CAPTCHA's or drag a slider or tick a box that says, "I'm not a robot." All of these actions are extensions of proof of work.

As the Internet started to enter every aspect of life and work, it also created a strange dichotomy with money. Although we could communicate in a decentralized way, we could not yet exchange value in a decentralized way. Banks were able to adapt their systems to this technology, but they remained as gatekeepers between two exchanging parties and charged us fees for their services.

This is not to say that the banks were mere functionaries in regimenting our affairs. The main purpose of the bank was to do two things: first, ensure that there was no double spend, and second, maintain a continuously updated ledger that detailed what was going on.

The first function is something that is truly the crux of the raison d'être of the blockchain. When an individual sends an email or a message to another person, there is nothing that stops them from copying and sending the same message to other recipients. However, if we were to do the same thing with money, it would be a big problem. When an individual sends a sum of money to another person, it is extremely important that it is this specific sum and not a digital copy of this sum that is sent. If we did not have a ledger that accounted for all the transfers that were being done and a way of measuring the total withdrawals and transfers going and coming to an account, then there would be no order or meaning to the exchange of value. This is primarily what the banks are doing and the reason we pay them fees. When a person wishes to send money electronically, the bank acts as a gatekeeper, who verifies that they can make the transfer of the desired sum and ensures that the account shows the true value of what is left in the account after the transfer has been made.

What Satoshi described in his paper was a way of working around this. Rather than using a bank and depending on their regulations and limitations to send and receive money, Satoshi created a value exchange protocol. Much like in the same way that TCP/IP breaks down a message and sends it to a recipient using the other nodes connected in the network, Satoshi devised a way that allowed for the same process to occur with a new value-exchange protocol.

Rather than depending on a bank, Satoshi proposed that we use the other nodes who are part of this value exchange network, which he called bitcoin. By harnessing the lessons learned from Back's proof of work and using the developments in cryptography and encryption, Satoshi created the bitcoin network which was essentially a peer-to-peer payment network. Specific users called "miners" would voluntarily participate to verify transactions when two counter-parties in the network decided to exchange funds (in this case Bitcoin). The way that this would work was genius in its ingenuity. The following points break down the process in a simplistic manner (*For a more technical understanding, refer the technical books cited in the notes at the end of this chapter*):

- Persons wanting to transact using this network would first need to create a wallet. This is akin to creating an account on a particular website. This can be done individually or via a wallet provider, based on the kind of role a person wishes to play in the network. Companies such as Coinbase simplify the wallet creation process and help individuals create wallets securely and within the norms of regulations: sign up, present the necessary documentation (such as passport/driving licence), take a picture, and presto…you now have a bitcoin wallet. Funds can then be added to the wallet via a regular banking account or from other bitcoin wallets.

- When a member of the network decides to send funds, they would follow a procedure similar to signing a check, except here the signing is done by using public and private keys. A public key is like an email address. A user would share it with others to send and receive emails, or in this case money. The private key is like the email password. It's what is used to "sign" the check when making a transfer. The keys are mathematically linked based on elliptical curve cryptography (ECC). Essentially they cannot be forged owing to this link (*Both Andreas Antonopoulos's and Pedro Franco's books provide excellent explanations of how ECC works*).

- For a transfer to occur, the sender would need to create a transaction in which they detail their address (public key), the recipients address (their public key), and the amount being sent. Once these details have been entered, the sender would then "sign" the transaction with their private key and the transaction is emitted to the bitcoin network.

- It is here that the miners come into play. Participants who are willing to act as miners have a dual role to play. First, they validate the transaction. As the transactions are signed with the mathematically linked keys, the miners can verify this transaction by using their computer hardware to do mathematical calculations. In this way, they confirm transactions and allocate the sum transferred to the recipients address. Second, after having done the transaction, they include the record of this transaction onto the Blockchain, which is the network's distributed ledger.

- The reason the ledger is called a blockchain is because every time a transaction is validated, it is added to a "block" that contains other transactions that have occurred recently. When the block reaches a certain size, it is compressed and added to the ledger, which consists of other older blocks. This process of adding a block to the previous blocks is based on the Proof of Work concept. It shows that the miner has done the necessary work to add this block to the existing blocks.

- The blocks are linked to one another with a time stamp. This is done for security purposes, as if a malicious network member wanted to change the address of a transaction to their address; then not only would they need to change the time details of the said transaction, but also every other transaction in the previous blocks. This is what gives the blockchain its superior security: it is immutable. It is also the reason that it is called the blockchain, for it is a series of blocks of transactions that are linked one after another.

- This ledger holds a record of every transaction ever done on the network and it is shared with the network, i.e., anyone who is part of the network can see the information in this ledger. Miners who do these two functions—verifying the transaction and recording it on the blockchain—are then rewarded with bitcoins for their effort. This is how bitcoins are "mined." Since the number of bitcoins is fixed to 21 million, it is like mining the bitcoins out of a reservoir. Hence the term miner.

Although these series of operations seem relatively straightforward, they include elements of cryptography, computer science, game theory, and classical economics. The above breakdown is certainly not enough to pierce the complexities of how blockchains work, but is portrays how this decentralized and distributed value exchange system works. More importantly, it helps us realize that the for the first time since the inception of banking, we now have a system to help us transact without the aid of banks.

Just as TCP/IP led to the creation of more subject-specific protocols, the advent of bitcoin has led to the creation of other value exchange protocols. Some of these differ in terms of the currency being used, while others differ in terms of how the validation process occurs. This is what has led to the creation of private and public blockchains.

It is reasonable to accept that not everyone would be thrilled to learn that some anonymous "miner" is verifying their transfers and playing a role in their financial dealings. As financialization is a cultural as well as an economic entity, individuals have developed trust relationships with large institutions. Furthermore, when a corporation or a business performs some consumer-unfriendly act, the aggrieved can pursue legal justification in order to set the matter straight.

These ponderations led to the creation of public and private blockchains. While a public blockchain, like bitcoin, is accessible to all, a private blockchain offers a degree of exclusivity. In a private blockchain, a financial institution (for example) could create a blockchain in which the miners are known, trusted, and vetted. As these blockchains are more reflective of the current financial system, a large number of financial institutions are keen on creating and using them. The recent R3 partnership (composed of 46 financial institutions as of June 2016), showcases the extent to which large institutions are seriously dwelling on the use of blockchains.

Smart Contracts

One of the most dynamic occurrences in the past few years has been the development of Apps. An App functions in very simple way: it is a piece of code that reacts to a certain input to provide the user with a certain output. Press this button on the screen and you are taken to a website or you can call an Uber to come pick you up where you stand. Apps use the information that is being exchanged on the protocol on which they run to perform these activities and deliver these outputs.

A smart contract, according to Ethereum's founder, Vitalik Buterin, *"is a computer program that directly controls some digital asset."* Smart Contracts are essentially the same as Apps, except they perform a different kind of automation. While the traditional Apps available on a Google Play Store or Apple App Store are useful for certain operations, Smart Contracts function as Apps that perform value exchange operations when they receive a certain input. Just as the blockchain is a digitally native protocol that is designed for value exchange, Smart Contracts are native to the Blockchain and perform value exchange operations based on the input signals that they receive from the Blockchain. This is currently one of the explosive areas of innovation and protocols developed by platforms like Ethereum are allowing the large scale deployment of Smart Contracts.

Whereas a traditional legal contract defines the rules regarding an agreement between multiple counter-parties, Smart Contracts go further and actually administer those rules by controlling the transfer of money or assets under precise conditions. Using Smart Contracts, an asset or currency is transferred into a program *"and the program runs this code and at some point it automatically validates a condition and it automatically determines whether the asset should go to one person or back to the other person, or whether it should be immediately refunded to the person who sent it or some combination thereof,"* (Buterin, 2016). Just as traditional legal contracts are standardized, smart contracts can be standardized as templates that users can choose based on the type of operation they want to automate. These operations can include real estate exchanges, automobile purchases, or even for making insurance payments. It is the ability to decentralize and automate these operations that makes Blockchain a technological skeleton key.

For example, in Sidebar 2-2, we had read about the rise of P2P micro insurance. Using the Blockchain, insurance firms can add the ability to efficiently bring a wider range of parties together online to tailor an insurance product to meet individual needs and reliably and transparently record the transaction. With the use of smart contracts, the firm can then automatically enforce and fulfill the obligations of the parties when the conditions of the contract are met. As a smart contract provides the ability to program a contract, payouts between parties can be made once certain criteria have been met, without involving a middleman. This could also be triggered from input signals that come from IoT devices that are used by the insureds. Just as Discovery uses information that comes from an insured's FitBit device, the same data can be sent to a smart contract in order to execute changes in premium payments as the client's health state changes.

These executions are recorded securely on the Blockchain as self-executing contractual states, thereby eliminating the risk of relying on others to follow through on their commitments. The advantage of a smart contract programmed into the blockchain is that it can be formed as an objective authority over the agreement, automatically releasing money and fulfilling other conditions when the terms and conditions are met without the intervention of third-party intermediaries. Thus, a complete end-to-end process can be managed by computers providing objective information and/or representing the interests of the parties.

The same rules can be extended to a range of applications. Investment operations performed on a Blockchain can be automated with Smart Contracts. While today's FinTech firms have already automated a large part of the operations, the settlement process still takes time, as the transactions need to occur on the SWIFT* interbank network. The result is that even if buy and sell operations occur in nanoseconds, the actual trade is only formalized after T+2 or T+3 time delays, as the current legacy infrastructure coupled with burdening regulatory obligations slows the transaction process.

Smart Contracts can be a workaround around this and payment houses are taking note. In August 2015, the SWIFT Research Institute sent out a call for papers under the appellation, "The Impact and Potential of Blockchain on the Securities Transaction Lifecycle," (The Swift Institute, 2015). Since the beginning of 2016, they have published two academic articles gauging the speculative and post- trade impact of this technology. Other incumbents such as Earthport have been quicker to move. At about the same time that SWIFT was putting a call out for papers, Earthport partnered with Ripple, a company that helps construct quasi-private Blockchains for clients, to implement an instant cross-border payment system. Using Ripple's blockchain-based RTGS**, Earthport launched the Distributed Ledger Hub (DLH), which provides its clients instant payments and liquidity, transaction cost efficiencies, a high standard of compliance control, and elimination of counter-party risk via pre-funding (Earthport, 2015). As stated by Jonathan Lear, Earthport's

President, *"The world is getting smaller and payments needs to move faster… The legacy way of making cross-border payments, well there is only one way to describe it—it's a real bloody mess…. The essential problem in moving funds from country A to country B is the network of bilateral relationships [that exist]—and that doesn't create transparency or predictability. It presents a very complex, costly, and cumbersome process [to move money around the world]. And we think there is a better way to address that"* (PYMNTS, 2015).

*SWIFT: Society for Worldwide Interbank Financial Telecommunication
**RTGS: Real Time Gross Settlement

Using the Skeleton Keys

What the condensed insights in Sidebars 2-2 and 2-3 provide is the evidence that the financial ecosystem is being transformed and fragmented by actors and technologies that are exogenous to the traditional financial sector. Mark Carney's statements about FinTech changing the nature of money and central banking thus hold sway as the fragmentation is happening at every level of this sector.

Moreover, the fragmentation process is occurring at two echelons. While FinTech innovations are more concentrated on providing front end solutions that offer better benchmarks for speed, agility, and user- friendliness, Blockchain and Smart Contracts are bringing about change at the infrastructural level by providing better security, transparency, and automation of operations. This two-sided attack from the front-end and the infrastructure side of financial operations are the reason why the fragmentation of finance is occurring at a blitzkrieging rate and why investment has been increasing in the sector.

It is for this reason that when we talk about the Blockchain, it is imperative that we also consider the other side of the FinTech coin. One of the first things I mention to students when giving lectures about the Blockchain is to tell them to "Cool it with the Blockchain," for as we have seen in Sidebar 2-2, there are a range of other mature technologies which are fragmenting and changing the financial sector in ways that are more significant at the current time period. The Blockchain is not a panacea; it is an infrastructural technology that should be looked at as part of a toolkit. This toolkit is made up of all the technologies cited in Sidebars 2-2 and 2-3, and when they are used together, they will create the infrastructural foundation for the next chapter of financial services.

Consider the case of the payments and remittances sector. As mentioned before, the cost of using a non- bank remittance provider can be frightfully expensive. If a user intends to use their bank for the transfer, then the average cost involved is 11.12% of the sum being transferred (World Bank, 2015). While it cheaper to use a post office (5.88%), it depends on the country where the money is being transferred. Sending money to countries in sub-Saharan Africa and China remain very expensive, and the average cost of conducting a transfer using any channel totals to 7.37% (World Bank, 2015), assuming that the receiver has a bank account. With over two billion people still considered unbanked, this is not always an assumption that can be generalized. With profit margins being this high, it is unsurprising to learn that the global payments market is growing at 5% a year globally. Yet inspite of these profits, micropayments are not feasible, owing to the fees involved in making payments, and as per Stephan Thomas, CTO of Ripple, 2% of wire transfers fail, take over two days to settle, and cumulate to an annual cost of $1.6 Trillion.

The reason for high transfer fees is because of the number of players involved in transactions and the regulatory compliances each player has to respect. Currently when making a transfer, apart from the sender's and receiver's banks, the flow of money includes the involvement of non-bank companies (such as Western Union), the correspondent bank which deals with foreign exchange, the clearing networks (such as SWIFT and ACH[21]), and regulators from central banks and financial authorities that monitor KYC and AML standards. As there are many separate players involved, the information about the sender needs to be verified by each participant, which results in repetitive business processes, accumulated costs, delays, errors, and multiple operations.

However, as we have seen in Sidebars 2-2 and 2-3, this system is currently in a state of flux. Companies like M-Pesa are allowing the unbanked to send and receive payments without depending on the traditional players, and companies like Transferwise[22] are reducing the FOREX risk that is involved in cross-border transactions. If the Blockchain were to be inculcated in this value exchange process, it would further streamline the entire transaction. Senders and receivers would still have to go through a KYC process to have a digital wallet and identity, but once this has been verified, there is no need to repeat the verification process at every step. A smart contract can be generated that stipulates the conditions of the transfer between the counterparties, and currency conversion can be done via liquidity providers who are willing to facilitate the conversion or by adopting methods similar to Transferwise. As the smart contract executes, the transaction would occur in real time and the entire history can be verified by a regulator on the Blockchain. This would automate compliance, insure trust, reduce settlement times by orders of magnitude, and reduce costs for the end users. The only losers in this process would be the current intermediaries who presently perform the role of inter-operators.

Lending institutions also face changes from the amalgamation of the technologies described in Sidebars 2-2 and 2-3. When business entities require loans to grow their businesses, they face similar procedures and obstacles, as seen in making transfers. The lender or lenders first need to conduct a manually intensive due diligence process to ascertain if the business is sound and financially healthy. This involves analyzing a multitude of data sources, which is time-consuming and prone to errors. As the

---

[21]ACH - Automated Clearing House. The ACH is the largest clearing house network and the backbone for the electronic movement of money and data in the United States. It transfers over $40 Trillion in value a year. The two main operators of the ACH network are the Federal Reserve and the EPN (Electronic Payments Network, a private institution). The ACH is administered by NACHA, which manages the development, administration, and governance of the ACH Network.
[22]Transferwise eliminates high bank fees from foreign exchanges by matching users based on the currency they are sending. If a user wishes to send money from Europe to India (Euros to Rupees), then the company finds another user who wants to transfer a similar amount of money in the opposite direction (Rupees to Euros). A simple, secure swap then takes place, allowing Transferwise to execute the transfer up to 89% cheaper than with a bank (http://www.telegraph.co.uk/money/transferwise/how-does-it-work-and-is-it-safe/).

underwriting process is often not integrative of the due diligence process and often involves depending on third-party providers, it leads to duplication of efforts, additional costs to the investors, and information asymmetries owing to the siloed structure of the entire operation.

However, companies like Kabbage are showing us that via the use of Big Data analyses, these steps can be automated. Based on the digital footprint of the company, the lending institution can use advanced analytics to perform its due diligence with a better understanding of the risk involved, with a higher level of transparency, and with less manual intervention at higher speeds. Apart from a better matching of counterparties based on acceptable risk levels, using a smart contract can further tailor partnering criteria based on programmable selection conditions, hence reducing the time for receiving a loan. Big data also allows the analysis of other attributes of financial information, which allows investors to gain a more holistic understanding of the company's character. Using smart contracts, this automated due diligence can then be leveraged to automate the underwriting process, which reduces execution time and reduces the number of supplementary intermediaries that are currently employed, thus reducing operational risks and information asymmetries.

The P2P lending sector is already making strides in this direction to connect savers and lenders. Companies like MoneyCircles connect savers with borrowers who are part of their social circles. Lenders can create or join circles based on their Gmail, Facebook, Twitter, or LinkedIn networks and loan money based on their criteria. The conditions are embedded into a smart contract and the transactions occur via a blockchain. The smart contract also ensures the disbursement of the principal and interest payments over the loan period. As the transactions occur in real time over the loan cycle, regulators are provided with a real-time view of the financial details, which simplifies the KYC/AML procedures. As it stands, MoneyCircles is regulated by the UK Prudential Regulation and Financial Conduct Authorities.

While machine learning and robo-advisors are changing the investment landscape, compliance, auditing, and regulatory costs continue to surge (Noonan, 2015). It is in this sector that banks, taxation bodies, and regulators stand most to gain by the adoption of Blockchain, as the technology has the potential to provide them with a heightened enforcement tool. As things stand, regulators and auditors are required to be provided with annual financial statements and access to systems to conduct risk assessments and stress tests. In case of any discrepancies, a process is launched to determine the scale of the issues. Based on the audit report, the institution then issues its quarterly/annual report to investors. This process is resource- and time-intensive, as it affects the day-to-day operations of the company. Owing to the lack of interoperability of IT systems, the auditing process is manually intensive and prone to errors.

However, with a Blockchain the process can be streamlined across multiple platforms. As auditors and regulators are provided with authorized access, the institution's employees and leadership do not need to be intrinsically involved in the auditing process. Using the data from the Blockchain, the auditing of the institution can be done in real time with a smart contract supplying the information to the auditors' reporting instruments at predetermined periods. This allows for faster assessment, precise tax determination, quicker detection of discrepancies, and easier enforcement of new regulations. As startups like FundApps provide regulatory information in machine-readable language, the next step in this direction would be to allow a smart contract to make changes in regulation as an input, and adjust the investment and reporting procedures based on these changes. This would reduce time delays in the execution of new regulations, provide greater transparency of financial records, and allow sovereign regulatory bodies with automated capital analysis. It would also allow investors to make more informed decisions. Chapter 3 of Dan Tapscott's book (see notes for reference), provides a detailed understanding of how auditing firms will be affected by the Blockchain.

One of the most important uses of Blockchain in investment markets will be in the area of asset rehypothecation. Financial institutions often participate in this practice wherein an asset posted as collateral by a client is used by the financial institution for its own purposes, such as getting a loan. Clients who permit rehypothecation may be compensated either through a lower cost of borrowing or a rebate on fees. However, there need to be limits to which this process can be done, as excessive rehypothecation creates a collateral chain, misallocates the asset, and attaches additional risks to the collateral. The ambiguity of ownership of the asset and the ballooning of counterparty risks thus requires a mechanism which allows for tracing the transaction history of the asset. However, today's systems do not provide this level of insight, as secondary trading markets are not required to detail the transaction history of assets. As a result of this lack of transparency, regulators are unable to track securities and investors are unable to determine the true value of an asset, as each rehypothecation leverages a percentage of the collateral. If there is a default, the snowball effect then corrupts the entire transaction chain and can have spill over effects in other sectors. This was seen in gargantuan proportions during the financial crisis.

The Blockchain's ability to tokenize physical assets is thus an invaluable tool to investors and regulators. As the asset is tokenized, its transaction history can now be traced on the Blockchain with a smart contract enumerating its value and ownership as it begins to get rehypothecated. Regulatory limits can be set and encoded based on the percentage value of the asset once it is rehypothecated a certain number of times, with the smart contract restricting additional rehypothecation when the limit is reached. This provides investors and regulators with a transparent view of the asset's real value and if the investment firm is violating any stipulations. In sum, it provides a clearer view of the derivatives market.

In the world of AI-led high frequency trading, generic algorithms might allow for the development of automated learning strategies and execute trades in nanoseconds. Yet the post-trade processes are time-intensive and take up to T+3 days to settle. As the trades are executed in bulk at the end of the day and involve the involvement of intermediaries such as custodian banks, clearing houses, and securities depositories, the efficiency of the trade between the buyer and the seller is adversely impacted. This time lag affects the actions that investors can take over this period.

The Blockchain is perfectly suited to overhaul this process, as the transaction of securities is tailored for a ledger. Counterparties can use a smart contract to "book" a trade, and the liquidity and the tokenized asset (bond/equity) can be transferred to the Blockchain. Once the conditions for the execution of the smart contract have been met, the smart contract would execute and the exchange of the asset for the funds can be conducted on the Blockchain. A real-time transaction notification can then be sent to the counterparties' banks and custodians, which would allow for faster settlement time, reduce operational complexity, remove intermediaries, and improve the efficiency of the clearing processes.

The unglamorous yet immense insurance industry is another financial sector where the Blockchain can have significant impact. As mentioned in Sidebar 2-2, fraudulent claims pose a significant risk in the insurance industry. While new P2P insurance models are beginning to address this issue, owing to the reputational effects within a group, the Blockchain can help in dispersing the same practice in other branches of insurance as well. Currently, false claims are related to the multiple versions of truth that are associated with claims. When an insured reports a claim, they normally have to interact with a broker who confirms the validity of the claim. This is followed by a second assessment by the insurer who verifies the associated documentation from the broker and additional sources. This multi-step process is customer-unfriendly and based on the "one-size-fits-all" package. Intermediaries are costly, and manual data verification from third-party data providers increases the risk of fraud, the amount of time, and the resources necessary to process a claim.

With the Blockchain and IoT, this process can be simplified to a great extent. Sensors (for life or property insurance) can submit data to trigger a claim based on predefined conditions. Using data analysis and smart contracts, the due diligence and analysis process can be automated, codified, and executed. When additional data sources (such as weather conditions) need to be verified, this can be included and automated as well. The payment can then be made via the smart contract if all conditions are met.

All in all, across the various financial services, the use of Blockchain and FinTech can lead to simplified operational procedures, lesser risk, lower liquidity requirements, fewer intermediaries, higher transparency, better regulatory oversight, and easier multi-stakeholder agreement.

In spite of this potential, the large-scale deployment of the Blockchain has been hindered for two main reasons. First, as traditional analyses of macroeconomics have been based on methodologies that do not consider the actions of the financial system, it is increasingly difficult for macroeconomists to gauge the consequences of these changes using the existing methodologies and theories. It is for this reason that we must tackle the task of understanding the future impact of these changes by depending on the learnings of other disciplines, such as evolutionary biology and complexity science, as they are more suited to this task in spite of their relative bifurcation from a subject matter context. This is why the findings regarding the behaviors of micro-groups in complex systems hold so much pertinence; for as the influx of investment and players augments, we require a new methodological process that helps us adapt to this change at a rate at which it can be cognitively absorbed. Without a firm understanding of new theories that provide this ability, we have no compass with which we can navigate these frothy waters.

Second, the large-scale deployment of the Blockchain also necessitates a conversion towards a more digital system. As we have seen, the current processes are largely manual in nature and still involve the use of physical documents and person-to-person interactions. For the Blockchain to be effective at a societal level, it needs to overcome these physical barriers, namely with respect to:

1. digital identity and KYC

2. scalability

Both these topics will be addressed in relative detail in the final part of this chapter.

The Enemy of my Enemy is my Friend

"Good derives its virtue from evil, just as it is the silent pause that gives sweetness to the chant."

—St. Thomas Aquinas

As the fragmentation of the financial sector continues, incumbents and startups find themselves as competitors in the same race as market share continues to be broken up. As per a recent PricewaterhouseCoopers report, more than 20% of financial services business will be at risk to FinTechs by 2020. The study also estimates that 28% of the banking and payments sector and 22% of the insurance, wealth management and asset management sectors will belong to the FinTech firms by 2020 (PwC, 2016). According to Autonomous Research, online lenders originated $22 billion in U.S. consumer and business loans in 2015. While this represents only 6% of the total volume for such loans, the sector is expected to grow 75% in 2016, the financial research firm estimates. Goldman Sachs analysts have predicted that banks stand to lose 100% of the student, consumer, and mortgage loan business to online lenders over the next five years (Crosman, 2016).

While 57% of incumbents are not sure or unlikely to respond to Blockchain technology (PwC, 2016), the remainder are taking bold steps to inculcate this technology for obvious reasons. Studies by Goldman Sachs estimate that Blockchain could reduce transaction costs in underwriting insurance by $2–$4 billion, just in the US. By applying Blockchain to streamlining clearing and settlement of cash securities (equities, repo, and leveraged loans), they estimate the industry could save $11–$12 billion in fees, OpEx, and capital charges globally (Schneider et al., 2016).). As the Blockchain also offers a tamper-proof way of storing records, it could ease the process required to know a customer and reduce the number of "suspicious" transactions, resulting in $3–$5 billion in cost savings for KYC (Know Your Customer) and AML (Anti-Money Laundering) compliance (Schneider et al., 2016).

As P2P platforms begin to the change the role of the consumer into a prosumer, the growth of business models that do not have to depend on a central point of authority is gaining stead. As the Blockchain is suited to this environment and is digitally native, its continued use in various forms is bound to increase. While the current total worth of bitcoin in the Blockchain is around $20 billion, the growing popularity and use of Ethereum[23] and Ripple is tipping the scale, and the World Economic Forum estimates that by 2027, up to 10% of the global GDP will be stored on the Blockchain (WEF, 2015). Some skeptics still stubbornly state that, owing to regulatory and operational limitations, this technology will remain on the fringes of finance and exist as just a cryptocurrency. But the evidence shows that it is much more. It is a protocol, a commodity, an automation system, a secure exchange, a ledger, and a community that is creating a counter-culture movement.

---

[23]On the 30th of April 2016, the founders of SLOCK.IT launched the DAO (Decentralized Autonomous Organization) on the Ethereum platform.

At the same time, incumbents and startups face different challenges. While banks invest more heavily in innovation (e.g., Bank of America has a $3 billion annual innovation budget), they still need to find ways to diffuse their innovation strategies across their organizations, yet retain market share. To this end, banks have begun to collaborate with each other to develop new platforms with similar standards to update their legacy infrastructure; one of the main objectives of the R3 consortium is to address the issue of standards for global cross-border Blockchain use. Startups, on the other hand, are trying to find ways to gain customers and scale their business while facing increased regulations, higher costs, and larger infrastructures that will be more difficult to change and manage.

As a result, just as it was mentioned in the evolutionary biology article, banks and FinTech startups are now working together to figure out ways to remain competitive but still (re)gain market share. At the end of 2015, JPM Chase partnered with OnDeck to begin providing quick, small loans to SMEs. In May 2016, UBS partnered with SigFig to provide robo-advisory services to their wealthy clients (Yurcan, 2016). While Kensho functions as an independent technology firm with partnerships with a host of banks, it was initially funded by Goldman Sachs and continues to provide services to them (Nadler, 2016).

As banks continue to evolve from their traditional nature towards a modern outlook, the partnering and alliances will still continue to fragment and metamorphose the sector. This will inevitably be accompanied by new risks and challenges. The hurdles are not just in term of regulations but also in terms of policies. As financial markets get increasingly fragmented by technology, they are also getting increasingly cashless. Thus, future policy for a decentralized and fragmented future needs to adapt to this facet.

In a cashless world, how are KYC and AML compliance measures to be administered when signing up to online platforms? What kinds of regulations need to be developed to aid FinTech firms to continue growing while giving them the leeway to innovate? How is the production of money going to be affected in the fragmented market? What kinds of regulations need to be put in place in order to stop TBTF and can these regulations be adapted to comprehend new technology? For example: Try going to a regulator today and saying, *"The exchange of this asset or product is sound and valid because its transaction was done on a cryptographically secure and time-stamped distributed ledger that exists on a hybrid permissioned-permissionless Blockchain."* In terms of adapting regulations to this new environment, regulators are going to be in need of a stiff drink.

But the sobering realization is evident: today we live in a financial quagmire that is besotted with institutions that are TBTF. As technology continues to converge with the changing mindset of society, the emergence of new enterprises is fragmenting the financial sector and calling for academics, organizations, and regulators to begin perceiving the economy via a new lens. This call has been heard by innovators and is now being echoed by central bankers such as Andy Haldane, Neel Kashkari, and Mark Carney. But the main roadblock today seems to be not with technology but in the way regulations and polices need to be structured in order adapt to this new environment. As stated by Jake Kendall, the former director of research and innovation at the Gates Foundation,

"... [in terms of scaling democratizing financial services], a lot of it is not a technology problem but a regulatory issue or a business model issue," (Microsoft Research Conference, 2016)

Hence, prior to answering the questions of how much debt should be issued and how big can a firm be allowed to become before it poses systemic risks, we need to understand how the regulations and policies that govern these institutions need to be fabricated while keeping our future cashless economy in foresight. This will be seen in the next chapter.

Challenges and Solution Pathways

As banks and financial institutions begin to gauge the applicability of Blockchain technology, both from the private and public utilization diasporas, the manner in which identity is verified and shared is found to be lagging in context. Know Your Customer (KYC) and Anti-Money Laundering (AML) procedures that are typically used by financial players and governments seem to be at odds with the anonymous and pseudonymous representative possibilities offered by distributed ledger technologies.

Likewise, the scalability issue is a priority technical concern and different efforts such as improving proof-of-work/proof-of-stake protocols, consortium consensus, construction of sidechains, and sharding are currently being explored. It is quite possible that given the investment and current interest in Blockchains that a solution might have been found by the time this book is published. Recent advances by Gavin Wood[24] with the Polkadot Framework (see "Polkadot: Vision for a Heterogeneous Multi-chain Framework") and ByzCoi.

The following two sections review these issues.

Digital Identity and KYC

There are a number of technological solutions that are currently being offered by a variety of players (refer to Table 2-2). Juxtaposed with this diversity of solutions is a rift in the opinions of policy makers. Some suggest that a centralized identity management system is the way forward, while others extol the virtues of leveraging the existing decentralized morsels of identity.

---

[24]Gavin Wood is widely known in the Blockchain community as the Co-founder and CTO of Ethereum and the Co-founder of Grid Singularity (a company that uses the Blockchain for decentralized energy data management)

Table 2-2. *Private companies that are providing identity and KYC/AML services via the Blockchain*

Company	Service	Solution
2WAY.IO	Identity	2WAY.IO transforms public nodes into private nodes by adding a permission layer and connects information silos and secure communication channels. They offer systems that are privacy-by-design and security-by-design that are both trusted third-party- and blockchain-agnostic.
ShoCard	Identity and KYC	ShoCard is a digital identity that protects consumer privacy. Their current products allow a user to integrate their driver's license and travel identities into the bitcoin blockchain, although they are also blockchain-agnostic. Their technology is optimized for mobile and secure for even banks to rely on it. A user's identity is encrypted, hashed, and then written to the blockchain, where it can be called up when needed. Users would, in effect, give banks temporary access to the private side of this blockchain record in order to verify identity. Once that is done, the bank creates its own record that can be consulted in the future to determine that a certain Joe Smith is really Joe Smith. Their recent project with SITA allows for an airline customer to tokenise. their identity in the form of a single use travel token which can be used by authorities to verify the client's identity and transport credentials.
Guardtime	Identity and KYB	Guardtime enables organizations to assure the integrity of their networks, prevent data loss of critical digital assets, and to verify enterprise behaviors. The platform records the state of all digital assets by registering them in a global blockchain, generating a mathematically verifiable image of the network.
Trunomi	Identity and KYC	Trunomi provides KYC without the blockchain and securely manages the consent to use customers' personal data. Trunomi connects financial institutions to their customers and allows the clients to manage and share their identification and personal data via a platform.
BlockVerify	KYB	BlockVerify provides a blockchain-based anti-counterfeit solution and is focused on the supply chain industry. This allows users to track products throughout the supply chain and to ensure that the consumers receive an authentic product.

(continued)

Table 2-2. (*continued*)

Company	Service	Solution
SkuChain	KYB	Skuchain is similar to BlockVerify and is targeting the supply chain industry as well, but with a focus on collaborative commerce. Their BRACKETS[25] technology makes smart contracts to govern all phases of a typical trade agreement from order, shipment, and invoice to final payment.
CredyCo	Identity and KYC	Created by Trustatom, CredyCo provides a cryptographic due diligence service built on top of Bitcoin's blockchain. They provide document verification "software as a service" (SaaS) which uses smart contracts and identity technology built on top of the blockchain to ensure the credibility and irrefutability of all statements. Primarily targeting the venture capital industry, the company seeks to automate KYC practices by allowing their customers to authorize transactions with cryptographic signatures.
HYPR	Identity	HYPR combines Bitcoin biometrics with blockchain security to provide an enterprise-ready multi-signature platform. HYPR-Secure's tokenization provides blockchain applications a viable solution for securing private keys behind a biometric authentication gateway.
Bitnation	Identity	Bitnation has worked out identification solutions, such as putting a passport and a marriage certificate on the blockchain. It aims to provide the same services that governments provide, but in a decentralized and voluntary manner, unbound by geography.
Cryptid	Identity	Cryptid takes data provided by institutions, encrypts it, and permanently stores it on the Blockchain. The user is provided with a password and a unique Cryptid identification number that points to the information on the block chain. The ID can be stored on almost anything from magnetic stripes to QR codes making it easier to use.
Case	Identity and KYC	Case is a multisignature, multifactor Bitcoin wallet, which is biometrically secured. A transaction can only occur if validation from two of three keys is confirmed. In a way, it is a collation of 2FA, biometrics, and Bitcoin technologies. By generating and storing each key in a different location they avoid any risk of single point of failure.

(*continued*)

---

[25]BRACKETS: Blockchain-based Release of funds, that Are Conditionally Key-signed, and Triggered by Signals.

Table 2-2. (*continued*)

Company	Service	Solution
kompany	KYB	By applying a hybrid blockchain to continuously monitor and note changes of official company information (e.g., address, managing directors, company registration number, company filings, changes in directors, etc.), kompany.com provides a verifiable source of actual and historical data of the company that can be auditable. They provide access to commercial registers, allowing user to search for official information on more than 50 million companies in 80 countries and jurisdictions. They thus address KYC, KYB and EDD[26] issues.
KYC3	KYC, AML	Another non-blockchain-based company, KYC3 uses big data and AI to offer SaaS solutions to financial and legal professionals that extend and improve risk-based approaches to the management of compliance and reputational risks. As of April 2016, KYC3 was selected as innovation partner by BNP Paribas Wealth Management.
Tradle	KYC	Tradle combines blockchain technology & smart contracts with KYC requirements. They use the blockchain to store data, offer transparency, and associate electronic identities with user addresses, thus simplifying the KYC procedure. The founder Gene Vayngrib states *"Instead of sending all the data to the regulators to prove that you have done the AML correctly, the bank can prove to the regulators that they have automatic procedures that do AML and do things like report suspicious transactions. The auditing of the bank by the regulators in such a way preserves privacy as much as possible. The regulator could get information about suspicious transactions without banks sharing a lot of raw, private data with them."* (IBT, 2015)
Polycoin	KYC, AML	Focused primarily on digital assets compliance management, Polycoin provides a blockchain-based accounting solution that balances compliance requirements but deals with the relative anonymity of transactions. Polycoin's platform analyzes transactions to try and identify whom they are from. Transactions are then ranked. Upon a transaction being deemed suspicious, the product sends compliance officers an alert to further investigate problems like AML breaches.

(continued)

---

[26]EDD: Enhanced Due Diligence.

Table 2-2. (*continued*)

Company	Service	Solution
Coinfirm	KYC, AML	Focused on the digital currency sector, Coinfirm uses the blockchain to provide KYC/AML reports on digital currency transactions and entities. The transactional data is analyzed to measure the client risk rating, transaction patterns, and to identity discrepancies. They also provide services to banks or financial institutions who want to adopt or assess the adoption of blockchain technology with respect to AML/KYC regulations and compliance. Using Coinfirm, institutions can accept clients utilizing digital currencies, depending on their AML/KYC procedures.
Coinify & iSignthis	KYC, AML	iSignthis provides automated AML/CTF KYC identity proofing by using real-time electronic verification of regulated payment instruments. They recently partnered with Coinify, a Denmark-based blockchain currency payment provider, to offer a new service connecting blockchain payments, identity verification and credit cards.
KYC-Chain	KYC	KYC-Chain uses the blockchain and smart contracts to provide a platform for opening accounts online, while complying with laws and regulations. KYC-Chain employs Ethereum and will work primarily via the use of "trusted gatekeepers," who can be any individual or legal entity permitted by law to authenticate KYC documents, for example, notary publics, people of diplomatic status, lawyers, governments, etc. A trusted gatekeeper would perform an individual check on a user's ID using KYC-Chain's platform and authenticate them. The verified files would be stored in a distributed database system, which can later be retrieved by the trusted gatekeeper, or the user, to demonstrate with certainty that the ID is genuine. (Palmer, 2016)

Irrespective of the reader's stance, it should be remembered that the objective should not be to side with any singular offer or approach. On the contrary, the diversity of the offered solutions helps us illustrate the richness of the challenges that we are faced with and thus allows us to realize that it is the environment in which a certain identity is used that defines the appropriate technology selection. In a world of increasing complexity peppered with multiple personality representations, it is the convergence of these apparently separated solutions that will allow us to find the best solution for this new era.

Nonetheless, the current dearth of digital identity systems limits the ability of regulatory institutions to deliver efficient and secure digital financial service offerings. To begin the conversation of what it required, it is first necessary to understand the ways in which the current systems impedes digital identity progression and reimagine the concept of identity.

To illustrate some of the problems currently faced by customers with respect to identity and KYC, let us begin with a true story of what a customer from HSBC faced when she wanted to open an account. A letter in the *Daily Telegraph*'s "Money" section on the 2nd of October 2009, exemplifies the problem of identity in modern life (Birch, 2014). The letter came from someone who had tried to open a bank account with HSBC, but who didn't have a current passport or driving licence.

She wrote: *"When I explained this at a branch, it was suggested that I ask the police station for proof of identity."* She dutifully went to the local constabulary, who told her that they had never heard of such a thing unless she had a criminal record. Thinking it seemed odd that you can only have a bank account if you have a criminal record, she returned to the branch to be shown a list of documents that the bank would consider acceptable for the purposes of account opening, and this time they suggested a letter from Her Majesty's Revenue & Customs (HMRC). She reports *"I duly went to the local tax office, where the assistant said she wished banks would stop sending people there… they would not waste public money providing such letters for banks."*

The letter goes on to list the documents that she had presented and which were subsequently rejected by the bank: an out-of-date passport, a birth certificate, a current payslip from an employer (the local council, for which she had worked for more than two decades), a work ID card (complete with microchip), utility bills, statements from another bank, house deeds, and a voting card. Any one of these would have been sufficient to procure a job with the bank, but apparently it seems, not an account. Although this problem may have been rectified since the publication of this letter, the story is still relevant to today's modus operandi seen in a number of banks and financial institutions. The issue here is not just about KYC, but about how identity is measured and what value is given to reputation.

It is at this juncture that we see the current flaws of the existing KYC procedural system. In a number of ways, most of the institutions don't really care about identity. They care about the credit history of whatever persona is presented to them. They comply with stringent "know your customer" regulations, although these have nothing to do with any real identity security. As things stand, if one were to open an account with, say, a passport, the bank cannot possibly know whether it is a genuine passport or not. But it does not matter, since the obligation on them is simply to keep a copy of it. If they do this, and the passport subsequently turns out to be false, it's *non mea culpa*.

Hence, in order to make KYC relevant to the digital economy, the concept of identity needs to be seen through a new lens. More importantly, it is essential for regulators and service providers (financial or otherwise) to consider the digitization of identity and the digitization of finance in order to create a verified channel of value exchange suitable to the future era. To do so requires not just an understanding of the way identity is changing in the context of decentralized technologies but also the way in which money and value transfer systems are being interpreted today. The digital economy, and the digital society that we are building on top of it, demand a convergent view on the way we think about identity and money.

Since the development of virtual avatars, our deep-rooted notion of identity has become tangential to what identity really is now in an online, interconnected, and networked world. A singular identity can exist in multiple states of simultaneous existence. Hence, what needs to be understood today is that identity exists in different forms. Demarking the kinds of identities a person can have in different networks and systems is thus crucial to understanding the rhetoric of reputation based on identity. It is, after all, the reputation of a person that is being judged in a KYC process. A person's Facebook account is not the same as their LinkedIn account. The way one represents themselves on these mediums is a direct representation of how they wish to be seen by the employer or their entourage or to the world in general.

By analyzing the different manifestations of identity, we realize that there are really three kinds of identity associated with people: the individual's own personal or psychological identity, their social identity, and their legal identity. The element of change is what differentiates individual and social identities from legal identities. Both individual and social identities are not fixed: they evolve and change over a person's lifetime. Legal identities, on the other hand, are fixed and are about the identifiability of the individual. Online, an individual can have multiple social identities that may be linked directly or indirectly to their legal identity. While some companies stick to using only legal identities for KYC procedures, an increasing number of new companies are comparing legal identities with social identities to determine risk associated with an individual.

For example, Kabbage, the online lending platform, provides financial services to small business. Known as the 6-minute loan, Kabbage uses real business data from eBay, Amazon, Shopify, Stripe, and Square (among others), to determine the risk factor of a potential borrower. On the basis of this score, the borrower is capable of then borrowing up to $100,000, within 6 minutes of launching the request for funds.

The above example is one of the many companies that are using multiple sources of identity to validate KYC and KYB.[27] By not depending on solely the legal identity, they are able to get a deeper understanding of the client by gauging their reputation and histories from the social and individual networks. Irrespective of the channel of identity that is used, the key element which requires this level of understanding is reputation. Identities and credentials are easy to create and destroy. Reputations, on the other hand, are much harder to subvert since they depend not on what anyone thinks, but on what everyone within a network thinks about an individual. When it comes to commerce, KYC, and ALM, the role of reputation precedes money for establishing transactions.

Trust is the link that unites the changing state of identities with the changing face of money in new value exchange platforms. In a trust-based network, reputation rather than regulation animates economic exchange. From the perspective of transactions, we get another tangent to the purpose of identity today. For example, as per a recent report from the Financial Conduct Authority, the UK government has forced banks to spend almost a billion pounds on the Current Account Switching System (CASS), in order to reduce the time taken to switch bank accounts from three weeks to one (FCA, 2015).

Yet if a customer from Bank A decides to open an account with Bank B, they will still have to produce a physical copy of their utilities bill and a passport, along with photocopies. Why is it that the client is unable to use their online banking identity provided by Bank A and open an account in Bank B, especially since they follow almost similar KYC procedures?

---

[27]Know your business.

The response to this question is multifaceted in nature, but the underlying issue is that subjects pertaining to identity and KYC cannot be resolved if banks do not have mutually beneficial circles of trust between themselves. The lack of shared narratives in this arena is impeding adaptation and progress in a world where customer-centric approaches to delivering services and products equate to value generation. Banks currently attempt to sidestep this issue by focusing on short-term profit maximization instead of dealing with the longer-term structural issue. What is therefore required is a merging of identities with value exchange networks.

The argument for a more inclusive way of looking at KYC is also one that needs to be looked at from a contextual scenario. What is required today is not just a dependence on the identity documents that we use to control our physical presence within politically established borders (passports, driving licences, etc.), but also our virtual borders. What is required is KYC infrastructure that allows the amalgamation of different kinds of identities, some of which are static and some of which are flexible. At the same time, the infrastructure needs to provide appropriate privacy and security at stringent levels without necessitating the need for a trade-off between these salient features while remaining cost effective so that it allows scalability.

With this preamble in foresight, and having looked at the evolution of identity from an empirical approach, a stark realization emerges. What is required today is a means that allows individuals to prove that they are entitled to perform certain operations—such as opening an account, receiving insurance claims etc.—without the need to divulge all elements of their identity at each interval. The ability to prove that an individual is entitled to do something is an entirely different issue from proving one's identity, and one that can be resolved without compromising on privacy by showing the details of one's ID at every point (Huckstep, 2016).

For example: Is it really necessary to show all our personal credentials to enter a bar? Would it be enough to have a certification that says, "Yes, this person is over 18" without showing all personal information. What is needed to enable transactions is not identity per se but the associated entitlements.

In order to achieve this objective, we need to have *economic avatars* based on **tokenized identity**. Avatars are a relatively well-known concept: these are two or more identities that are connected to one another. A person can have a primary, verified real identity and then have a pseudonymous identity that is linked to the original identity. Having this form of two-way linkage gives individuals a means to engage in economic and social transactions whilst using the pseudonymous visage of themselves to control their privacy in the transactional world. It also allows for an easier method of assimilation with Blockchain technology.

The concept of tokenizing identity needs to be broken down into two aspects:

1. Simplify the KYC process so that it makes the absorption of virtual identities and the sharing of information regarding identity much easier. That way an individual does not need to prove their identity at each impasse if it is already done once.

2. Allow someone to use one's identity to generate "economic avatars" that can be used to prove that a person is entitled to perform certain tasks or receive services/benefits, without needing to reveal all traits of their identity in the process.

To achieve this objective, we can use tokens. The following hypothesized flow of events shows how this can be achieved: Let us say that one wishes to transact with a merchant, but does not want to show all details of his/her identity. At the same time, the merchant needs to know that the person is legit and not involved in illicit activities. To address this, when a client opens an account, their bank creates an electronic wallet and generates a token that it digitally signs and provides to the client. The token is tied to the client's account at the bank. However, the bank does not know who this token is going to, only that it is going to someone who has already opened an account with them, and who has gone through their KYC process. To pay the merchant, the client must submit the token. The merchant can then easily check the digital signature from the bank that proves that the provider of the token does have a verified account, yet allows for pseudonymity.

By tokenizing a client's identity, the bank can be sure that they are a customer, but neither they nor the merchant knows who the client actually is. This brings up a key point: For pseudonyms to have a value, they need to be underwritten by trusted institutions. If the client does something that is against the law, a court can then order the service to turn over the true identity of the client. Apart from providing a secure way of hedging against counterparty risk, the sense of privacy in a networked world is addressed through personal control. It should be underlined that transactions ought to be private, not anonymous, and this is why the infrastructure for pseudonymity is the most important feature of transactional systems.

The advantage of the model of tokenized identities is that it is agnostic to the kind of institution that issues identity in a country. The way identity is formalized varies from country to country. In the developed world, there are essentially three models in place (Birch, 2014):

1. the Scandinavian model: where banks provide identities that are used by business and government;

2. the Continental model: where government identities are used by banks and business;

3. the Atlantic model: where banks and business provide identities that are used by each other and by government.

The Atlantic model is most pertinent to use in countries like France, as different instructional bodies currently exist that issues bits of a person's identity (e.g., the post office, government agencies, etc.).[28] In essence, an individual could have three or four identities given by different identity providers, much as we have different bank cards. A person could hence have a bank identity, a residential identity, an education identity, and a travel identity, for example.

Each of these identities may be given by bodies that specialise in a certain function. The postal service, for example, might be the preferred provider of the "address" attribute. A bank identity and a travel identity might both use this attribute in creating their identity. By letting each individual body specialize yet transmit their confidence in the person's identity (based on their KYC procedure), we can stimulate the conversation

---

[28]In the UK, there are currently eight such providers approved by the government, including PayPal, the Post Office and Experian.

between different actors which, as we described in the previous paragraphs, is one of the current limitations of the system.

As identity and identity attributes are bound together in digital credentials, it is these credentials that must be verified to support transactions. If a person is required to prove their age, then they may present the certified credentials that contain the attributes that affirm that the identity being presented is verified to be over a certain age (say over 18). The fact that the verified certification comes from a provider that another party can recognize and trust is further bolstered by its ability to be checked automatically. The advantage of using these kinds of frameworks is that they resemble those frameworks which are central to much of modern Internet cryptography. By using a public-key certificate (PKC) and a public- key infrastructure (PKI),[29] information that is digitally signed by third parties can be verified.

The reason for putting forth the tokenization of identity in reference to the Atlantic model is because it reverts to the concept of decentralized identity, which has been a topic of debate since the advent of the Internet. Due to the recent advancements in cryptography, most of the solutions currently being explored are with regards to a public-key infrastructure, where people could store a private key safely and identity will be decentralized as only those with the keys would be able to access it.

Bitpay, a US-based bitcoin merchant processor, was one of the first companies that launched a project in this space with the release of BitAuth, a project that leverages bitcoin technology to facilitate a decentralized authentication system. The system uses cryptographic signatures in place of server-side password storage, thus solving a common security problem[30] for IT administrators (Cawrey, 2014). BitAuth uses Bitcoin's technology to create a public-private key pair using secp256k1. By providing the user with a system identification number (SIN) that is a hash of the public key, it allows for password-less authentication across web services. It uses signage to prevent man-in-the-middle (MITM) attacks, and a nonce to prevent replay attacks (Raval, 2016). The private key is never revealed to the server and can be stored safely and securely. Identity is decentralized, so instead of having to trust a third party to store identity, a user can store it themselves.

The OpenID protocol, developed by the OpenID Foundation, is also pioneering this concept. OpenID is a decentralized identity protocol that uses existing web protocols like HTTP, SSL, and URI. The basis for this technology is that as identity is fragmented across the web, by using the OpenID protocol, users can transform existing URIs into an account which can be used at any site that supports OpenID. By allowing the user to store their identity at a trusted source, the service provider can carry the identity across multiple providers. Google, Yahoo, and Twitter have been OpenID providers. But OpenID still creates a potential security vulnerability, as it requires trusting a service provider with data (Raval, 2016).

---

[29]A PKC is an identity with some other information (such as an expiry date) that is put together and digitally signed by a third party. The attributes might come from a variety of sources. If you send me such a certificate, I can use the PKI to check the digital signatures so I can trust the contents.
[30]Because a breach can potentially leak customer authentication information.

Namecoin was designed to overcome this limitation (also referred to as Zooko's triangle[31]). While OpenID solved security and human meaningfulness attributes of Zooko's triangle, Namecoin completed it by including decentralization. Namecoin used the blockchain[32] as an intermediary between the user and the service requesting their identity. Using Namecoin, a user can register their name into the Namecoin blockchain by sending a transaction with their name embedded in it under the /id namespace. When the user sends the transaction, Namecoin stores it if it's unique. Hence, as users create and select their own identities, the user gets a new namespace for a new service.

An evident question that offshoots from this development is how would authentication and authorization work in this fragmented system? To respond to this concern, NameID was created, which can be described as the sum of Namecoin and OpenID. While Namecoin allows users to register arbitrary online identities in a decentralized and secure manner, NameID allows the user to turn their Namecoin identity into an OpenID, and use it to readily sign into thousands of OpenID-enabled websites.

There is nonetheless a caveat to be remembered with the decentralization of identity, which is, the user is still required to store their encrypted private keys locally. In order to help users address this issue, Coinbase, which acts as a bank for Bitcoin holders (and is hence the opposite if decentralization), provides private-key storage as a service.

Following on the path set by Coinbase and other early entrants, there has been an increasing number of companies that have been created in recent times that are providing decentralized identity services. A growing number of these are leveraging the Blockchain, as it allows for the storage of all types of data and transactions in a secure and open way, while combating identity theft.

At the same time, combining the decentralized blockchain principle with identity verification gives users greater control over who has their personal information and how they access it. Consumers can now log in and verify payments without having to enter any of the traditional username and password information. Through some blockchain solutions, consumers can use an app for authentication instead of using traditional methods, such as a username and password. The companies also provide solutions that store their encrypted identity, allowing them to share their data with companies and manage it on their own terms.

Given these multidimensional attributes of identity, it is unsurprising to see regulators struggle with creating new standards for identity and authentication. Moreover, as the complexity of transactions grows with the volumes being transferred, regulators are obliged to demand greater granularity and accuracy of identity, especially as the increasing sophistication of technology also allows bad actors to exploit weak identity systems. In light of these challenges, some governments have begun the drive to create new digital identity systems (e.g., Estonia's e-Residency[33]). However, most efforts have been focused at the regulatory level and thus do not offer commercially viable solutions.

---

[31]Zooko's triangle is a conjecture that unites the three desirable traits of a network protocol identifier: human-meaningful, decentralized and secure. The conjecture states that in a system that is meant to give names in a protocol, only two of the three desirable attributes can be achieved.
[32]The Namecoin blockchain was one of the first forks of the Bitcoin blockchain and is still in existence.
[33]offers every world citizen an Estonian government-issued digital identity and the opportunity to run a trusted company online

As identity is a vast-ranging subject, it will be necessary to have a certain amount of division of labor in order to create a ubiquitous identity system. For this reason, government and private institutions need to work together in defining the concept of digital identity. Given the technology solution providers and the landscape of the technology companies, it can be said that financial institutions are best positioned to drive the creation of digital identity systems. Financial institutions store client data for their own commercial purposes and are thus better positioned to develop identity toolkits without extensive incremental effort. However, they still need the involvement of the government, and it is only through symbiotic collaboration while keeping the citizen/user in mind that progress can be made. Tables 2-2 and 2-3 detail some of the progress being made with respect to digitizing identity from private and public actors respectively.

Table 2-3. *Government digital identity programs*

Country	Program	Initiative details
UK	Public - Private	The Verify program is an external authentication system which allows UK citizens to access government services online. Users verify their identity online with the credentials provided by one of the nine certified identity providers. Once they are authenticated, they are granted access to the government service they are trying to access.
Canada	Public-private	SecureKey Concierge is a digital authentication system that allows individuals to choose a trusted credential they already have with one of a set of financial institutions to access government services online. The users log in with their online banking username and password and are authenticated by their bank. Once authenticated, the users are granted access to the service. No attributes are transferred in the system. The SecureKey Concierge system allows Canadian citizens to access government services online by authenticating through any of a large number of financial institutions with which they already transact.
Netherlands	Government	DigID is a digital authentication system for Dutch residents who are accessing government services online. Individual attributes are held in a national citizen registry; these attributes are used to authenticate users when they apply for a DigID. Individuals can then use their DigID username and password to authenticate themselves to government agencies. Their national identifier number is transferred from the national citizen registry to the relying parties.

(*continued*)

Table 2-3. (*continued*)

Country	Program	Initiative details
Finland	Government and Private sector solutions	The Population Registry is a national database that is owned and maintained by the Finnish government. The government acts as the identity provider, transferring attributes to public and private relying parties. The purpose of the system is to collect data that can be used for elections, tax filing, judicial administration, etc. Private relying parties may also access this data if they pay a fee and have received user consent. TUPAS is an identity system in which over ten banks act as identity providers. Individuals can log into a wide range of services with credentials from their bank. The users' full names and National ID numbers are transferred from the identity provider to the relying parties. The user has visibility into which attributes are being requested by the relying parties, and must provide consent for the exchange to occur.
Denmark	Private sector	NemID is an electronic ID, digital signature, and secure email solution that provides individuals access to public and private services. The government tendered the system to the private sector. Users use a common NemID login and password, as well as unique one-time passwords to authenticate themselves to online services. User attributes are stored in a central registry.
Sweden	Public-private	Sweden has established an eID system that provides citizens and businesses access to over 300 public and private services. Digital identities are issued by a set of private entities, including large banks and a major telecommunications provider. The public sector buys identity validation services from the private sector. Private sector service providers can join the BankID system by signing contracts with eID providers for authentication. The solution has been very successful; over nine million citizens currently use the service.
South Africa	Public-private	The South African Social Security Agency, Grindrod Bank, and MasterCard have issued biometric-enabled debit cards to over 22 million social security recipients. The SASSA card holds an individual's personal information on the chip, is authenticated through biometrics (fingerprint and voice pattern) or a personal identification number (PIN), and is linked directly to a bank account where social grants are deposited. The end result is over five million people becoming financially included, and huge efficiencies in the distribution of social grants in South Africa.

(continued)

Table 2-3. (*continued*)

Country	Program	Initiative details
India	Government	The Aadhaar program was introduced in India to increase social and financial inclusion by providing identity for all Indians residents, many of whom previously had no means of proving their identities. The Unique Identification Authority of India (UIDAI) acts as the central identity provider, controlling who has access to the data that they collect and store. To receive a card, individuals submit various documents to a local registrar. If they are unable to provide documentation, an "introducer," such as an elected representative or a local teacher or doctor, can vouch for the person's identity. This parallel process decreases the chance of UIDAI storing inaccurate information or providing social services to illegal immigrants or other illicit actors. The UIDAI has a database that holds information such as name, date of birth, and biometrics data that may include a photograph, fingerprint, iris scan, or other information. The Aadhaar program has been very effective in increasing financial inclusion with over one billion people enrolled for accounts; however, there are still some outstanding concerns about information protection and privacy.
Estonia	Government	The Estonian government is currently setting the standard in terms of digital identity systems: The government of Estonia has created a digital interface between citizens and government agencies. The government holds citizen information in a centralized Population Registry and acts as the identity provider and governing body, transferring reliable and trusted data to relying parties. Citizens are each assigned an eID identifier that they can use to log on to the State Portal, which provides access to dozens of services, from voting, to updating automobile registries, to applying to universities. The government transfers the attribute information needed to complete each transaction from the Population Registry to the relying parties, and citizens are able to see what entities have accessed their information.

(*continued*)

Table 2-3. (*continued*)

Country	Program	Initiative details
		Citizens of Estonia have the ability to view who has accessed their records, how often, and for what purpose. This transparency allows citizens to feel ownership over their data, as they are able to see how the information is being used.
		A compelling example is the Electronic Health Record, a nationwide system that integrates data from various healthcare providers into a single portal. Users are able to log on to a Patient Portal to control their treatment and manage their healthcare information.
		Estonia is also creating a digital identity system that is built on a common technology framework, called XRoad. This framework creates interoperability between different databases, hugely increasing the digital identity system's functionality and effectiveness.
		Finally, the government's e-Residency program is opening borders to outsiders. The e-Residency program allows non-Estonian citizens to get a digital ID card that enables them to use Estonian private and public services and to use secure digital signatures. The purpose of the program is to create a virtual business environment and continue to position Estonia as a hub of the digital world. Since its inception in December 2014, almost 10,000 people have applied for e-Residency and over 400 have established companies domiciled in Estonia.
EU	Public sector solution	The EU E-Identity legislation sets requirements for member states issuing identity to citizens to ensure mutual recognition and scale of identity systems across Europe.

Source: World Economic Forum—A Blueprint for Digital Identity,2016

Scalability

While networks such as SWIFT, ACH and Earthport are capable of transmitting a large number of transactions, the same cannot be currently said for all Blockchain networks. Open networks such as the Bitcoin Blockchain are only capable of confirming 3.3—7 transactions per second. On the other hand, the Visa credit card network is capable of confirming a transaction within seconds, and processes 2,000 transactions/sec. on average, with a peak rate of 56,000 transactions (Croman et al., 2016). Thus, the large-scale deployment of Blockchains requires the technology to be massively more scalable than the current limits that support Bitcoin.

At the current time there are a number of technical solutions being pursued by a variety of actors. One approach being explored is the sharding of Blockchains and replacing a single Blockchain with many independent blockchains, interoperating in a semi-trusted manner via cross-chain miners (James-Lubin, 2015). Another possibilty being explored involves techniques from advanced cryptography, called "zero- knowledge proofs." These proofs allow quick verification of transactions without running the actual computation. However these techniques are still in a state of exploration and no concrete large-scale deployment is yet to be seen.

Private Blockchains, such as those designed by Ripple, are constructed to be more efficient and scaled to handle high transaction volume. Both Ethereum and Ripple are capable of verifying transactions much faster than the bitcoin Blockchain. However, as Ripple transaction validators are private enterprises, they have regular IT systems with various limits. One interesting workaround of this limitation has been the development of the InterLedger Protocol (ILP) by Ripple. The ILP itself is not a ledger, as it does not seek consensus toward any state. Rather, it provides a top-layer cryptographic escrow system which allows funds to move between ledgers with the help of intermediaries it calls "connectors." As stated by Ripple CTO Stefan Thomas, *"As long as your ledger supports [Interledger], you can participate in a payment and someone will be able to provide liquidity. It can be PayPal, Alipay, bitcoin, bank ledgers or Skype, anywhere people hold balances, they have a ledger"* (Rizzo, 2015)

CHAPTER 3

■ ■ ■

Innovating Capitalism

As stated in the previous chapter, the most pressing issue facing the adoption of technology to address TBTF and the fragmentation of the financial services is the existing regulatory and policy framework. We have also seen that although finance becomes increasingly cashless, the validation and auditing operations of financial firms are still largely dependent on manual and/or archaic processes. However, this operating methodology is attuned to the current regulatory settings and, in part, is the reason for its continued existence. Furthermore, the disconnect between finance and macroeconomics has resulted in the execution of unsatisfactory monetary and fiscal policies that have been unable to adequately address the growing debt of nation-states and have been unsuccessful in detecting, let alone addressing, systemic risks posed by large institutions. Thus, prior to establishing a new framework for a cashless age, we need to determine what are the obstacles and limitations of the current regulatory and policy frameworks. It is only by identifying the pain points in the current system that we will be able to determine if today's monetary and fiscal policies are out of ammunition and instigate changes and alternations for the next epoch of capitalism.

Reviewing the Current Definition of Capitalism

Let us begin by first asking what is the definition of capitalism? To me, owing to the intimate role of money in every aspect of our lives, capitalism is as much a cultural construct as it is an economic paradigm. As per empirical studies and philosophical interpretations, a capitalist society is one in which markets consist of multiple players who are all performing efficient value exchange operations under the premise of allocating scarce resources for their most optimal function. In such markets, regulations and policies act as levers which are to be used appropriately, based on clear rules, to achieve outcomes of prosperity for a society at large.

However, the precipitate of the analyses depicted in the previous two chapters indicates that the increased financialization of society has tarnished this definition. Today, capitalism has gone from a society that uses markets to reach certain shared prosperity objectives, to a society where everything is for sale, including risk. It can almost be said that we have gone too far with capitalism and that we have overused the three governing levers of capitalism—markets, regulations, and policies—to create matrices of inequality grounded on an unsound or misinterpreted understanding of efficiency. It is thus not surprising to find that no historical definition of capitalism encompasses all three levers.

© Kariappa Bheemaiah 2017
K. Bheemaiah, *The Blockchain Alternative*, DOI 10.1007/978-1-4842-2674-2_3

Hence, to construct an updated definition of capitalism, we need to have a clear and discursive understanding of the current limitations of the three levers and the roles that they play. When redefining the role of markets, we need to inculcate the concept of inequality and ask ourselves whether the distribution of income and wealth governed by markets is a problem. Inequality by itself is not a fallacy; it is a motivational tool which allows for the development of skills and knowledge, which in turn uplifts marginalized peoples to previously unbeknownst levels of prosperity and happiness (sometimes referred to as the famed "middle class"). Inequality can thus be looked at as a catalyst for initiating a transitionary process that allows for the development of robust economies; the evolution of China over the past three decades is a good example of how the opening up of markets coupled with a combat against inequality can lead to transformative outcomes. Indeed, over the past thirty years, the increasing momentum of globalization has allowed for the use of societal inequalities as a catalytic agent to elevate close to a billion people from poverty (Olinto &Uematsu, 2013). But inequality can also be too much of a good thing. When inequality reaches a certain threshold limit, it leads to less social mobility and affects the future growth of the economy, as it alienates poorer sections of society from developing knowledge and skills that are germane to innovation (Chetty et al., 2015). Thus, while the market lever of capitalism has solved many problems with regards to poverty, the sub-factor of inequality has created new ones. Today we bear witness to the disenfranchisment of people across various strata of society. When inequality undermines the lever of markets itself, we must acknowledge that we have a problem.

The lever of regulation is a much more multifaceted hydra, as it variates at sectorial and societal levels. There is a rhetoric that it is crippling regulation that is currently stagnating the progress of society and infringing upon the waves of productivity. While there is evidence to support this claim, it belies what regulation is all about. Regulation allows a society to use market mechanisms to achieve outcomes, but in a way that is conducive to society at large, while allowing for fair game between market players. The process of regulation is to determine what is the ideal cost-benefit trade-off for what we want as a society and what markets need to do in order to help us get there. This encapsulates a plethora of societal concerns ranging from the destruction of monopolies to protecting the environment. It is needless to say that regulation is important. But, as we have seen, the current regulatory structure has led to the creation of banking oligopolies and is limiting the progress of technologies such as the Blockchain. As regulation is constantly evolving with a significant time lag when compared to the quickening frequency of technological waves, efforts need to be made to address this chasm. This is a complex and complicated endeavor and, in a later part of this chapter, we will discuss an alternative way to view regulation.

As markets and regulation are interwoven into the fabric of policy, the final lever of capitalism is the fundamental tool that guides the development of society. From an all-encompassing view, it can be said that today's policies are inefficient in execution, as they fail to englobe the looping behavior of technology. As it has been seen in Boxes 3 and 4, the fastest branch of technological progress is software. Software excels in looped behavior. By using code to perform repetitive tasks, software allows for large-scale automation of tasks that were previously the domain of skilled workers. In the past, technological evolution posed threats to manual jobs. But as machine learning, neural nets, and AI continue to make significant and rapid strides, the threat is now faced by skilled personnel who were employed to perform cognitive tasks (Refer to Sidebar 3-1). As Marc Andreessen said, *"Software is eating the world."* Today, software is increasingly threatening anyone whose job function involves a repetitive framework. With automation and financialization posing the biggest risks to industrialized economies, policies are needed that address the changes in productivity gains. Hence, it must be understood by policy makers that we have an ailing self-organized society that needs more direction in order to combat and adapt to the future technological changes. To do so requires policy makers to think about initiatives related to the development of a cashless society, technological unemployment, increasing life spans, and their macroeconomic impacts.

All in all, it must be understood by the helmsmen of the three levers that the future definition of capitalism cannot be based on theoretical abstractions, but by understanding the complexity and dynamism of future societies. As the fragmentation and digitization of society accelerates, we are witnessing the growth of multi-player relationships between real and virtual economic actors whose behavior is not portrayed by theorized ideal agents. While macroeconomists frequently talk about the economics of innovation, they often fail to consider the innovation of economics. Just as our institutes are predicated on growth expectations, it is imperative that there be a steady stream of innovation, even at the academic and theoretical levels. The laws of economics are not like the laws of physics, where a set of commandments works universally. What we will see in the next portions of this chapter is that, owing to the different kinds of economic and financial transitions, there are several variations of capitalism. Hence, rather than constructing a universal definition of capitalism, what is required is a buffet of theories. Prior to attempting this multi-theory development exercise, we first need to understand how technology in redefining work, income, and productivity in capitalistic societies as markets, regulation, and policy are intertwined with these factors. Sidebar 3-1 offers some insight.

SIDEBAR 3-1: HOW TECHNOLOGY IS REPLACING SKILLS AND TASKS

Source: "Inequality, Technology and Job Polarization of the Youth Labor Market in Europe" (Bheemaiah & Smith, 2015).

The growth of information and communication technologies (ICTs) has had broad encompassing effects on various sectors of employment, education, and societal structures. Understanding the dynamics of technology's impact on the future of employment thus requires a holistic analysis of the range of tasks currently being automated in various sectors of employment. This in turn provides us with a heuristic connection between education, employment, income levels, and ICT.

The impact technology, and more specifically ICT technology, has had on inequality and changing the structural foundations of the labor market, has been a central theme for researchers for quite some time (see, Acemoglu, 2010; Autor et al., 2003; Michaels et al., 2010). These studies have focused on understanding the impact of advancing technology on skills, education, and job structures. In this regard, a number of arguments including the skill-biased technological change (SBTC) hypothesis and the Autor-Levy-Murnane (ALM) hypothesis have underlined how advancements in technology reduce the demand for unskilled labor and increase the income compensation for skilled labor.

While researchers and economists from MIT, notably Daron Acemoglu, established the correlation between skill acquisition and technological change, others, notably David Autor, were able to show that improvements in technology were leading to the creation of a polarized labor market, where growth was seen in jobs sectors that required high skills. Autor also found that an increasing demand was seen in jobs that involved "cognitive flexibility," while at the same time, the demand for low-skill jobs requiring "non-routine manual tasks" also grew, creating a dip in the demand for jobs that involved tasks attributed to medium skill sets. However, more recent research from Beardy et al., 2013, has shown that there is also a reversal in the demand for jobs requiring cognitive flexibility, owing to the advancement in ICT.

As technology continues to replace labor it also contributes to enlarging the inequality gap. Greater inequality has been shown to make a greater proportion of the population vulnerable to poverty (Jaumotte et al., 2008), and in the aftermath of the crisis it becomes increasingly relevant to analyze social exclusion from the perspective of Kuznets Hypothesis*. While previous literature focused on the causes of inequality have compared globalization (both trade and financial), offshoring, and technology as the three most common contributors to inequality, the dominant view among labor economists has been that technology was more important than trade as the driving force behind changes in the structure of employment ((Desjonqueres et al., 1999); (Katz & Autor, 1999)), and that technological change was biased towards skilled workers, leading to the hypothesis of skill-biased technological change (SBTC).

More recently, studies have also focused on the role played by wage premiums associated with higher education and cognitive ability (Frey & Osborne, 2013); (Autor, 2014) and the effect of technology in offshoring employment. To gain a better insight into the role of technology, offshoring, and globalization in accentuating inequality, studies such as those done by Jaumotte et al (2008), have examined survey data of the subcomponents of trade and financial globalization, including comparative analysis of exports of manufacturing versus agriculture, and portfolio debt and equity flows versus foreign direct investment (FDI). They found that while trade liberalization and export growth are associated with income inequality, increased financial openness was associated with higher inequality.

----

*(An economic hypothesis which states that as an economy develops, market forces first increase and then decrease economic inequality, following a bell curve trajectory.)

However, the main finding of this line of research has been that the combined contribution of these factors towards income inequality was much lower than that of technological change, both in developed and developing countries. While the spread of technology is by itself related to increasing globalization, the study found that technological advancement was seen to have a unique and identifiable effect on inequality, especially in terms of wages, with greater technological progress increasing the premium paid on high-skill inputs and lowering the premium paid on low-skill inputs.

Technological change was thus observed to affect a significant segment (manufacturing and services) of the economy in developed countries by increasing the relative demand for higher skills and thereby intensifying income inequality. The study also found that better access to education and training could allow for sharing the benefits of globalization and technology as increased access to education was directly associated with more equal income distributions on average.

The results of these studies indicate that the rise in inequality is largely attributable to technological change and that the results of globalization are relatively minor in comparison. However, both technological progress and globalization were seen to increase the relative demand for skills and, as a result, the main effect technology was having on the work structure was the creation of a polarized workforce, in which employment shares for high- paid managers and low-paid personal services workers was rising, while the employment of shares of manufacturing and "routine" office workers was seen to be falling.

The link between the relative demand for skills and technological advancement, in particular the "skill bias" of technical change (SBTC), was first established with Tinbergen's (1974, 1975) founding work and the development of the canonical model (Acemoglu & Autor, 2010), which offered a structure to measure the changes in the return earned by workers with respect to their skill. The canonical model was especially useful in measuring the skill attribute of earnings, as it offered a model to conduct comparative analysis of different worker groups simultaneously. The empirical success of the canonical model helped account for salient changes in the distribution of earnings (Autor, 2010). However, despite the model's applicability, modern changes in labor markets and employment trends motivated the creation of a new model more attuned to the modern era, as one of the shortcomings found in the canonical model was its lack of a concrete definition for "tasks."

A task, as per Autor and Acemoglu (2010), is defined as a unit of work activity that produces an output, i.e., good or service. In contrast, a skill is a worker's endowment or capability to perform a task or various tasks. These researchers determined that the distinction between skill and task needed to be formally addressed, as a worker's skill to perform a task(s) was directly related to the quality of the good or service being produced, and hence to the wages earned by the worker. They have further gone on to state that a worker's wages were thus related to his or her ability to perform multiple tasks, and to be able to change their skill-set based on the changes in the labor market and the introduction of new technologies.

(As per the European Migration Network (EMN), workers with a high skill level are those that create significant economic value through the work performed (human capital). Skilled labor is generally characterized by high education or expertise and high wages. Skilled labor involves complicated tasks that require specific skill sets, education, training, and experience; may involve abstract thinking; and are seen as complementary to ICT capital and the organizational forms that go with it. Examples include physicians, plumbers, attorneys, engineers, scientists, builders, architects, and professors. Low-skilled or unskilled labor includes the segment of the work force associated with a skill level of limited economic value for the work performed (human capital). Unskilled labor is generally characterized by low education levels and small wages).

The classification and distinction between various tasks performed by workers was formally addressed by ALM in 2003. Their paper categorized tasks as "routine" and "non-routine," with routine tasks being defined as cognitive and manual activities that could be accomplished by following explicit rules, while non-routine tasks were defined as those tasks that required problem-solving and complex communication activities. Using this classification, they subdivided all tasks performed by workers into four separate categories*: (1) non-routine cognitive tasks, (2) routine cognitive tasks, (3) routine manual tasks and (4) non-routine manual tasks.

Using this classification, ALM proposed the "routinization" hypothesis and continued to argue convincingly that modern technology was capable of replacing human capital in routine tasks, i.e., tasks that can be performed via step-by-step procedures or rules, but could not replace human capital in non-routine tasks. Furthermore, they provided evidence to support the fact that demand for labor input of routine cognitive and manual tasks in the US economy had declined, while the demand for labor input of non-routine analytic and interactive tasks had risen.

By distinguishing and measuring the relative demand and supply mechanisms for tasks, the routinization hypothesis went on to prove that the effect of these demands on the labor market had led to the creation of a "polarized" work environment in which expansion was seen in the demand of high-skill and low-skills jobs, but coupled with a fall in the demand for routine or "middle-skilled" ** jobs, and that job polarization was leading to a shrinking concentration of employment in occupations in the middle of the skill distribution. The polarization effect also had an impact on the polarization of wage growth, with a relative growth in upper-tail and lower-tail earnings, relative to median or middle earnings. More recent research also shows that this process has gained pace in recent years, as per capita employment in middle-skill jobs continues to disappear (Jaimovich & Siu, 2012).

The growing body of empirical evidence exacerbating the leveraging effect technology has on inequality merits scrutiny in order to identify which gamut of technology is having the most influential role in this transitional shift. In this regard, work done by Michaels, Natraj, and van Reenen (2010), has attributed the dominant effect to ICT on the changing educational composition of employment at the international scale. The authors also found that industries and countries with faster growth rates in ICT also experienced an increase in demand for college-educated workers relative to workers with intermediate levels of education and that the falling quality-adjusted prices for ICT had a significant impact in causing this shift. The researchers concluded that both ICT and research and development (R&D) had raised the relative demand for college-educated workers and that, consistent with the ICT-based polarization hypothesis, this increase had come mainly from the reduction in the relative demand for middle-skilled workers rather than low-skilled workers (Michaels et al, 2010).

(As per the Occupational Information Network (ONET) database, non-routine or abstract tasks are those that involve critical thinking, judgment/ decision making, complex problem solving, interacting with computers and thinking creatively. Routine task measures are by arm-hand steadiness, manual dexterity, finger dexterity, operation monitoring, and estimating the quantifiable characteristics of products, events, or information. Service tasks are further measured by social perceptiveness, service orientation, assisting and caring for others, establishing and maintaining interpersonal relationships, selling and performing for or working directly with the public.)

**(Based on education and training levels, middle-skill jobs are those that generally require some education and training beyond high school but less than a bachelor's degree. These postsecondary education or training requirements can include associate's degrees, vocational certificates, significant on-the-job training, previous work experience, or some college, but less than a bachelor's degree. They are represented by routine cognitive and manual tasks which were defined earlier.)*

The effects of technical change (proxied by ICT and R&D) on employment is consistent with other literature (see Draca, Bloom and van Reenen, 2009) that found that technology had a more explanatory capability in affecting skill demand. While the analysis by Michaels et al. further bolstered the routinization hypothesis, other work by Jaumotte et al. (2008) had also shown that some of the key control variables in determining inequality included technological development (measured by share of ICT capital in total capital stock) and access to education (measured by years spent in education by people 15 years and over and share of population with at least a secondary education).

Measuring this form of skill-biased employment adaptability was the primary outcome of the work carried out by Autor and Acemoglu in 2010, 2013; where they introduced a framework to systematically understand the recent labor market trends and the impact of technology on earning premiums and employment opportunities. By building up on previous work (ALM, 2003); the authors explained that the necessity to create this new framework was quintessential to understand the effects of technological developments, and particularly the impact of (ICT), on middle-skill workers. This symbiotic relationship of technical change, skills, and education is relative to the task dimension of employment and continues to be a significant predictor of employment flexibility and inequality. Thus, this makes the effect of ICT on education and employment a non-trivial effect (Goos et al., 2014).

Although these studies establish the link between the effects of ICT on education and employment, the relationship between education and earnings is more nuanced. The polarization of employment coupled with the polarization of wages (Autor & Acemoglu, 2010), suggests that a worker's occupation is the main determinant of their wages. This would suggest that a worker's educational level had a weaker role in determining occupation and earnings.

In order to gauge the explanatory power of educational attainment on wage determination, Autor and Acemoglu (2010), conducted their study by taking into consideration four control variables, which included years of schooling, educational attainment (some high school, high school grad, four-year college, post-college degree, etc.) and dummy variables for ten occupational categories* as well as 11 industry categories**, for both genders. By measuring the change in trends over a forty-year period, they concluded that the occupation plays an increasingly important role in the evolution of both employment and earnings and that it was simply not a proxy for either education or industry (Autor & Acemoglu, 2010).

The results of these findings allow us to draw parallels with the SBTC and ALM hypotheses, along with other task-versus-skill literature. According to the SBTC hypothesis, technology increases the demand for skilled labor and reduces the demand for unskilled labor, thus lowering the wage compensation for the latter. The ALM hypothesis, on the other hand, explains the routinization and polarizing effect of technology, while the Acemoglu and Autor (2010) study shows that it is skills and occupations that determine earnings and not just education. The pivotal role paid by education has been documented by various studies. But the results of recent studies show us that, in the light of increasing technological change, skill adaptability and cognitive flexibility has an increasingly influential role in the inequality debate.

(The occupational categories were selected as per the four task levels, namely: Non-Routine Cognitive Tasks: Managers, Professionals, Technicians; Routine Cognitive Tasks: Sales, Office and admin; Routine Manual Tasks: Production, craft and repair, Operators, fabricators and laborers; Non-routine Manual Tasks: Protective service, Food prep, buildings and grounds, cleaning, Personal care and personal services.)

**(The industry categories were subdivided as per the four tasks categories as well, namely: Non-Routine Cognitive Tasks: Professional, Managerial, and*

Technical Occupations; Routine Cognitive Tasks: Clerical, Administrative, and Sales Occupations; Routine Manual Tasks: Production, Craft, Repair and Operative Occupations; Non-Routine Manual Tasks: Service Occupations)

While the subject of inequality often looks at the "top 1 percent," this approach overlooks the earning capacities of the remaining 99 percent and, more specifically, the dramatic growth in wage premiums associated with higher education and cognitive ability. The past three decades of computerization and the profusion of ICT in organizations have increasingly raised the criticality of cognitive labor as it complements educated workers who excel at abstract problem solving and creative tasks. But when combined with the polarization effect, the net result is an increase in demand for formal education, technical expertise, and cognitive flexibility, and a devaluation of the skills of workers without a post-secondary education (Autor, 2014).

However, recent research (Beaudry et al., 2013), is now indicating that although the supply of higher-skilled workers has grown, a gradual slowing down in the demand for these workers is currently occurring. As a result, an increasing number of higher-skilled workers are now performing tasks that qualify them as underemployed, while simultaneously pushing lower skilled workers out of the occupations that are associated with these tasks and, in some cases, even pushing them out of the workforce completely.

By creating a model that emphasizes technological change, the authors found that the skills downgrading process which forces high-educated workers into accepting routine jobs is because, as technological progress has positive impacts on the productivity of cognitive tasks, it eventually leads to a decreasing path for the cognitive task employment rate. This contrasts with the evidence of an increase in demand in this sector (Autor et al, 1998).

The authors coin this development as a "de-skilling" process, since it involves cognitive workers with experience and already in the job market being obliged to move down the ladder in order to stay in employment. This has serious implications for new job seekers as not only is the entry bar raised higher for new entrants, but the number of opportunities available to them is also reduced (Beaudry et al., 2013).

As individuals in routine cognitive occupations incur a higher probability of unemployment than individuals employed in non-routine cognitive occupations, the unemployment gap between these occupations is attributed to advancements in technology. However, more importantly, the question to be raised is if skill-biased technological change is being replaced by skill-substituting technological change and, if so, is education the sole answer to this change?

In light of the evidence provided in Boxes 3 and 4, the answer to this question will not be relegated only to the creation of value from education. There is no doubt that education will play a pivotal role in helping knowledge and manual workers prepare for the future demands of the economy. But markets, policies, and regulations will also play equally important roles, for it must be remembered that markets by themselves do not aid in the development of skills and growth. Growth results from the co-evolution of technologies, firms, and industry structures and the social and public institutions which support them, connected by complex feedback processes (Jacobs & Mazzucato, 2016).

It is only with an understanding of technology's effect on inequality, the situation of labor markets, the polarization effect of technology on tasks, and the changing demands for skills, that we will be able to begin the redefinition of markets, regulations, and policies for tomorrow's cashless and entrepreneurship-driven knowledge economy.

■ **Note** While the SBTC assumes that wages are determined through the forces of supply and demand in the labor market, some ongoing research is challenging this paradigm by stating that the primary determinant of wages on a sustainable basis are the employment practices of major business enterprises. Refer: "*Skill Development and Sustainable Prosperity: Cumulative and Collective Careers versus Skill-Biased Technical Change*" (Lazonick et al., 2015).

A Changing Market Structure

The information revolution is reversing the industrial revolution and changing the structure of markets in the process. While the industrial age allowed for people to team up in large, mechanistic, organizational hierarchies to create factories and companies, the information revolution is in the process of breaking down communication barriers and creating technologies that reduce intermediaries to create smaller and more interconnected teams (Ravikanth, 2015). As technologies such as the Blockchain begin to remove central points of control, the evolving digital and decentralized structure of markets today are challenging the predefined theories on productivity, risk allocation, and labor requirements. Increased automation, propelled by rapid advancements in machine/deep learning, mobile payments, robotics, and the exponential increase in the computerization of tasks, is leading to the development of networked, on-demand businesses which are transforming and reorganizing firms and establishing new skill requirements across the entire economy. As tasks are digitized and operations are networked, processes can be codified and then replicated. As a result, these changes are beginning to challenge our relationship with technology, as machines that were created as tools to increase the productivity of workers are now turning into the workers themselves.

Although the majority of these technologies were created in an effort to challenge the existing incumbents, it is interesting to note that those firms that were created to utilize these technological changes have begun to create winner-take-majority effects, changing the market share decomposition in the process. While the rise of companies such as Uber or Airbnb have been amply discussed and function as effective success stories, these changes can also be seen in other sectors as well. Consider the case of

AngelList, the successful fundraising platform, in its rise over the past few years. Founded in 2010, AngelList is a Silicon Valley-based community-styled company where startups meet investors. The company is responsible for moving millions of dollars in investment and does so with a team of only 22 personnel. Almost every operation including fundraising, recruiting, engineering, systems operations, product development, customer service, marketing, inbound deal processing, and deal closing is done in code. Of the 22 personnel, 16 are coders or have coding experience. (Slayton, 2014).

As digitization leads to massive increases in efficiency and network effects, markets are getting more Schumpeterian in the sense that those market players who are capable of digitizing business models are capable of overtaking existing incumbents and gaining larger portions of market share.

In *The Wealth of Nations*, Adam Smith famously said that the division of labor is limited by the extent of the market. Thus, as digitization overcomes the physical barriers to access markets, we notice that it is creating room for specializations that address granular subdivisions in existing and niche markets. Moreover, as the barriers of technical know-how and location get porous, the impact on strategy has been the obsession on customer focus. Offering unique and customizable services inherently entails a certain amount of risk on the part of the entrepreneur, as success is dependent on the willingness of future clients to move away from existing offerings to new ones. As a result, experimentation and risk- taking are now increasingly touted to be the pillars of innovation by the stalwarts of entrepreneurship. But what this is also doing is creating new risks across the business diaspora.

As it has been seen in previous sections of this book, the world of finance and economics is not oblivious to this phenomenon. However, from a market risk perspective, the world of finance is still plagued with the inherent dichotomy that is seen between economics and finance. While governments have been focused on increasing regulatory measures for financial institutions following the crisis, less attention has been given to the development of sensible and effective regulation for private financial services providers. As finance increasingly migrates to the online world, it becomes increasingly necessary for governments to ensure that economic growth is curtailed from systemic stability while allowing for the long-term scaling of democratic value exchange networks for maximum social utility.

It must be remembered that this new financial market is a scalar in construct, owing to the diversity of technology. But, as new innovations are launched, the regulatory responsibility is often not consistently defined across geographies and business functions. As a result, it is often seen that the regulatory stipulations are at odds with the company's legal description and the financial activities that it engages in. The current rigidity of regulatory remits therefore does not allow for a holistic supervisory view, which in turn reduces the expansion of these business models and asphyxiates innovation.

For example, although consumers today have better access to alternative sources of credit, a lack of understanding of these new products and insufficient validation from regulatory bodies can shift the risk involved to the end investor. While the use of data provides the delivery of customizable financial services, these data-imbued services also entail cyber-risk, cyber-crime and data privacy issues. Hence, the establishment of standards in terms of safeguarding information has to be a quintessential safety objective to counteract any predatory misconduct and allow for large-scale adoption.

However, as technology has changed the risk profile of the market, it has also enabled the creation of techniques that can be used to enhance market stability. Thus, from a regulatory standpoint, the risks posed by technology can be addressed with a market framework that allows for the leveraging of technology to address these issues. The scalar configuration of the financial market requires for this fight-fire-with-fire approach to be deployed at multiple levels, based on the sector of financial services. We have already seen how different market sectors are changing with Blockchain and FinTech in the previous chapter. Hence, we will review today's market structure by focusing on the two primary functions of a market: getting access to funds/credit (lending and payments market) and the exchange of goods (trade finance market), to see how Blockchain can be used to redefine market operations and thus provide a primer to the necessary policies required for scaling this change.

Lending and Payments

The lending and payments sectors share some common traits. First, increasingly these functions are moving out of the purview of the banking domain and into the commercial sphere at both the business and operational levels. Second, as more private market players get involved, there is an increasing tendency for the use of "private regulation"[1] between businesses and customers (notably for SME's). The increased use of private regulation is leading to the sharing of risk exclusively between the client and the financial institution. The reason behind this practice is relatively straightforward. As FinTech firms use technology to create proprietary algorithms and software to address customer needs, the rate at which their offers proliferate the market is outpacing the adaptive abilities of regulators. As a result, we are faced with a scenario in which the regulations do not cover the consumers' interest as they do with traditional channels.

The lending practices of large banks are mostly executed in the offline world and, as a result, are subject to more regulatory scrutiny. For example, in the US, an established firm that offers loans is subject to at least two regulatory control bodies. While commercial banks in a certain state are subject to local regulators, national banks (which function as member banks of the Federal Reserve), are subject to examination by the US Treasury Department. If the bank is considered a SIFI, then they are supervised by the Financial Stability Oversight Committee (FSOC) and may even have government representatives involved in their business and compliance operations (Murphy, 2015). When these institutions provide loans to businesses, they are further required to participate in the 5-step CAMELS evaluation,[2] and if they were to receive a rating of 3 or more, would be subject to regulatory corrections. In addition to these regulations, following the crisis, the Dodd-Frank Act reforms and new Basel III stipulations require

---

[1]In terms of IT systems, data sharing, authorization, fraud, and arbitration.
[2]Since 1979, banks have been rated using the interagency Uniform Financial Institutions Ratings System (UFIRS), recommended by the Federal Reserve and other banking agencies. This system evaluates six components: Capital, Assets, Management, Earnings, Liquidity and Sensitivity to Market Risk and is referred to by acronym CAMELS. A Rating of 3, 4, or 5 may subject the bank to enforcement actions, enhanced monitoring, and limitations on expansion. *Source : https://www.fedpartnership.gov/bank-life-cycle/topic-index/bank-rating-system*

banks to hold significantly larger capital requirements and issue debt also in the form of contingent convertible (CoCo) bonds[3] (see notes).

The result of these regulations have definitely led to a safer lending sector. But at the same time they have created adverse side effects. As commercial banks continue to settle lawsuits following subprime mortgage transgressions, they have unsurprisingly adopted more conservative tactics when making loans to riskier borrowers. As stated by John Shrewsberry, Wells Fargo's chief financial officer, *"[the bank is not interested in making loans to riskier borrowers, even those who meet Federal Housing Standards]. Those are the loans that are going to default, and those are the defaults we are going to be arguing about 10 years from now. We are not going to do that again"* (Koren, 2015).

These above-cited reasons have, however, not restricted the entry of the new entrants. On the contrary, the current climate and the lack of oversight has allowed them to thrive to a certain extent. In the mortgage industry, for example, 42% of mortgages issued in 2014 were issued by new lending firms as compared to 10% in 2009, and these firms currently account for 4 in 10 home loans (Koren, 2015). But all that glitters isn't gold. As most of the new FinTech lending platforms provide smaller amounts of credit (less than $100,000) they are better suited to serving the SME loan market.

But as these credit providers are not defined as banks, they are not subject to the same regulatory pressures. In most cases these lenders may be required to register with a regulator and subject to examination, but this is not set in stone. As a result of this oversight, the new lending platforms have begun to participate in riskier business practices. Some Fintech lenders do not even ask for a business plan or future cash projections. All that is required to get a loan of less than a $100,000 is that the company needs to be in business for over 24 months, have at least $75,000 in annual sales and have no recent history of bankruptcy. If a large bank were to execute a similar practice, it would be criticized for being lackadaisical. This is not to say that there is not oversight at all. Lending Club, the well-known peer-to-peer lending company, is overseen by the US Securities and Exchange Commission, but this is mainly because it has now grown so large and receives a majority of funding from institutional sources (e.g,, insurance firms, banks like JPM Chase, etc.). In that sense, it can be seen as more of an exception to the current rules.

It can be argued that, owing to the small size of these new firms, subjecting them to the same stringent regulations as large institutions would be overkill and would thwart innovation. To a large extent this would be correct. But it must be remembered that as things stand, FinTech firms do not have to adhere to capital requirements. Hence, if the economic conditions were to take a downturn, these firms are ill-suited to respond to a cessation of credit supply. As an increasing number of consumers and SMEs turn to FinTech firms for borrowing money, such an occurrence could have disastrous effects for a number of SMEs. And as the current regulation is largely "private" and involves contractual agreements between provider and consumer, the liability ultimately falls upon the consumer, leaving them unprotected.

---

[3]CoCo bonds are financial instruments that can be converted to equity if certain capital ratio conditions are met (e.g., when capital falls below 7.5%). This allows banks to increase their capital ratio if it falls below a predefined threshold. Refer notes: CoCo bonds and the Blockchain.

The payments industry is facing a similar conundrum as lending services, with the sector witnessing dramatic technological changes over the past few years, notably with the Blockchain. These changes reflect the altering needs of households and companies, and new payment providers have stepped in to address these needs. In a way, regulators have been more responsible in this arena and the recent launch of institutional networks such as CHAPS, the ACH network, and the Real Time Gross Settlement (RTGS) system, which currently transfer immense amounts each day (in the UK, RTGS settles around £500 Billion between banks every day—that's almost a third of the UK's annual GDP), shows how institutions have been able to adapt.

The growth of payment API's and the rise of mobile banking (e.g., Atom Bank), has enabled non-bank entities to deliver better services using the payments infrastructure, and allowed these providers to grow without building an extensive network. Although this has provided the end user with benefits and savings, it has led to the creation of new risks. First, real-time payments make it harder to implement effective defenses against money laundering, terrorist financing, and various kinds of electronic fraud. The more connected a payment system, the higher the threat from cyber-attackers and the greater the risk of contagion. Second, traditional payment providers have direct access to payment networks and hence have to adhere to their regulations (Shafik, 2016). However, this is not the case with FinTech firms who normally use correspondent banks or alternative payment channels. Hence, the question needs to be asked as to whether regulation needs to be passed to include the new entrants into the existing payment platforms.

All in all, the lending and payments industry of today suffers from three fundamental limitations. First, the new entrants in these markets are not subject to the same regulations and supervision as their larger counterparts. This puts a greater amount of risk on the consumer, affects the scalability of new business models, and makes these sectors more vulnerable to systemic risks. Second, companies can only enhance their performance when immersed in a stable regulatory environment. A lack of this environment creates higher levels of profit uncertainty. Third, as the pace of technology outstrips the pace of regulations, supervisors have very little time to adjust and adjust at different paces in different areas. As a result, this is leading to imbalances of control within the system, which in turn increases the system's vulnerability as weak links are created within the networks. To address these limitations, regulators have to extend their practices across all market participants while ensuring that the rules can be modified according to the role and the type of financial institution.

Furthermore, as mentioned in the previous chapter, the lending sector is beset by rehypothecation, which uses the channels of shadow banking to convert secure collateral into risky debt instruments and structured investment vehicles. Coupled with excessive borrowing and poor information available to investors, these shadow banking investment products were the source of the global financial crisis in 2007. Hence, apart from the three fundamental limitations, regulators also need to ensure that borrowers and investors are protected from debt maturity mismatches that are characteristic of shadow banking products, if they intend to avoid history repeating itself.

It is in responding to these limitations that the Blockchain offers a solution pathway. A lender or sender is essentially doing a simple operation: they are exchanging capital for an investment in an asset or transferring value from themselves to another. Thus, at a fundamental level, lending and payments involves a record of a transfer of existing capital for assets among a set of identified owners. This is the very definition of what a Blockchain does. It sends value across a network and records every movement that occurs in this space. The codified execution of smart contracts is another benefit for regulators. In the context of loans, the pre-determined terms such as loan amount, loan maturity, interest rate, principal, and interest payment schedule and permitted flexibility can be encoded in a smart contract. This allows regulators to verify if a firm is behaving in a predatory manner and creates better circles of competition within the sector. As actions can now be verified and challenged, assets can be tracked and their true value can be verified by following their exchange between market players. This in turn can lead to better consumer protection and a safer environment.

What regulators need to decipher are the advantages that are gained from the use of cryptographic laws instead of regular laws. Regular laws can be seen as "code" that is extrinsic to the system: the rules can be broken, but consequences flow from that breach to ensure compliance (UK Government Chief Scientific Adviser, 2016). Cryptographic law, on the other hand, is intrinsic: if any action goes against the code/rules, then an error is returned and no activity occurs. Thus, compliance is guaranteed through the operation of the code itself.

In light of the aforementioned challenges and advantages, government institutions ought to seriously consider the employment of the Blockchain. As stated before, one of the Blockchain's main advantages is that it is an infrastructural tool. The fact that it offers public and private operational features also makes it relatively malleable. We can imagine a scenario in which a newly created firm approaches a government institution and applies for a licence to trade on its sovereign Blockchain, much like in the same way that a firm has to register its company status. Once the KYB (Know Your Business) process is done, the firm begins to transact and the validation of these transactions can be done by registered governmental bodies or private enterprises that offer this service and which have a license to perform this function. This idea is not a far stretch from the existing practices, and Blockchain-based initiatives like this are already being deployed.

Consider the case of Ripple. In the Ripple protocol, the validation is done by a process called consensus, rather than proof of work. Consensus is different from proof of work in the sense it that depends on a system of voting. Every transaction is verified by the authorized transaction validators and the registered Ripple validators include reputed institutions such as Microsoft and MIT. When a supermajority (>70%) is reached by these validators, the transaction is deemed sound, verified, and added to the Ripple Blockchain. The advantage of this process is lower verification time and higher verification of transactions per second (TPS). It is for this reason that the Ripple protocol has been adopted by the Earthport payments network, which processes 150 million transactions per day.

Hence, from a technical standpoint, the solutions are present and worthy of exploration. What is required is the engagement of governments in order to achieve scalability and mass adoption. Institutional engagement will also spur innovation and also allow for the creation of Blockchains that are suited for specific operations. Using concepts such as a Sidechains and the InterLedger Protocol (ILP), usage-specific Blockchains can then be linked to the sovereign Blockchain, providing regulators with the necessary oversight.

But the efficient working of such a control system requires the deployment of the Blockchain at an institutional level. As things stand, most governments are focused on the risks of introducing this new technology into the financial sector and considering what steps need to be taken to limit or control it. In light of the potential of the Blockchain to foster prosperity, inclusion, and stability, perhaps the greatest risk is that conflicting government inertia could prevent it from fully reaching its potential.

Thankfully, there are some exceptions and some governmental bodies are seriously beginning to consider these ideas. In a recent speech given at the Bank of England, the Deputy Governor of the Bank of England stated her interest in using the Blockchain (or distributed ledger) to create *"a [new] blueprint for the Bank's settlement infrastructure."* If such a plan were to materialize, then it would mean that the events on the Blockchain could be supervised by the legal and regulatory systems under which banks and financial firms operate. This would in turn require that relevant legal and regulatory structures recognize the Blockchain as an authentic record of value exchange. It would also mean that sovereign currency would need to be tokenized so that their exchange on a Blockchain has legal status. The tokenization of sovereign currency will be addressed in the section dedicated to policy at a later part of this chapter.

The good news for governments is that the blooming of the Internet has already provided them with a historical frame of reference to tether their introspection. The Internet was able to grow thanks to the collaborative efforts of government, academia, and the private sector. Just as open standards like TCP/IP and HTTP led to the advent of the connected age, standards like Ripple are supporting market competition and liquefying the Internet of value. What is thus needed by governments is the definition of global standards, so that inventions like Ripple can work hand in hand with societal stakeholders to strengthen the fundamental principles and guide policy-making efforts. At an international scale, what is required is an ICANN-esque equivalent for the Blockchain.

Trade Finance

Trade is the oldest form of value exchange that human societies have engaged in. Today, the movement of goods across borders is carried out through supply chain management and trade finance. Supply chain deals with the processes that document the flow of goods from producer to consumer. It encompasses a wide range of procedures and structures that govern manufacturing, inventory management, and quality control. This involves a number of intermediaries and the transactions between them have to be documented to ensure the integrity of the trade process. The key word to remember is documentation. Today's trade transaction and associated processes involves the transfers of records such as purchase orders, invoices, bills of lading, customs documentation, certificates of authenticity, etc. Most of these transfers are recorded on paper and unstructured electronic databases.

The other side of trade involves the financial institutions. While trade represents billions of dollars in revenue, it also entails significant risks related to time delays, condition of goods, Forex, political instabilities, and, of course, liquidity and cash flow limitations. Banks aid trade by providing companies with capital for production and manufacturing, aiding with regulation compliance/ prevention of fraud, and guaranteeing the creditworthiness of businesses that do not have well-known working relationships (KYC/AML regulation compliance across borders). Banks also provide services such as factoring, wherein a bank pays the seller of goods before the buyer of those goods makes the payment. In doing so, the bank takes on the risk of buyer payment delays or default, but charges the supplier a rate of 4% to 8 % for this service, eating into the supplier's margins in the process. Banks thus play a central role in enabling these cross-border trade flows through payment execution, risk mitigation, and financing. In light of these services, banks have functioned as intermediaries that offset risk by acting as catalysts of cross-border trading. This has given rise to trade finance, which is a major source of revenue to banks. Trade finance is safe bet, as it provides a source of revenue that is independent of interest rates, provides cross-border payment fees, and has a low rate of default (up to 10 times lower than for traditional corporate lending (Accenture, 2016)).

Together, supply chain management and trade finance provide market players with capital to produce and sell products and services within territories and across borders. However, in recent times, supply chain management and trade finance have come under increased scrutiny, which has resulted in processing delays and additional risks. Institutions are unsatisfied with the current trade finance instruments, as they involve relatively high fees, involve complex procedures, and entail large time delays owing to their dependence on paper documentation. Furthermore, there are interoperability issues between banks and clients: banks require a complete view of a company's transaction flow to provide value services at key points of the value chain. However, as a large number of the processes are still manual in nature, there are a spate of platforms that provide individual solutions but with low interoperability. This lack of interoperability reduces transparency, creates a higher risk of fraud and higher fees, and does not allow for the development of network effects that can transform the industry.

In order to respond to these limitations, an increasing number of institutions have opted for the use of open account transactions, where the exporter supplies the goods and the importer pays for them on reception or based on pre-agreed payment conditions. In recent times, open trade accounting has become increasingly popular and currently makes up 90% of global trade (Euro Banking Association, 2016). In doing so, institutions are moving away from the banks' intermediated products, even though this comes at the price of reduced financing options. Institutions are responding to this loss by digitizing and improving the efficiency of the supply chain process, in terms of transaction services, risk mitigation, data transfer and matching, reporting, forecasting, Forex, liquidity, and cash management. As the shift from letters of credit to open account transaction continues, this digitization has led to the creation of new trade instruments (such as the Bank Payment Obligation[4]), digital trade documents (such as essDOCS[5] /Bolero) and new ERP's (SWIFT MT798[6]).

---

[4]The Bank Payment Obligation (BPO) is a payment technique developed in 2012 by Swift and the International Chamber of Commerce (ICC). The BPO is an irrevocable commitment given by a bank to another bank to make a payment on any date after an event. This event has to be proved by the electronic reconciliation of data produced by the Swift TSU (trade services utility).

[5]essDOCS is a UK-based trade services company that provides paperless trade documentation services, such as Electronic Bills of Lading (eB/Ls), Electronic Barge Nominations & Documents, Bank Payment Obligations plus (BPO+), eDocs, eDocumentary Collections, Electronic Bunker Receipts, etc.

[6]SWIFT's Trade for Corporates, the MT798, offers corporates the use of established interbank industry standards in trade finance through structured messages.

In spite of these changes, the complexity of regulation from border to border has meant that the interoperability problem still remains an issue and large-scale network effects remain elusive. Banks have adapted by providing online portals which allows their clients to replace paper documentation flows with digital data flows and provide added value services such as invoice matching, forecasting, and balance sheet and cash flow analysis. But even these changes have been insufficient in addressing the problem.

The existence of this prevailing setback has resulted in new entrants trying to find solutions, which in turn has increased competition. As the competition between banks continues to ascend, new logistics companies, alternative supply networks, and niche trade finance companies that focus on commodity trade finance or which exclusively focus on SME's have begun to fragment the market in recent years. (For example, Alibaba has entered partnerships with two UK startups to provide financing to small British businesses looking to buy from Chinese suppliers (Accenture, 2016).) As Basel III regulations have limited the supply of credit from large banks, these new entrants are capitalizing on these regulatory changes to offer better services for a plethora of trade finance clients.

But these new players have their work cut out for them. While all the services they provide can be grouped under the umbrellas of financing and risk mitigation, the fact that regulations can vary from geography to geography (and the lack of interoperability) means that there is always a dependence on intermediaries and repetition of processes. As stated by Lamar Wilson, CEO of Fluent, a Blockchain network for financial institutions and global enterprises,

"Currently, bank-run trade finance programs require a tremendous amount of resource-intensive due diligence, document collection, and processing, including coordination of remittance information. Financing rates are high for the businesses despite the low and shrinking margins for the financing provider. This is especially true at smaller banks who lack this infrastructure and must outsource these services for their larger clients," (Harris, 2016).

The final limitation of the current state of affairs of the trade finance sector is its lack of inclusiveness. While new players are entering the market and providing services to SME's, this trend cannot be generalized globally. It is important to take this into consideration as SME's provide employment to large swaths of populations in less developed countries. Across the OECD area, SMEs account for approximately 99% of all enterprises, and 2/3 of employment (OECD, 2010). In Western Europe, Japan, and USA, SMEs account for 55%–80% of total employment, while in Pakistan and Kenya, SMEs contribute to 80% and 60% of total employed population, respectively (Katua, 2014). Yet owing to a shortage of working capital to finance exports, limited information on markets, lack of standardized interoperable systems, inability to contact potential oversees customers, and inability to obtain reliable foreign representation, SMEs in these parts of the world are unable to participate in the global trading arena. The net result is that there is a US $1.4 trillion unmet global demand for trade finance[7] (Asia Development Bank, 2015) (WTO, 2016).

---

[7]Asia represents US $400 billion of this figure, while Africa represents US $120–225 billion.

In light of these limitations, regulators and policy makers need to look for technical solutions to overcome these shortcomings. Evidently, the objective should be to create a more interoperable system with specific standards to ensure trust and augment inclusiveness. It is here that the use of the Blockchain would make most sense. With the majority of trading occurring on an open account basis, the Blockchain can be used to gain real-time transparency of trade transaction documentation, including invoices, payments, change of ownership, customs documents, and bank-related data. This would not only streamline the trade process but also allow for better data matching, better dispute reconciliation, and better credit risk management. The transparency of the Blockchain would also allow for better audit trails, which in turn would help in credit risk assessment and fraud prevention, thus creating a more level playing field for all exporters and importers.

The automation provided by smart contracts will also help in reducing the number of intermediaries in the trade process. As transactions and documents get exchanged on the Blockchain, the transfer of ownership can be used as a trigger to execute the next leg of the trade process. As one party initiates a payment, the smart contract can be used to change the ownership of the goods to the other counterparty. The ability to link smart contracts to black/sanction lists and embargos will ensure that trade occurs within the norms of regulation and policy. As the shipping industry turns a technological corner and adds tracking chips to containers, the Blockchain will allow another level of IoT integration in the trade finance process. As smart contracts allow for immediate triggering effects, funds can be released sooner, thus enabling more granular payments. For example, if a smart contract between an exporter and an importer stipulates that, say, 15% of the funds are to be released to the exporter once goods have been cleared by customs, it would reduce the risk spread of the transaction, provide the exporter with some access to funds (which means more working capital), increase liquidity within the supply chain, and counteract duplicate invoicing, leading to the creation of a better level of trust within the market. Finally, if Blockchain and Smart Contract were to be used at a market level, it would allow for an upgrade of the existing IT systems and address the interoperability issues that currently challenge this market.

Just as digitization is changing the trade finance space, the Blockchain offers regulators a means by which they can construct a new framework of trade finance to improve efficiency, reduce the use of paper documentation, increase interoperability, automate processes, stimulate competition, and include a greater part of the global economy. Some critics might say that the scalability and the current scope of the Blockchain is ill-suited to this task. This is true to a certain extent, but as we have seen, progress is being made in many diverse ways (see Notes: "Scalability"). A more important question that these critics need to ask is if they ought to be content with the current provisions offered by the SWIFT system following recent events. In February 2016, hackers exploited weaknesses in local security systems, compromised networks, and sent fraudulent messages requesting money transfers on the SWIFT network. The hackers tried to pull off 35 bank transfers and, while a majority of these transfers were blocked, the hackers were still successful in transferring $81 million USD. Network members were asked to upgrade their security systems, and the worst was considered to have passed as the investigation commenced. However, at the end of August 2016, a letter was issued by the SWIFT network informing clients that new cyber-theft attempts—some of them successful—have been surfacing since June.

"Customers' environments have been compromised and subsequent attempts (were) made to send fraudulent payment instructions," according to a copy of the letter reviewed by Reuters.... "The threat is persistent, adaptive, and sophisticated—and it is here to stay." (Finkle, 2016)

As it has been repeatedly mentioned, the immutability and protection that is offered by the Blockchain is the most promising alternative in terms of addressing security concerns of this ilk. A Blockchain-based trade finance system would reduce the number of intermediaries and still perform the same functions, but in a safer and more transparent manner. Figure 3-1 provides a summarized graphical representation of what this would look like.

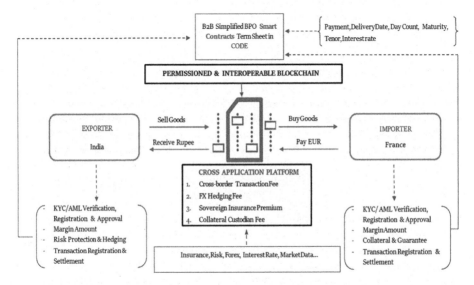

Figure 3-1. *Blockchain-based trade finance product and revenue model*

But as was mentioned in the lending and payments market section, for such a system to work would require the deployment of the Blockchain at an institutional level. More than a technical challenge, the real obstacle is once again regulation. As long as trade finance institutions are unsure of how regulators view the use of the Blockchain, they are unlikely to make it the interoperable backbone of their processes. What is required by regulators is the provision of concrete rules and standards that will help reduce the risk of regulatory violation and thus scale the use of this technology with all its benefits. This is not to say that the technology is ready for deployment. There are a number of hurdles that have been cited in this book. But regulators need to acknowledge that there is proof in the pudding and determine how to act.

Thankfully regulators do not lack of a reference of how this can be achieved. Just as the evolution of the Internet provides a historical frame of reference, the ongoing development of the R3 consortium's prototype platform, Corda (see Sidebar 3-2), can provide regulators with a current operational model of how the new market structure can look.

SIDEBAR 3-2: R3 CORDA™ : A FINANCIAL SERVICES BLOCKCHAIN THAT SERVES AS A FUTURE MARKET FRAMEWORK

Source: "Corda: An Introduction," R.G. Brown, J. Carlyle, I. Grigg, M. Hearn (August, 2016)

The 2011–2013 period was a turbulent year for the bitcoin Blockchain and the damaging reputational effects that it gained during that time have left its mark on this technology. As investors lost their investments in the Mt. Gox bitcoin exchange (mainly due to bad management and underdeveloped security systems), the Silk Road was posted on the cover of most news websites as the illicit substances hotspot.

If there was one positive effect of these events, it was the publicity that it received. As the management flaws of Mt. Gox were reviewed, an increasing number of entrepreneurs realized the mistakes that had been made and the potential of the Blockchain. As early adopters and angel investors started to get involved and build businesses, VCs were soon to follow. In a very short time (by 2014), even VCs like Andreessen Horowitz began to invest in this technology.

As VCs began to gravitate to these new businesses, it was no surprise that banks and Wall Street also began to follow suit and in 2014, the R3CEV LLC. was founded with the aim of creating financial innovation with the Blockchain. The R3 Consortium is a partnership with over 50 of the world's leading financial institutions (including all the TBTF banks) who are working together, and independently, to create "distributed ledger technologies" for the modern financial market. Banks have realized that if they are to gain the benefits of this technology, then it is imperative that common standards and shared platforms be established. Corda is the underlying distributed ledger software which functions as a universal platform.

It is important to state the distinction between the term "Distributed Ledger Technology (DLT)" and Blockchain. Distributed ledgers and cryptocurrency systems are different in the way transactions are validated: While Bitcoin uses pseudonymous and anonymous nodes to validate transactions, distributed ledgers require legal identities (permissioned nodes) to validate transactions (Swanson, 2015). Hence the jargon of DLT is related to its context. It is specifically designed with permissioned Blockchains in mind.

The underlying principle of Corda is universality. Rather than have a set of disparate ledgers working independently and serving a subset of market players, Corda aims to function as a global data platform that records all transactions occurring on it. This allows for markets to collaborate and maintain accurate, shared records, making duplications, errors, and reconciliations a thing of the past. If we are all on the same platform and have access to the same data, then why do we need to keep separate copies individually? With Corda, authorized parties can connect to the ledger, create an agreement (in the form of Smart Contracts), and the record this agreement on the ledger. Furthermore, only the counterparties (and others with a legitimate need, like regulators) may have access to these transaction details.

To increase the wide-scale adoption of the platform, portions of the system are open: open source, open development, and open standards. As a result, Corda allows for existing and new providers to compete in developing new services at different levels, promoting choice and competition.

As per Richard Brown (CTO of R3), the key features of Corda will include (Brown, 2016):

- no unnecessary global sharing of data: only those parties with a legitimate need to know can see the data within an agreement;

- choreography of workflow between firms without a central controller;

- consensus between firms at the level of individual deals, not the level of the system;

- a design that directly enables regulatory and supervisory observer nodes;

- transaction validation by parties to the transaction rather than numerous unrelated validators;

- a system that supports a variety of consensus mechanisms;

- creating an explicit link between human-language legal prose documents and smart contract code;

- industry-standard tools;

- no native cryptocurrency.

The ultimate objective of Corda is to create a future financial market, where *"financial agreements are recorded and automatically managed without error, where anybody can transact seamlessly for any contractual purpose without friction."*

Corda is soon to be launched and at the time of writing this short summarized note, only an introductory white paper that explains the scope and description of the platform has been made available. 2017 promises to be an interesting time for DLT, R3, and markets in general.

Capitalistic markets are a source of value creation, the means of prosperity dispersion, and thus the lifeblood of human societies. But the current impact of technology and the form that it is taking requires that we update our understanding of markets. Till today, markets have been defined as a medium where the exchange of goods and services takes place as a result of buyers and sellers being in contact with one another, either directly or through mediating agents or institutions. But as decentralization becomes a salient feature of today's markets, we will need to ascertain what this means to our conceptualization of markets and what regulations are required to make this new market framework more inclusive in nature.

Regulating Regulation

The period after the crisis has been rife with regulation as bank and market-focused rules have been/are in the process of being implemented, notably in the US and in the EU, e.g., Dodd-Frank Act (2010), Volker Rule (2013), Third Basel Accord (2013), EU Commission's Liikanen proposals (2012), European Market Infrastructure Regulation (EMIR) (2012), etc.... These regulations target liquidity and collateral requirements, money market funds, taxation, derivatives, and consumer protection rights, among others. As the scope of regulation is large, we will focus on the concept and role of regulation in the context of market players rather than entering the intricacies of specific regulations on different sectors.

Markets are often cited to be the whipping boys of regulation. Time and time again, terms such as "stifling regulation" or "excessive regulation" are cited by the media as impediments to innovation and economic growth, and regulators are portrayed to be "asleep at the wheel" or detached or aloof from the markets that are in their supervisory charge. Unfortunately, there is some truth to these statements, and this is partly due to the time lag between technological evolution and regulatory reform. Owing to this time lag, businesses are burdened to deal with time-consuming red tape; costly, outdated stipulations; and cartel-like turf wars. But in a number of ways, this view is a simplified misinterpretation and harshly diminishes the true function and importance of regulation.

Regulation exists to protect the rights and safety of citizens in a market economy by ensuring the fair delivery and exchange of goods and services. Rather than overwhelming businesses, the true function of regulation is to underpin the proper functioning of economies by acting as a balance between capital creation and investor protection. In performing this balancing act, the key objective for regulators is to increase the effectiveness of the financial system to absorb shocks and maintain financial stability.

But in the shadow of the global financial crisis, the effectiveness of regulatory frameworks has come into question. Repeatedly, we find ourselves asking the question that, in spite of all these regulations, how did we not see the crisis coming? While previous parts of this book provide some clues to this why this occurred, a large part of the problem lies in asymmetric information. As markets, investors, and regulators were exposed to different amounts of information, the lack of knowledge, and hence oversight, led to blissful pre-crisis ignorance. Thus, if we are to regulate sensibly, we need to go to the crux of the subject and focus on the data, rather than the legalese. It is only by being fully informed that we can ascertain risk, identify opportunity, and enact appropriate rules that are upstanding to the purpose of regulation. It does not work the other way around.

Accounting Jiggery Pokery

Recent times have been peppered with a number of financial scandals caused by "cooking the books" and inefficient business control systems. A prime example of this was the 2001 Enron scandal, where company executives and managers, in a blatant display of rule-flouting, used accounting loopholes, special purpose entities, and false financial reporting to hide billions of dollars of debt incurred by botched deals and projects. The Enron scandal had two primary outcomes. First, it led to the passing of the Sarbanes Oxley Act (refer to Notes at the end of this chapter). Second, it showed us the difference between the *reliability* and the *relevance* of financial data.

Financial data is important to investors, as it allows them to make decisions. It is based on this data (relevance) that investors can decide as to the future growth of a company and whether it will be a good investment or not. But just because data is relevant, it does not mean it is reliable. As seen in the Enron scandal, investors were provided with relevant false information or bloated figures, which encouraged them to continue investing. But in the meantime the reliable data (i.e., precise information that is free of bias and manager manipulation) was kept in the hands of the executives and obscured from view.

The dichotomy between the reliable and relevant reported data stems from the conflicting interests of businesses and investors. The source of the contradiction is not double-entry bookkeeping, but rather it is due to bias. Information producers, in this case managers and executives, are constantly faced with a conundrum: do they provide the most objective and true version of the information regarding their business (income and cash flow generation capability, assets and liabilities, etc.), or should they only provide the most relevant information that investors would normally seek? If they were to provide all the information, could it lead to a hampering or destructive effect? Would it not be a better idea to distort the economic reality of the firm to a certain extent in order to accomplish short/medium-term benefits for a group of large shareholders and thus protect the firm in the long term?

Information bias and cooking the books is not a recent phenomenon and the Enron scandal is just one example of this practice. The 2014 investigative documentary, *The Price We Pay*, by Harold Crooks, shows how companies like Apple, Google, and Amazon (among many others) shift profits to offshore tax residencies and tax havens, such as the Cayman Islands, beyond the reach of regulators and tax authorities. By undertaking such practices, managers are able to provide an alternative picture of their company's obligations and liabilities, leading to substantial medium-term cash flow competitive advantage (Cilloni and Marinoni, 2015).

In the past, and till today, one means of controlling this behavior has been the use of private auditing firms. Private auditing firms are employed to make judgements on the potential information asymmetries that exist between the company executives and the stakeholders. By using an external auditor, the goal is to expose such information gaps. But this method of supervision is questionable, as private auditing firms, just as private companies, can also be inclined to provide partial information for their best interests. Today, we are familiar with the auditing firm oligopoly which goes under the moniker of the "Big Four"[8]. But prior to the Enron scandal, the sector was made up of the Big Five, the fifth member was Arthur Andersen who, in 2002, surrendered their Certified Public Accountant licenses after being found guilty of criminal charges relating to their handling of the auditing of Enron.

Private or self-regulation will always be subject to biases for two reasons. First, auditors for a company are selected by the company itself. As a result, when selecting an audit firm, managers will prefer selecting one that is inclined with their business interests. Second, while in principle companies are supposed to rotate their selection of auditing firms, the fact that the sector is dominated by an oligopoly of four private firms means that the people carrying out the auditing activities do not change, to a large degree. This reinforces the practice of bias, as the participants in these circles have tight bonds and in-group obligations and preferences. In short, it compromises objectivity, as there are mutually beneficial alignments of interests.

In light of these limitations, following the crisis, legislators have attempted to address the manipulation of financial information and ineffective business controls, by increasing the number of laws and corresponding organizations. But as stated in the beginning of this section, these attempts are not always conducive to innovation or business growth.

What is required today is a change in the perception of regulation. Rather than being seen as a balancing act between investor protection and capital generation, regulation needs to use investor protection as the foundation upon which capital generation is built. Regulation needs to be perceived as a public obligation and not simply as a private responsibility. For this to occur, we would require the existence of a public body that is focused on the objective analysis of companies in order to reduce the effects of bias seen in mutually beneficial oligopolistic structures. Regulation, in essence, needs to move from being a private business function to a social entity. Such a system would be more respectful of the citizens' interest and be focused on long-term economic health and stability, rather than short-term profit maximization.

In order for such a public function to exist, regulators have to be equipped with a control mechanism that is governed by a suitable public authority. This public authority should consist of a Securities Exchange Commission-type board with the power to implement a system of independent auditing via the appointment of auditors in order to reduce bias. Unbiased trust has to be the center of regulation, as it is only by providing investors with the confidence they need to invest that regulation can allow for capital formation to flourish. Such a framework will have transparency and public interest as the tenets and allow for a tiered system of compliance rather than overarching sectorial rules.

The Blockchain can be used as a tool to construct such a framework, as its transparency provides a way to address the information asymmetries that have been described above. We can imagine a sovereign/institutional-level Blockchain that is capable of interoperability with other Blockchains that are used by private firms. (Such a composite Blockchain framework would be an amalgamation of the salient features of Corda and the InterLedger Protocol.) If companies were obliged to transact over such a framework, then a permanent record of their transactional activities would be visible to regulators in real time. As privacy will always be paramount, the ideas proposed by the Corda platform

---

[8]The Big Four consists of PricewaterhouseCoopers, Deloitte Touche Tohmatsu, Ernst & Young, and KPMG. These four auditing firms provide auditing, tax, and consulting services to large corporations and currently share the vast majority of the sector's market share.

of secluding visibility of transactions to those who need to see it would be a concept to be indoctrinated in creating such a framework. This in turn would provide a rebuttal to the reliance-relevant debate, as in such a framework, the reporting and manner of analyzing the activities of firms is no longer cloaked by the judgment of firm interests.

However, this is only part of the solution for reforming regulatory practices. The second issue with regulation is the asymmetry between legal code and technical code in digital markets and increasingly cashless societies. As noted by Lawrence Lessig, of Harvard University, in a digital environment both laws (legal code) and computer code (technical code) need to be used to regulate activities (UK Government Chief Scientific Adviser, 2016). Thus along with the information gaps that we are currently faced with, a new public regulatory framework has to be able to inculcate this feature as well. Not only will this make the framework more suited to our digitized markets, but it will also reduce the effort that is required by regulators to determine if firms are respecting the rules.

This aspect of regulation in a digital environment was admirably and succinctly analyzed in Chapter 3 of the UK Government report, "Distributed ledger technology: beyond block chain" (2016), where it states,

> *"One fundamental difference between legal code and technical code is the mechanism by which each influences activity. Legal code is "extrinsic": the rules can be broken, but consequences flow from that breach to ensure compliance. Technical code, in contrast, is "intrinsic": if its rules are broken then an error is returned and no activity occurs, so compliance is ensured through the operation of the code itself. Another characteristic of software is that a machine will rigidly follow the rules even where that compliance produces unforeseen or undesirable outcomes. This leads to some striking differences in the operation of distributed ledger systems compared with the current financial system."*

What the report helps us see is that the elements for the construction of a new Blockchain-based regulatory framework (BRF) are starting to get in place. Financial markets are already administered by a combination of technical and legal code. However, the regulations such as those cited at the very beginning of this section (Dodd Frank, Liikanen proposals, EMIR, etc.), are largely legal in nature and regulatory compliance is tracked via legal code. As market players must provide the information to the regulator, it is inherently subject to the biases mentioned before. But with a BRF, this problem is overcome, as enterprises would need be operating on a Blockchain that is under the purview of regulators. Smart contracts or compliance software can then be provided to participants to issue transactions. As the code will not execute if a condition has been breached, this would reduce the need for external auditors. The role of these actors in such a system will inevitably change. They could go from being verifiers of transactions to verifiers of code, ensuring that the BRF is in tune with the dynamic changes of the market. This is a role that is of primary importance, as today's regulatory framework is not capable of respecting the heterogeneity of the market.

While current regulations have made markets safer, there are two pitfalls which need to be taken in view first. Regulations can be constructed to protect incumbents and erect barriers of entry to newcomers. This stifles innovation and does not allow for the evolution of an industry. Second, in an attempt to counterbalance the first pitfall, regulators might go too far and issue policies that do not capture the risks of new technologies and new firms adequately. This brings us back to the problem of not safeguarding consumer interests, as seen in the lending and payments industry.

The BRF, and the smart contracts that it creates, thus has to have a multilevel approach. Rather than passing overarching rules for an entire sector, the BRF should aim to construct multiple standards for companies on a risk-oriented basis, where equals are treated as equals, and where the issue of concern should take priority over the size of the firm. For example, data privacy is not a concern for large firms alone. Hence all-encompassing rules related to data privacy can be established as a norm, such as the current European approach of defining harmonized EU-wide standards to combat data privacy breaches.

On the other hand young tech-led firms, such as FinTech companies that are still in their infancy, have small side effects and pose less systemic risk. Hence, regulators need to create their smart contracts with this in mind and define appropriately structured responses. The key is to be technology-agnostic when looking at innovation and concentrate on risk. The transaction data from the company can be used to determine the risk profile of the company and, based on this and a selection of sector-specific rules (such as leverage employed), a company would need to respect specific regulations.

A consequence of this kind of a regulatory framework would be that the role of existing auditing firms would change and they would function more as a consultancy than an audit firm. But for a large part this that is already the case, as all Big Four audit firms have well-established consultancy services. From a strategy perspective, it's more a question of adaptability than it is of transformation. This could be good news for the Big Four for, as we know, adaptability is closely allied with further earning power.

Regulators are not incognizant of these possibilities, and an increasing number of them are seriously beginning to look at the Blockchain as a solution to the current problems. Sidebar 3-3 provides a summarized list of a few comments made by J. Christopher Giancarlo, the present Commissioner of the U.S. Commodity Futures Trading Commission (CFTC) at the recent Consensus conference (May 2016) and offers regulators some Blockchain food for thought:

SIDEBAR 3-3: PERSONAL OPINION STATEMENTS MADE BY J. CHRISTOPHER GIANCARLO, COMMISSIONER OF THE U.S. COMMODITY FUTURES TRADING COMMISSION (CFTC)

Source: Consensus conference, May 2106, presented by CoinDesk

Conference videos accessible at: `http://www.coindesk.com/events/consensus-2016/video/day2/`

■ **Note** These statements were made in response to several questions related to the future of regulation with the Blockchain and were made at different intervals of the conversation. However, this does not mean they are taken out of context, as the conversation was centered on this topic.

"[Let me] take you back to a moment in time where it became clear to me that something like this [the Blockchain] was tremendously necessary. In Sept. of 2008, days before Lehman Brothers collapsed, I was a senior executive at the world's largest trading platform (electronic and voice), for OTC swaps, particularly CDS (credit default swaps). Days before Lehman Brothers fell, we were watching credit spreads on Lehman and a number of the world's trading banks' gap-out basis points indicating real stress in their viability…."

"… We were in conversations with bank prudential regulators who were asking us questions as to what we were seeing in the market place, where were the credit spreads, how much stress were the trading counter parties under, whether certain counterparts were not trading with other counter parties …basically what signals was the market giving the trading platforms that the regulators didn't have in their data sets…. It became clear to me, [that] at the core of the financial crisis was a lack of visibility by regulators into the counterparty credit exposures of the world's largest trading banks between each other…."

"… Now, the regulatory solution to that in Dodd Frank was to create swap data repositories where information can be gathered and then reassembled to somehow look like the actual trading ledgers of the different financial institutions…and eight years after the crisis, that's where we are. We're trying to gather that information, clean that data and reassemble ledgers… and we'll be doing that for a long time to come…"

"… the world is divided into regulatory regimes by natio-state as well as by asset class…for example, we at the CFTC have the responsibility for credit default indices, while the SCC has the responsibility for CDS….two products that trade in tandem in the real world but are separated in the regulatory world. The point is [because of this separation] we will be assembling data, cleaning it, and trying to reassemble trading ledgers forever, I think, without really being able to see what it is (and here's the point) that potentially the Blockchain can provide for us. And so there are many reasons for further development of the Blockchain, but one important one is it can provide regulators with something they didn't have during the financial crisis, which is real time visibility…. I don't believe that visibility will provide risk avoidance, but it is certainly a risk response methodology that's very central."

"What we have today is ex post facto data or data after an event. We have data sets that various degrees of completeness to them. We have good data of cleared swaps and lacking data of uncleared swaps. Sometimes a trading book that we see may look terribly unbalanced because it might show cleared swaps on the ledger but not the uncleared swaps. With the remaining information it might be a much more balanced portfolio… We are trying to assemble trading ledgers between parties…"

"What the potential of the Blockchain is to see real ledgers in real time, across markets (and) across asset classes. That is a tremendous step forward. That would be information that we didn't have during the crisis. That would be information that, in the event of a future crisis, would allow regulators to be more precise and calibrated in their response to the crisis conditions. It does not necessarily avoid a failure…. but it would give them the transparency into the issues in question in order to make a decision whether to allow that firm to fail or prevent it from failing…."

"Now, that's only one part of the promise of the Blockchain. In the wake of the financial crisis, the G20 nations have imposed a whole host of regulatory mandates and requirements and capital requirements on financial institutions, created enormous amounts of operational complexity of capital constraint and capital complexity. There, too, the Blockchain offers the promise of being able to transcend some of that regulatory and operational complexity that regulators have imposed."

"I think regulators have their own reasons that help them fulfill their mission to taxpayers, to citizens, and to market participants to see this technology thrive, to allow regulated entities to meet their obligations under regulatory reform measures…."

The comments in the box above thus help us see to what extent a regulatory structure like the BRF would reduce information asymmetries and help in centering the direction of regulation towards investor protection. Such a system would have a number of advantages including:

- lower compliance cost, which can help funnel more funds for R&D and innovative projects at firms;

- greater transparency, which is a boon for investors and regulators;

- reducing the bias of firm managers and executives, making them more accountable. This would create a safer business environment and could aid in reducing systemic risk;

- faster identification of systemic risk and deployment of countermeasures by regulators;

- tailored regulation that is based on the risk-profile of a firm rather than the overarching sectorial rule compliance obligations. This can be beneficial for newcomers and startups, allowing them to experiment and scale faster;

- standardization of data. The ability of regulators and auditors to analyze and compare data between firms and the assets they own is a challenge today, as the information is not standardized. Moving to the BRF and establishing stipulated data standards will be able to combat this discrepancy;

- less work for regulators. Using a combination of technical code and legal code, regulators would be able to govern with less manpower and in a more robust manner;

- better oversight of tax revenues;

- finally, (and, once again, because it's worth mentioning it twice), better citizen protection.

The effective working of the BRF would require the need for a sovereign Blockchain that is capable of interoperability and which needs to be deployed across different geographies if this is going to become a worldwide mechanism. This is a point that has been repeated at different points in this chapter. Hence, as we move from markets and regulation to the topic of policy, we will concentrate on the subject of sovereign blockchains and inquire what the benefits of such a system could be for society in general.

Policies for a cashless future

A review of markets and regulations in today's economic landscape has shown us how changes are occurring and what challenges authorities are currently faced with. We have also seen that the Blockchain offers solution pathways that would be beneficial to investigate, and are being considered by certain authorities. But if markets and regulations are the pillars of an economy, policy is the base on which it is built. Governments pursue monetary and fiscal policy objectives to adapt to the changing market conditions and use the lever of regulations in order to ensure the proper functioning of their economies and hence improve the everyday lives of businesses and citizens.

As we have seen in Chapter 1, monetary and fiscal policy has often excluded the role of financial markets. Markets were seen as a porous shroud whose function was to ensure the discovery of prices and the right allocation of resources. By "outsourcing" this function to markets, policy makers could focus on the bigger task of maintaining economic growth by controlling interest rates and inflation. This in turn would ensure steady nominal demand growth for current goods and services, which in turn would ensure apt employment levels and a balanced level of inequality, and maintain societal prosperity.

But this operating thesis has been challenged since the crisis as excessive leverage, and the trade of financial assets which hold no intrinsic value have proliferated the market and changed its very structure in the process. Being more concerned with inflation and interest rates has caused central banks to ignore the creation and allocation of private credit, leading to rapid credit growth and excessive leverage. Today's economies are faced with excessive debt levels that are projected to grow and exceed the productivity (GDP) of nations forever. Coupled with technological advances, increased globalization, and dropping productivity levels, the spread of inequality is on the rise.

A primary reason for this phenomenon has been the way that debt has come to be regarded in modern economies. Debt and credit by themselves are important levers of prosperity generation. By allowing individuals to borrow against future projected revenue growth, debt instruments allow households and businesses to achieve immediate levels of prosperity, hedge against fluctuations of income, and leverage new opportunities to ensure a safer and more prosperous future. But what has been seen in the past three decades is that the instruments of debt have now become commodities in and of themselves. Rather than directing credit to investments with productive ends and which have the greatest potential to push forward economic growth, credit instruments have been transformed into derivative assets that are exchanged based on speculative inferences.

This transformation of credit has reduced its social value. While derivatives are said to enhance better price discovery, better risk transfer, and economic efficiency (refer to the quotes of Alan Greenspan in earlier chapters), it has also led to large-scale betting. Price discovery is, of course, a useful function. But what is the social gain of exchanging these derivative products on a nanosecond-to-nanosecond level? What is the social-economic benefit from indulging in trading activities that exploit interest rate differences and future value expectations of these derivatives? If anything, this practice has led to the false allocation of resources[9] (especially talent) and created a system where commercial banks can indulge in short-term profit maximization and increase the financialization of markets. As stated by Keynes in *Treatise in Money*,

> *"[There are] two types of transactions: First, those that involve the purchase of current goods and services whose value will be a fairly stable function of the money—value of current output (GDP). Second, those that involve speculative transactions in capital good or commodities... these are pure financial transactions and they bear(s) no definite relation to the rate of current production... the price level of the capital goods thus exchanged may vary quite differently from that of consumption goods."*

Financialization has transformed credit from being a means of achieving future prosperity, to a commodity that can be exchanged for value. At the base of this transformation is a conflict of categorization. While debt has come to be regarded as an

---

[9]The false allocation of resources has led to an increasing amount of capital being diverted to investments in financial instruments instead of actual business creation. Another side effect of this practice is the diversion of capital to real estate, especially in advanced economies which are witnessing technological advances. As ICT continues to change the role of tasks and jobs in the market, physical assets are becoming less important than software. There is one exception however: real estate. As the price of technology continues to fall, it is seen that the price of land continues to rise as investors can always be certain of the demand for land. This demand for land is not just in terms of the area of land but also its location. As the amount of land in desirable locations is already fixed, the only thing that can change is the price. It is for this reason that the price of real-estate has continued to rise and why most bank lending today is not allocated for the creation of new businesses but for residential mortgages. As per the Bank of England, 65% of bank lending is directed to residential mortgages while only 14% is directed to non-real estate business creation (Bank of England, 2012).

asset, it is characteristically different from an actual good or service. Money and credit are in a different product category altogether, as their creation results in purchasing power, which in turn has macroeconomic consequences. This is not the same with creating a new product or services based on technological advances. A new product or a service affects productivity curves and creates economies of scale which reduce prices. Thus, any gains in purchasing power are a consequence and not the cause of their creation. Money and credit, on the other hand, offer immediate purchasing power improvements just by being created. It is for this reason that applying the free market principles that govern the creation of goods and services to credit and money supply is an excruciatingly delicate exercise.

Hence, we need to question the very mechanism by which money and credit is created and ask ourselves who needs to be at the helm of its production? Today, in any economy, money can be created in two ways: either the government takes on the role of creating fiat cash or we depend on the fractional banking system in which money is created through private credit issuance. But, as seen in the previous chapters,, leaving the creation of money (based on debt) to commercial banks has led to significant social problems, such as increased financialization, banks getting TBTF, and excessive debt levels at the sovereign level. In light of technological unemployment and the fact that private debt ultimately becomes pubic debt and creates debt overhang effects, what needs to be considered is the role of the state in money creation and if it is a better idea to only let the state control the production of money. If this seems too centralized and dictatorial, then the second option is to think about the creation of multiple forms of money that are created by different actors and all of which are recognized and accepted by citizens within a sovereign nation.

Both these money creation methods are not new concepts and have been explored and utilized in the past. The difference this time, however, is the cashless form of today's money and the repercussions an entirely digital money or monies may have. Both these options will have significant impacts on the functioning of central banks and monetary and fiscal policy. Nevertheless, there are advantages and by adopting the right option, policy makers might actually be able to address the issue of debt-based growth in their economies. Let us thus explore both these options in order to determine which is the best way forward. We begin by looking at the concept of government control over money issuance. In this regard, it would be advantageous to familiarize ourselves/refresh our knowledge about the Chicago Plan. Sidebar 3-4 offers a summarized note:

SIDEBAR 3-4: THE CHICAGO PLAN

Source: The Chicago Plan Revisited, *Jaromir Benes and Michael Kumhof, IMF, 2012.*

■ **Note**   The conclusions in this box are a diluted summary of the findings of the above cited source.

The private issuance of money is embryonically linked to usury in two ways: the supply of money and the yield obtained from it. Let's first look at supply. Under the fractional banking system, as private entities are capable of creating money and thus influence the quantity that is in circulation, they can increase the quantity of cash in good times, leading to credit creation and higher prices. In times of economic contraction, the opposite occurs. History has shown (refer Zarlenga, 2002 and Graeber, 2012), that these expansion and contraction cycles ultimately lead to systemic borrower defaults and the concentration of wealth in the hands of the lenders, who in this case are the issuers of money.

The second form of usury pertains to the yield or the benefit that is attained by the issuance of money. As we have seen in the fractional banking system, private money has to be lent into existence and is issued with a positive interest rate. The interest rate, in part, is attributed to the risk premium of lending money. But this interest rate value is also based on the immediate purchasing power creation ability of money. As money can immediately offer liquidity to the borrower, the borrower pays interest also, in part, for money's liquidity benefits. The result is intense rent-seeking behavior by those who have the privilege of issuing privately created money.

The Chicago Plan was a formulation to address these key issues of monetary economics. Following the Great Depression, American macroeconomists such as Henry Simons of the University of Chicago (hence Chicago Plan) and Irving Fisher of Yale University, proposed fundamental monetary reforms and called for the separation of monetary and credit functions of commercial banks. They proposed that private banks should have 100% of their deposits backed by government-issued money (base money (refer to Chapter 1)), and that new commercial bank credit should only be issued based on the earnings that have been made by the banks (which are held in the form of base money), and not by the creation of new deposits, as seen in the fractional banking system today. Fisher (1936) claimed four advantages for this plan:

1. As commercial banks would no longer be able to expand and contract the supply of cash (the first form of usury), it would allow for better control of credit cycles.

2. It would allow governments to issue money at zero interest (the second form of usury) rather than borrowing cash from central banks. This in turn would reduce interest burdens on government finances and reduce sovereign debt.

3. As money would no longer be created by the issuance of private debt, it would reduce private debt levels (and public debt as well since, as we have seen in Chapter 1, private debt ultimately becomes public debt).

4. It would eliminate bank runs.

The issue of cash supply expansion and contraction is of primary importance. As discussed in the beginning of this box, money creates purchasing power. Hence, expanding and contracting the supply via credit is not driven by the fundamentals of the real economy, but changes the very fundamentals by itself (Benes and Kumhof, 2012). As under the fractional banking system (broad) money can only be created by the creation of credit, the willingness of banks to issue loans not only creates excess or shortages, but also drives nominal aggregate demand.

But under the Chicago Plan, the creation of money and credit are separated and can be governed independently of each other. Doing this would reduce the role of banks to what they are primarily supposed to do: be pure intermediaries that receive funds and lend those funds to borrowers. This is a crucial point that merits emphasizing in light of the increased financialization of markets. Debt cannot be reduced by issuing more debt. We need to grow our way out of it.

The feature of debt and the second advantage of the Chicago Plan is hence another key factor which merits discussion. Today, the total liabilities of the financial system (thanks in part to shadow banking), are far greater than the government's liabilities. As the plan calls for commercial banks to have 100% reserves to back their liabilities, government-issued money allows for these liabilities to be converted into assets for the government. Since the liabilities of the financial system are greater than the liabilities of the state, the conversion of private liabilities into assets would mean a reduction in the total amount of liabilities for the state, as the assets they acquire would be more than the current liabilities. Fisher proposed that this could be done via bonds. As private banks own government bonds, the state could buy back the bonds and cancel their debt in the process.

Benes and Kumhof argue that this proposal by Fisher to reacquire bonds and cancel debt, albeit sound, is outdated for today's economy. When Fisher made this proposal in the 1930s, commercial banks in the US held a major portion of their government's debt. As today most government debt is held outside the nation's commercial banks, Benes and Kumhof state it would be a better idea for the government to issue state money and "*leave the separate gross positions outstanding.*" Irrespective of the approach, the result is the same: net government debt is dramatically reduced*.

As commercial banks would need to convert their liabilities into reserves at the treasury, the third advantage of the Chicago Plan to reduce private debt levels is of particular importance. As we have seen in Chapter 1, private debt does not go away and ultimately becomes public debt (see Sufi & Mian, 2014; Turner, 2015). Hence, reducing private debt levels is crucial to reducing public debt levels. As the Chicago Plan requires commercial banks to have full reserve backing at the treasury, this inflow of cash coming in from the private sector can be used by treasury to buy back any government debt that is currently held by the private sector. This influx of cash could also be used to cancel any credit that has been issued by the treasury to the private sector. In essence, this practice of holding reserves gives us options to reduce the debt on the balance sheets of both the private sector and the public sector. In the simulations performed by Benes and Kumhof, buy-back of private bank debt (except finance investment in physical capital) was the operating assumption.

Based on these principles and assumptions, the authors of the paper created and tested a theoretical model based on state of the art DGSE models (more on this in Chapter 4). They found strong evidence that supported Fisher's claims and found that monetary policy based on debt-free government-issued money would reduce debt levels across the economy and ensure smoother business cycles. Some other points worth mentioning include:

- The Chicago Plan creates longer-term output gains: Lower debt levels in the economy cause investors to demand lower real interest rates. This makes borrowing money less risky and can help in spurring investment. As the government is also capable of gaining a higher Seigniorage income, it can offset distortionary tax rates that are paid by citizens, giving them more income to save or invest. Finally, as money can now be created debt-free, there is a reduced need to monitor the creation of those loans whose primary function was to create an adequate money supply. This in turn leads to lower credit monitoring costs.

(It should be remembered in viewing this plan that money is not looked at as a debt instrument issued by the government (as is currently done in the fractional banking system). Rather it is to be seen as equity. The money being issued is an asset for the holder and not a liability to anybody, as it is not based on the creation and issuance of debt.)

- Inflation can drop to zero and not cause monetary policy issues: Most of us are familiar with the practice of central bankers trying to stimulate the economy by keeping inflation at around 2% per year. The reason for engaging in this practice is multi-fold. Firstly, having a slightly positive inflation rate makes it easier to service debts. If prices were to fall, then the value of the debt would increase and reduce investor investment. Second, if prices were to fall, i.e., inflation is too low, then borrowing goes down and it becomes difficult for the central bank to stimulate the economy with low interest rates (see the note below on liquidity trap*). The only option in this situation would be that central banks would begin to apply negative interest rates. But if consumers can convert their bank funds into cash, such a measure would turn out to be ineffective. This is known as the *zero lower bound* for interest rates and can cause a liquidity trap. Hence a consensus merged that inflation needs to be low, but positive – at around 2% which would be accompanied with a nominal GDP growth rate of 4-5% (Turner, 2015).

For several decades prior to the crisis, this is what was seen: nominal GDP did grow at an average of 5% per year and inflation near 1–3%. But this growth was accompanied by private credit growing at 10–15% (Turner, 2015). If the central bank increased the interest rate, then credit growth slowed down and so did investment. This would make it seem that we required an annual credit growth rate of 10–15% to hit an inflation target of 2%. But as we have seen, growing debt levels are exactly what we need to avoid today, as it leads to a host of other issues.

Creating monetary policies based on the Chicago Plan offers us a solution to this quandary. As money and credit are no longer intertwined, the government can now increase the quantity of broad money without depending on the private bank's willingness to issue/refuse loans and thus have better control over stimulating nominal demand via their control on the money supply.

Furthermore, the central bank can also loan money based on the purpose of investment. One of the reasons for rampant credit growth in the period prior to the crisis was due to increased investment in real estate and speculation activities. By getting control on the supply of money, central banks are now in the position to ensure that credit facilities are accessible only for specific activities such as investment projects (for example). Hence, interest rates can become zero or even negative without any practical problems. In fact, one of the crucial conclusions of the author's model was that by using separate policy control instruments, especially in terms of controlling money supply, the quantity of bank lending and the interest rate at which the government lends money to banks, the central bank has a better grip on controlling inflation and interest rates and would be able to address the zero limit bound problem and eliminate the liquidity trap. In their words,

"…a zero bound does not apply to this rate, which makes it feasible to keep steady state inflation at zero without worrying about the fact that nominal policy rates are, in that case, more likely to reach zero or negative values."

(The liquidity trap is a situation in which cash injections from the central bank to the private sector fail to decrease interest rates. Consumers prefer to save rather than borrow and invest, as they believe that the interest rates will soon rise and it is just a matter of time. As a result, monetary policy becomes ineffective.)

The authors concluded that none of these benefits would change the role of commercial banks but would not diminish the role of these institutions in the economy. They would function more as effective payment systems and enable effective capital allocation to support investment in those activities that would be socially useful. What they would no longer do, however, is create money that is based on the issuance of credit. Money supply would essentially become debt-free and the ability to create new purchasing power, which is currently the privilege of private banks, would be returned to public authorities.

A Pinch of Salt

While the Chicago Plan provides evidence to reduce private and public debt levels, it is necessary to add a note of caution. First, just having 100% reserves at central banks will not solve the problem of excessive private credit creation. Debt is important, as it allows the mobilization of capital and maintains a lifestyle based on future income growth projections. If consumers are constrained by new policies, then they will create and use innovative financial instruments (as seen before the crisis) that circumvent the formal banking system. Second, as the authors state, existing debt would be replaced by newly created reserves. This in theory is a great idea, but it also means that there will be winners and losers. How this can be tempered is anyone's guess. Third, if governments are in the money-creation driver's seat, then what will restrict them from using this power to ensure short-term political gain? The conclusion is stark: we cannot have any form of extremism with monetary policy under the fractional banking system or the Chicago Plan. A sweet spot needs to be found which will allow us to coerce and manage the quantity and type of debt being created in an economy.

The question thus becomes how can money be created, who should create it, and how much should be created? Should we depend on state-controlled money issuance or on multiple forms of money, or on a mix of the two? To answer this question, let's continue our dissection of monetary and fiscal policy from these vantage points, but in the context of an economy that is increasingly getting cashless.

Centralized Government Money Issuance and the Cashless Economy

When was the last time you remember seeing an advertisement that was exclusively marketing money? It would seem strange, would it not, that while almost everything today is advertised and marketed using customer segmentation behavioral analysis, the underlying unit of transfer is never advertised to help you get more luxury, feel better, look great, secure your children's future, etc....

While the idea of marketing money might seem absurd, it represents our innate sense of belief in it. Money is as much a part of our lives as is eating food to sustain living. We grow up learning how to earn it, use it, and save it. This makes money a social necessity whose value is of social importance and the reason why its production has to be entrusted in the most responsible hands. This function today is supposed to be that of the state. But with fractional banking, this exclusive privilege has been handed over to commercial banks, which is why they command such power in our societies.

Understanding the source of the value of money is key to understanding its role. In the past, the value of money was based on its link to a certain commodity (mostly gold or silver in human history). But money is essentially a state-backed utility, whether it is fiat-based or commodity-based. It could be argued that fiat money derives its value from the state, while commodity money gets its value based on its link to a certain commodity. Nevertheless, in either form, there is an active participation of the state. Purists may argue that the value of commodity money is not as easy to manipulate as fiat money. But in making this statement, they overlook the fact that the commodity is managed, monitored, and manipulated by the state (Desai, 2015). As money becomes increasingly cashless, new purists purport that the Blockchain (and virtual currencies such as bitcoin) will replace the existing monetary system. But irrespective of any view, we remount to the same conclusion: money is a store of value, a unit of account, and a means of transfer which needs the backing of the state to ensure trust and widescale adoption.

In light of the discussion of the Chicago Plan and the fact that economies are now increasingly cashless, central bank-issued digital currency or fiat money issued on a Blockchain is a subject worth discussing in the context of monetary and fiscal policy. In recent times, no one has been more vocal about this subject than Andy Haldane, the chief economist of the Bank of England. Haldane makes a number of arguments as to why we should move to scraping physical cash altogether, and a number of his arguments echo the conclusions of the Chicago Plan.

First, he argues that moving to a cashless system would give governments more flexibility in the event of a financial downturn. Second, Haldane states that a cashless system would allow us to manage inflation better, as it would allow us to bypass the zero lower bound—the working assumption being that if a central bank introduced negative interest rates, then people would convert their savings into cash. But in a cashless system, that would not be possible. In his words,

> *"Central banks may then need to think imaginatively about how to deal on a more durable basis with the technological constraint imposed by the zero lower bound on interest rates ... That may require a rethink, a fairly fundamental one, of a number of current central bank practices... [and] It would allow negative interest rates to be levied on currency easily and speedily."* (Giles, 2015)

While these possibilities seem worthwhile pursuits to central bankers, it would be prudent to check how far away are we from becoming a cashless economy and analyze if embarking on such a change is a worthwhile endeavor.

In terms of becoming a cashless economy, the situation is complex. It is true that, since the introduction of credit and debit cards, our use of cash has been in decline. The Bank of International Settlements states that the while the amount of outstanding cash in circulation in the largest 19 economies was 8.4% of GDP in 2010, it fell to 7.9% of GDP in 2014 (Tett, 2016). However, this decline has not been even across all economies. Owing to mistrust in banks, financial crises, threats of negative interest rates, and illegal operations (especially terrorism), the circulation of cash has actually increased in Japan, Switzerland, the EU, and the UK (Tett, 2016). But the future seems poised to change some parts of this trend. Growing dangers of terrorism and crime are urging policy makers to remove large denomination bills. As of May 2016, the ECB has stopped the production and issuance of the €500 banknote in an attempt to address these illegal activities.

But apart from the reasons stated by Haldane and the motivations of the ECB, there are other reasons why moving to a cashless system could be beneficial to society. First, there is the issue of cost. As per a recent report by the Imperial College and CITI, $13 trillion—almost 18% of global GDP—is withdrawn from ATMs annually. These and other such cash operations entail significant costs. The authors of the report state that moving to a cashless system could provide *"up to $400 billion in annual savings, as well as powerful social benefits, by moving even a quarter of paper-based transactions to digital"* (Davé, 2016).

Second, there is the issue of tax evasion. Cash allows us to make transactions anonymously and conceal our activities from the government. Bribes or payments made to illegal workers in cash, allow perpetrators to create an underground economy, avoid laws, regulations, and taxes, while continuing other forms of criminal activities. Research done by Harvard economist Kennett Rogoff, provides evidence that a large percentage of currency in most countries, generally well over 50%, is used precisely to hide transactions (Rogoff, 1998, 2002). This is a big difference from most forms of digital cash that, in principle, can be traced.

If we are to talk about tax evasion, then we also need to relook at the role of physical cash in crime and felony. Cash is used in two environments today: the legal domestic economy and the underground economy. Recent studies from central banks show that the amount of cash consumers admit to holding accounts 5–10% of the total currency in existence (Stavins & Schuh, 2015). A 2014 study done across seven countries (Canada, Australia, Austria, France, Germany, the Netherlands, and the United States) by the Federal Reserve of Boston showed that cash is by the most common means of payment vehicle for small size/low-value transactions ($5, $10), but for larger payments it is increasingly insignificant.

However, the same cannot be said for the underground economy. The underground economy includes not only illegal activities such as terrorism, drug trade, bribery, human trafficking, and money laundering, but also tax evasion via cash payments and employment of illegal immigrants. Some crimes are more serious than others, but irrespective of the type of crime being committed, it is the size of the underground economy and especially the impact of tax evasion that are truly noteworthy.

Studies done by the US Internal Revenue Service (IRS), show that business owners and corporations report less than their income to evade taxes. As of 2015, one study found that this led to a tax gap (difference between taxes paid and taxes due) of $500 billion in federal taxes in 2015 alone (Rogoff, 2016). A part of this sum is related to the cash that is stored in tax havens (refer to Harold Crooks), but this amounts to around 20% of the total sum (Zucman, 2015). Over 50% of the outstanding amount is related to cash-intensive activities (Rogoff, 2016). In other countries, a similar occurrence is seen. Although the figures may not be the same, the fact that EU countries have stricter tax laws means that the percentage value in comparison to GDP is much more significant. Figure 3-2 helps us see the gravity of the situation.

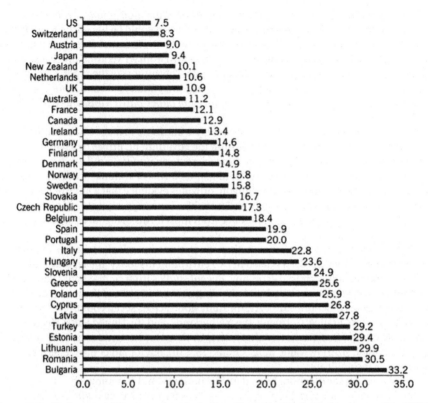

Figure 3-2. *Underground Economy (not including all criminal activities) in terms of % of GDP Source: IZA World of Labor, Data and Calculations—"The shadow economy" F. Schneider (2013)*

More serious crimes, like terrorism, bribery/corruption, and drug and human trafficking are very serious crimes that are mostly cash-based and involve large amounts of money laundering. But in comparison to tax evasion, that sum is relatively small.

In light of these practices, the obvious question is, why are central banks still printing cash even though they are aware of the benefits it provides to malicious and ill-intentioned members of society? The answer in a word is Seigniorage.

Seigniorage is the difference between the value of money and the cost to produce it. When commodity money was used, Seigniorage was the difference between the face value of the minted coins and the actual market value of the metal they contained. If the Seigniorage was positive, then the government made a revenue that was essentially a profit. However, with fiat money, the same formula does not apply. With a fiat money system, Seigniorage revenue is three-fold. First, revenue is obtained from the physical production of money. While it costs 10.6 cents to print a $50 note,[10] the actual value of the

---

[10]See the cost of printing money at: http://www.federalreserve.gov/faqs/currency_12771.htm

note is $50. Between 2006 and 2015, the US government earned 0.40% of GDP per year by printing new notes and spending them, while the ECB earned 0.55% per year (Rogoff, 2016). Second, when commercial banks require cash, they purchase it from the central bank via the reserves that they need to hold at the central bank. This is turn is a source of revenue to the central bank and the Seigniorage is earned from the reduction in the central bank's interest costs, as interest is payable on reserves but not on cash. Third, commercial banks can also purchase cash by entering a repo agreement with the central bank. In exchange for cash, the central bank buys securities from the commercial bank. But the commercial bank has to buy back the securities at a later date (hence a repo agreement). Seigniorage is thus made by the central bank during the repurchase phase of the repo agreement (Dyson and Hodgson, 2016).

As governments have complete monopoly over the printing of money, they enjoy considerable profits from its production. Remember that a commercial bank can issue money via offering a consumer a loan. But the physical printing of cold hard cash is still the right of the government, and the revenues from paper currency are considerable enough to offer the biggest counterargument to moving to a cashless system. But in light of the costs of the illegal activities that cash facilitates, the profits earned by Seigniorage are a pittance in comparison. As stated by Kenneth Rogoff in *The Curse of Cash* (2016),

> *The "profits" governments reap by blindly accommodating demand for cash are dwarfed by the costs of the illegal activity that cash, especially big bills, facilitates. The effect of curtailing paper currency on tax evasion alone would likely cover the lost profits from printing paper currency, even if tax evasion fell by only 10-15%. The effect on illegal activities is probably even more important.*

Taking a stand against crime and taxation evasion alone, would seem motivation enough to move to a cashless economy. Critics to a cashless system abound and immediately after Haldane's remarks to move to a cashless system were announced, other members from the Bank of England (including former members of the Monetary Policy Committee) were quick to criticize him, and some journalists cited that such a move was an "echo of Maoist China" (*FT*, 2015). It is sure that even if we were to move to a completely cashless economy, it would not be the answer to all our problems. But, nevertheless, there are advantages and possibilites that can be achieved which are not possible today, or can only be possible with increased regulation, oversight, and government cost. To ascertain if moving to a cashless sytem is a move that needs to be contemplated and how cashless do we need to be, let us review what could be the consequances of moving to a monetary system based on government-issued fiat currency on a Blockchain.

Fiat currency on a Blockchain

If central banks were to have complete control of money creation instead of the private sector, they would be in the position of providing individuals and companies with official digital money (as they already offer cash and coins) instead of deposits with commercial banks. There are two ways in which this can occur Either a central banks offers deposit accounts directly to the public or, instead, commercial banks offer accounts fully backed by central bank reserves (which is similar to the 100% reserve banking model discussed before).

The question becomes why should we indulge in such a transition? The response is multifold. Evidently, it would allow governments to address the problems of tax evasion and other such crimes that were discussed above to a certain extent. But for the formal economy, the consequences would be more far-reaching. Such a monetary model would destroy the private banks' debt-based deposit-funded model and change their function in society. They would still function as direct intermediaries between lenders and borrowers and offer investment products to households and corporations, but the broad money supply would now be more directly controlled by the central bank, making it independent of private lending decisions. The greater the quantity of broad money supply, in the form of sovereign digital cash or fiat money on a Blockchain, the greater the ease with which a central bank can use tools such as negative interest rates or helicopter drops (discussed in detail in the section on Universal Basic Income). It is important to highlight these two economic tools. Negative interest rates and helicopter drops are old theories and have been studied and critiqued for a while. But in light of technological unemployment and ageing societies, they might become quite indispensable in the future.

Building such a framework has become a resolutely mainstream subject in the past few months. In July 2016, the Bank of England published a 90-page report titled, "The macroeconomics of central bank issued digital currencies." The authors, John Barrdear and Michael Kumhof (co-author the Chicago Plan report described in Sidebar 3-4), looked at the creation and consequences of a permissioned monetary system which issues a central bank digital currency. The author's DGSE-calibrated model is based on the New Keynesian monetary model[11] (with nominal and real interest rate and inflation effects), but differs in two ways.

The first point of differentiation is that it incorporates the fractional banking system and acknowledges the existence of debt-based money. The authors argue that this has been done *"because of the key role of [commercial] banks as providers of the monetary transaction medium that would compete with central bank digital cash in the real world."* The authors thus state and acknowledge the demand for private sector monetary transactions as their model encompasses the spending and investment traits of households, financial investors, unions, and banks (in tandem with a government that determines monetary and fiscal policies). Private money exists in the model in a 1-1 exchange rate with government money (100% reserve).

The second point of differentiation is that their model disregards government money as being exogenous to the economy. The authors state that their model allows for central bank digital currency to be held by the non-bank private sector (which is not the case today) and unlike regular cash, this digital currency is interest-bearing. As a result, it can compete with endogenously created commercial bank-issued money.

---

[11]The New Keynesian model is the most popular alternative to the real business cycle theory among mainstream economists and policymakers. Whereas the real business cycle model features monetary neutrality and emphasizes that there should be no active stabilization policy by governments, the New Keynesian model builds in friction that generates monetary non-neutrality and gives rise to a welfare justification for activist economic policies (Sims, 2012)

Having created the digital monetary framework based on these assumptions, the next question was the quantity of digital currency to be issued. Their model showed that if we were to manufacture and inject a sovereign digital currency equal to 30% of the GDP, it would result in a 3% increase in GDP, owing to reductions in interest rates, tax rates, and transaction cost savings (they chose 30%, as it was similar in magnitude to the QE conducted by central banks over the last decade. Their DSGE model was calibrated to match the US economy in the pre-crisis period).

Furthermore, the authors found that such a regime would offer policy makers with a new tool to stabilize the business cycle. As the quantity and/or price of the digital currency could be tempered by the government, it would allow them to leverage this flexibility in a countercyclical manner to the changing business cycle. While the supply of money today is dependent on private lending decisions, having a policy instrument that controls the price and quantity of cash becomes especially effective in times of economic shock when private money demand fluctuates. In this way, a sovereign digital currency offers better financial stability. Through further experimentation (the report is very detailed) the authors were able to identify a number of consequences that would arise with the introduction of a sovereign digital currency:

1. Government bonds purchased with digital currency could reduce interest rates: When a central bank exchanges money for government debt/bonds, it receives interest payments. However, if these interest payments are greater than the interest expenses (which it is on average), then it makes a profit.[12] As profits made from the central bank are remitted back to the government, it makes the government's stock of debt more sustainable, which in turn lowers the government's interest rate burden.

    With the introduction of a "central bank digital currency" (CBDC), the authors state that retail transaction balances will gradually switch from bank deposits to CBDC. As a result, a large portion of bank financing will be dependent on market prices. As the interest rate on government debt is the ground on which we structure the entire economy's interest rate structure, as the interest rate on bonds goes down, it would reduce the spread between bond interest rates and bank deposit interest rates. The overall result is lowered borrowing costs and declining real interest rates.

2. Lower interest rates provide fiscal benefits: The authors find that as a consequence of reducing interest rate expenses, the establishment of a CBDC framework would also allow for increased fiscal income and state that the output gains would be almost as large as the lowered interest rates. This increase of fiscal income would allow governments to either spend more or lower tax rates.

---

[12]This is known as the net interest margin (NIM). **NIM = (Investment Returns – Interest Expenses) / Average Earning Assets**.

3. New control levers: As mentioned before, a CBDC also allows for the government to develop a policy instrument that can be used to temper the policy interest rate. The central bank could either calculate the quantity of CBDC relative to GDP or by adapting the spread between policy interest rate and the CBDC rate. Either way, the government is in a better position to control interest rates and respond to shocks in the economy.

4. Transaction cost reductions: The authors question whether official CBDC should be implemented via a central bank Blockchain or, as it is currently, through centralized registers held by the money issuers. They contend that a permissioned distributed architecture would provide improved efficiency in terms of settlement and improve resiliency. The net result is a reduction in costs.

5. Increased competition in accounts services: Non-physical official money could also allow central banks to offer deposit accounts to the public like commercial banks do. In some ways this is similar to 100% reserve backing, where commercial banks fully back their deposits with central bank reserves. As the CBDC would be comparable to the establishment of an "online-only, reserve-backed, narrow bank alongside the existing commercial banking system," the authors state that this would result in an expansion of competition in the deposit account market.

   Second, there is the issue of risk with regards to deposit insurance. Currently, consumers and companies can only make payments via commercial bank deposits. Owing to this critically important role, governments underwrite insurance policies that guarantee bank deposits (up to €100,000 for regular deposit accounts and small business accounts). In doing so, commercial banks enjoy the extraordinary privilege of having their liabilities backed by a central bank. This is the primary reason for TBTF. In essence, this form of deposit insurance creates the impression that deposits are risk-free; in reality, they are risk-bearing, with the risk falling upon the taxpayer (Dyson and Hodgson, 2016). By issuing a CBDC, a government can provide depositors with a real risk-free asset which is connected to the government and not commercial banks.

6. Increased competition and better resilience in payment services: A primary function of today's banks is transaction verification. While the pricing in the existing system is governed by the member institutions, a lower entry barrier to becoming a transactions verifier in a CBDC environment would mean that more players would enter the payment services market and lower the price of transaction fees so that it is more representative of the cost of verification.

Second, current payment systems are subject to operational risks. If a bank or payment institution were to shut down even temporarily, all payments need to be routed via other channels. This could in effect cut off the end user from the payment system till they find an alternative. However, with a Blockchain[13]-based model, this problem is avoided, owing to its distributed architecture.

The real advantage in terms of payments is with reduced collateral and settlement sums. Currently, any payment involves risk: credit risk (in case the bank goes bust) and liquidity risk (in case one of the counterparties does not have assets that can be turned liquid in case of nonpayment). To hedge against these risks, payment systems require that collateral be provided with assets that have a high liquidity and low credit risk, prior to engaging in a transaction. But with a CBDC system, settlement can occur directly between the counterparties across the central bank's balance sheet. Thus there would be lower collateral requirements and greater amounts of liquidity in the market.

7. Better payment infrastructure can reduce TBTF: Financial settlement systems currently used by central banks (such as CHAPS, BACS, FasterPayments, Fedwire, TARGET2, etc....) are expensive, have large downtimes, and are stagnant are in terms of innovation (Danezis and Meiklejohn, 2015). Moreover, while some central banks already use an electronic equivalent to cash in the form of reserves (e.g., the Bank of England), these reserve accounts are only available to licensed commercial banks and a small number of financial institutions (Dyson and Hodgson, 2014). As a result, commercial banks have become the gatekeepers to the payments system, and have the capacity to become systematically important nexuses within the economy. As a result, new entrants, smaller banks, and other payment service providers have to enter the payments space via a licensed bank even if they are able to provide better payment services. Moving to a Blockchain-based payment infrastructure could provide a single solution to these multiple latencies and thus increase competition in the payments space. If a CBDC payment system were to be constructed alongside the existing system, it would provide an alternative payment network in case of the failure of a systematically important bank.

---

[13]Note: The authors systematically refer to their model in terms of the CBDC. The word "Blockchain" is never used anywhere in the report except for two exceptions: first in the keywords classification in the abstract and second in the references, as one of the papers cited has the word "Blockchain" in the title.

8. Better response to shocks: The comments of J. Christopher
    Giancarlo, Commissioner of the CFTC (refer to Sidebar
    3-3), showed us the importance of having real-time access
    to information. Hence, a key feature of using a CBDC is the
    access it provides to transaction verifiers and to the public
    parties regarding historic and current transactions. This
    would in turn provide more data to policy makers about the
    interconnectedness of the financial system, allow for the use
    of smart contracts, and be a step forward in macroeconomic
    stability creation and response.

    The issue of holding deposits directly at the central bank is of
    relative importance to financial institutions such as pension
    funds and insurers. Currently, these market operators have to
    hold their deposits at commercial banks, but the government
    deposit insurance (see point 5 above) does not apply to them.
    If they were to hold their deposits directly at the central bank,
    they would be less affected by shocks on the financial system.

9. 24X7 operation: Commercial banks and payment systems
    might operate all day and all night, but central banks do not
    operate all day long and mostly function between 6am to 6pm
    (for IT maintenance). This arrangement exposes banks to
    overnight risks and is the reason why overnight transactions
    are limited in value. A decentralized architecture helps us
    work around this limitation.

The authors also look at some of the cons that a CBDC could create and state that
there is a danger of a bank run from commercial bank deposits to CBDC, as consumers
could prefer holding CBDC deposits instead of bank deposits. They also look at transition
risks of moving from the status quo to a CBDC regime. Although they state that they
have not looked at these cons in great detail, owing to the scope of the report, they
acknowledge their presence and state maximizing the benefits of the CBDC would
require *"an appropriate choice of CBDC issuance arrangements, CBDC policy rules,
and fiscal policy choices [along with] the need for a thoroughly tested and reliable digital
infrastructure, including cybersecurity and protection against hacking, appropriate prior
training of the human operators of such a system, careful analysis of the legal implications
(including, if necessary, introduction of additional legislation), appropriate changes
to financial sector regulation, full coordination with foreign central banks and foreign
financial institutions, and many others"*.

The conclusion of the report, like most good research, raises new questions worthy
of exploration. While the authors did find a number of pros and a few cons with the
introduction of the CBDC, they state that further research is needed to ascertain what
the policy implications will be. They ask whether new policy rules should be based on
inflation targets or should new information of financial variables be included, since
a cashless regime would allow us to have more data and a better view of markets and
financial institutions. But their overall consensus is that the pros far outweigh the cons.
Issuing a sovereign currency on a Blockchain can widen the range of monetary policies,
help address TBTF, encourage innovation and competition in account and payment

services, provide real time information to regulators, and aid in identifying systemic risk thus making the financial system safer.

While the Bank of England report offers policy modifications in consideration of the coexistence of two currencies (traditional debt-based money created via fractional banking and CBDC), they do not address the topic of the infrastructure that would be required to implement such a system in relative detail. But some recent research done by Positive Money, a non-profit organization based in London, has looked at what kind of framework would be required to implement government-issued digital cash.

In the report, titled "Digital Cash: Why Central Banks Should Start Issuing Electronic Money" (2016), Ben Dyson and Graham Hodgson state that governments have two options when it comes to providing CBDC. The first option is to provide citizens with accounts at the Central Bank. Via this direct approach (which has already been put in place by the Central Bank of Ecuador via their Sistema de Dinero Electrónico), every citizen would have an account at the central bank and the bank would take on the burden of providing all the functions of a commercial bank. This idea, although possible, is not a worthwhile solution as it nationalizes the entire banking system and puts a huge burden on central banks, not to mention the detrimental effects it will have on innovation and customer service.

The second option is based on the 100% reserve backing model as described in the Chicago Plan (refer to Sidebar 3-4). Here, central banks would create and hold digital cash, but all the operations related to transactions, payments, and investment would be provided by commercial financial institutions. However, these commercial financial institutions would need to hold 100% of their reserves at the central bank. The institutions would provide the statements, payment cards, mobile banking services, and customer support much like today, with the difference being that all the funds in their care would be held in equivalent as central bank deposits. This would also make the account holder's deposits fully liquid and permit banks to repay customers the totality of their funds at any given time—largely different from today's system, which only allows partial reimbursements. Commercial banks would thus become administrators of accounts but never actually own the deposit and would not be able to partake in fractional banking as is done today.

As the central banks would possess all the funds, the liabilities of the central bank would rise. However, the authors state that this can be offset by equivalent assets in the form of perpetual zero-coupon, i.e.., non-interest bearing bonds which would be issued exclusively for this function. As there is no interest or repayment date on these bonds, there is no additional debt incurred by the government.

In such a framework, commercial banks would no longer be able to issue loans or overdrafts. The authors are cognizant of this fact and state that an alternative can be arranged. Commercial banks wanting to provide credit facilities would need to fund loans by using CBDC borrowed from customers exclusively for this purpose. Such a system of credit issuance would be akin to how lending is performed in mutual building societies and credit unions. They state that such a method of providing credit would not necessarily increase the demand for credit overall, but will affect the demand for bank credit.

The question then arises with respect to the supply of credit. As banks cannot lend by creating new deposits, as they do with fractional banking, their loan portfolio will be affected. But the authors argue that the net effect on the supply of credit will not be significant. First, they state, that since reserves are zero-weighted for the purposes of calculating capital requirements for banks, moving from bank deposit accounts to 100% reserve accounts would not affect the capital requirements of banks. The level of money creation is based on the bank's loss-absorbing capital, rather than the amounts of its reserves. Hence, in terms of capital requirements, the net effect on banks providing loans will not be affected by moving to 100% reserve accounts. Second, they state that, as reserve accounts become available to all licensed commercial financial institutions, new entrants, smaller banks, and other providers able to deliver better lending services would be able to enter the lending space directly and cut their ties with commercial banks (see point 7 above). Thus, as bank deposits are converted to reserve deposits, loans could be funded by money markets as well. As cash becomes available from digital cash lenders alongside bank credit, the supply of credit could actually increase.

The ideas and methods described in these two recent works allow us to gain a picture of how monetary policy could be executed if we were to move to a Sovereign cashless Blockchain-based infrastructure and adopt a 100% reserve system. They would apparently be able to provide us with significant answers to the gridlock that is faced by policy makers today in terms of improving the productivity and efficiency of executing their duties. They will also allow for better financial inclusion and greater transparency, and reduce systemic risks. But there are reservations that need to be considered with moving to a 100% reserve-backed system. Some of these reservations have been described in the concluding section of Sidebar 3-4, where we read about the Chicago Plan. First, just having 100% reserves at central banks will not solve the problem of excessive private credit creation, for if consumers feel constrained, they could create and use new financial instruments to bypass the system. Second, even if existing debt was replaced by reserves, it also means that there will be winners and losers. Third, governments have an unflattering track record of being in charge of money creation, and there is the danger that they would use this power to ensure short-term political gain. We need to find a way to allow us to manage the quantity and type of debt. Rather than depending on a central full reserve banking model, would the answer lie in multiple currencies existing together?

Multiple currencies in a cashless environment

There is a large amount of literature concerning the issuance of private money. One of the most vehement supporters of private cash was the Austrian economist, Friedrich Hayek, who argued that private agents could use markets to create currencies which were a store of value and a unit of account. According to Hayek, private actors could create a stable monetary system without the need for government intervention. As per his view, the government ought to let citizens use a currency of their choosing and permit entrepreneurs to innovate in the monetary sector by creating digital currencies and minting commodity money (Hayek, 1976).

But currencies such as Ethereum and Bitcoin are not commodity monies. They can be considered as privately issued fiat currencies which are fiduciary in nature, i.e., they are not commodity-backed and cannot be redeemed for any other asset. Although these currencies are effective ways to transfer value on a decentralized network, from an economic perspective, their ability to fulfil all three functions of money[14] has been questioned due to their differences in comparison to a regular fiat currency. These include:

Volatility: The price swings of currencies like Bitcoin has been a subject of constant debate and had led analysts to comment that the currency will never be a good store of value since it is subject to large price swings. This is true, but if one were to look at the volatility over the past five years, the volatility has become less erratic. At the time of writing this chapter (September 2016), the 30 Day BTC/USD volatility was at 1.16%, while the 30 Day USD/EUR volatility was 0.32%. Between Sept 2015 and Sept 2016, the BTC/USD volatility swung from a high of 4.93% to a low of 0.32%, while the USD/EUR volatility stayed in the range of 0.67% to 0.32% (Figure 3-3). Effectively, bitcoin is yet to become as stable as a state fiat currency, but it is in the process of becoming less volatile as the network effect and user base expands. What was interesting to note was the surge in the price of bitcoin when the Brexit was announced (Figure 3-4). The changing value of cryptocurrencies still is a subject of concern, as it undermines their purchasing power ability and ability to function as long-term savings instruments.

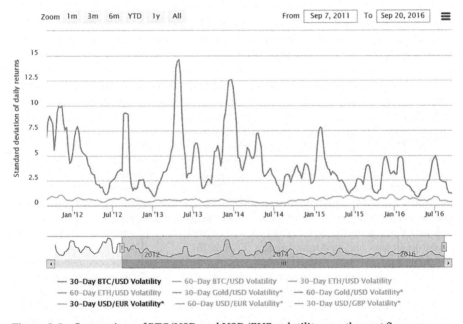

Figure 3-3. *Comparison of BTC/USD and USD/EUR volatility over the past five years*
Source: The bitcoin volatility index (https://btcvol.info/). Accessed September 2016

---

[14]The three functions of money: i) medium of exchange (money is used as a trade intermediary to avoid the inconveniences of a barter system); ii) store of value (money can be saved and retrieved in the future); and iii) unit of account (money acts as a standard numerical unit for the measurement of value and costs of goods, services, assets, and liabilities). Source: (ECB, 2015).

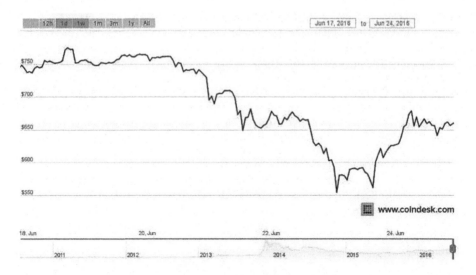

Figure 3-4. *Bitcoin price surge soon after the Brexit announcement (June 23, 2016)*
Source : CoinDesk (http://www.coindesk.com/bitcoin-brexit-ether-price-
rollercoaster/). Accessed September 2016

Legal status: As per the ECB, from a legal perspective, a currency refers to a specific form of money that is generally used within a state/country. As cryptocurrencies are not widely used to exchange value, they are not considered money and not currency either. They conclude that no virtual currency is a real currency.

The legal definition of what is an acceptable currency seems to be based on how it is legally interpreted as a way to transfer value. Money to be used for payments include euro banknotes and coins. These are considered as "legal tender" in the EU countries and therefore, by law, must be accepted as payment for a debt within those territories. However, bank money in euros or electronic money (e-money) in euros are not considered legal tender. Nevertheless, these forms of money are widely accepted for all kinds of payments **by choice**. The euro as a currency may therefore take the form of banknotes, coins, and electronic money. (ECB, 2015).

In spite of this choice-based interpretation of what can be legally accepted as money, the same rule is not extended to cryptocurrencies, as they use their own denomination, i.e., they are not electronic, digital, or virtual forms of a particular currency. They are different from known currencies and, as none of them have been declared as the official currency of a state, they do not have a legal tender capacity. Thus, no creditor is obliged to accept payment with it to discharge a debtor of its debt (ECB, 2015). This means that virtual currencies can be used only as **contractual money**, when there is an agreement between buyer and seller in order to accept a given virtual currency as a means of payment (ECB, 2015).

The legalese revolving around cryptocurrencies is even more complicated in the US, where it differs according to how it is being used (does it fall under the purview of the SEC, the CFTC, or FinCEN?), where it is being used (depends on the state. NY, for example, has begun providing a business license (BitLicense), which obliges virtual currency companies to adhere to a specific licensing regime), and who is using it (miners, banks, users, exchanges…). In other countries, the situation is the same and at present there is no legal consensus as to the status of cryptocurrencies.[15] The definition and legal acceptance of cryptocurrencies is a primary impairment to its widescale use.

Apart from these two impediments, there are also other differences between cryptocurrencies and state fiat. Staying with the legal angle, it is the acceptance of legal tender that determines the use of a currency. Central banks already compete with currencies issued by other central banks within their own states and, to a domestic central bank, a private money is essentially a foreign currency as its monetary policy is governed by an entity that is outside the domestic government's jurisdiction (Andolfatto, 2016). But the devil is in the fine print. Currency issued by a central bank is legal tender and is coupled to laws that certify its acceptance within a state. If parties within a state decide to use another currency instead of that which is issued by the central bank, then the laws do not apply. Hence, the state is absolved from any legal recourse in the case of any default of debt (for example) if the parties have entered a contractual agreement using a currency other than that of the state.[16] This is the underlying thesis of *Gresham's law*: bad money drives out good money and is the reason why central banks have a monopoly privilege in supplying money and why the production and supply of cash occupies a central function in monetary policy.

The supply of private fiat cryptocurrencies, however, is calculated in another way. As the private currency creators are essentially issuing tokens, which are intrinsically valueless, the value of these currencies is based on their scarcity, utility and reputation. As the tokens are unique and non-falsifiable, every user within the network is capable of verifying the total quantity in circulation and witnessing the flows between users. Thus, money supply is determined by profit maximization. As users witness the transfer flows of other users, they form belief systems about the exchange value of the private fiat and alter their behavior (save/spend) in order to protect their own individual interests. Profit maximization thus serves the same purpose as monetary policy with private monies (Fernández-Villaverde and Sanches, 2016).

The difference in the way the supply of private and state fiat currencies occurs is a key issue to determining how they can compete within a common state, and some recent work from researchers at the Federal Reserve Bank of Philadelphia and the University of Pennsylvania have highlighted the consequences of this difference. In a paper titled, "Can Currency Competition Work?" (April 2016), Jesus Fernandez-Villaverdea and Daniel Sanches use a quantitative model[17] to investigate the monetary possibilities with hybrid private and government monies.

---

[15]Refer to the article "Is Bitcoin Legal" (2014), on Coindesk: `http://www.coindesk.com/information/is-bitcoin-legal/`

[16]There are a number of countries where multiple currencies are used simultaneously albeit unofficially, e.g., Singapore (Brunei dollar & Singapore dollar), Ukraine (Ukrainian hryvnia & Russian rouble);, and Zimbabwe (Botswana pula, British Pound, Chinese Yuan, Euro, Indian Rupee, South African Rand and USD). Some currencies may peg their values to another, but this does not mean that the pegged currency is an official currency. It may be preferred by businesses, but taxes are rarely paid in foreign reserve.

[17]The authors use the Lagos-Wright model, which is a framework for monetary theory and policy analysis.

First, the authors found that when only multiple private monies exist within an economy (as proposed by Hayek in *Denationalisation of Money: The Argument Refined*), an equilibrium point could be reached at which the real value of private currencies remains constant. However, this equilibrium state is temporary and, over the course of time, the value of private monies begins to decline. Furthermore, owing to profit maximization efforts of private actors, purely private monetary systems were also susceptible to hyperinflationary episodes much like state-issued money. The conclusion was that a purely private monetary system would not provide the socially optimum quantity of money.

Second, when the authors modified their model to simulate the coexistence of both private and government fiat, the price stability of both private and government monies could only be attained if the government maintained a constant supply of its money. In the real world, a government would need to indulge in expansionary and contradictory policies in order to react to market and political changes. As a result, the government would be obliged to deviate from this practice of maintaining a constant supply, which makes the coexistence of private and government monies an unstable means of exchange.

The volatility, legal issues, and supply complications of functioning with multiple currencies are further compounded with taxation challenges. When governments issue currencies, they also pass legal tender laws. These laws provide licencing requirements for money transmission to indirectly regulate the threat from competing currencies, and hence make it easier for governments to combat tax evasion and money laundering (Raskin and Yermack, 2016). If multiple currencies were to be used, then there would need to be a surveillance system which would allow for proper taxation based on all the currencies in use.

The existing evidence on sovereign cash and multiple currency hybrid systems seems to indicate that if we were to move to a cashless monetary system where currency was issued via Blockchains, then a single currency would be easier to adapt to. This, of course, is a working hypothesis based on existing data. As network effects and the scale of use of cryptocurrencies continues to augment, there is a possibility that we will need to revisit this hypothesis and adapt it to changing market trends.

There are critics who believe that private currencies like bitcoin will soon cease to exist. But there is no evidence to certify this opinion and the website "Bitcoin Obituaries[18]" provides some entertaining evidence of how such opinions have been proved wrong. There is some new research (see Notes—Multiple Currency Mechanisms), which are being explored in the field of network science with regards to multiple currency operations. Nevertheless, from the perspective of large-scale Blockchain adoption, at the current time it would be more sensible to continue investigating the use of a single government-issued fiat currency on a Blockchain.

On a personal note, the bias of continuing with an approach centered around a single sovereign currency issuer is due to my personal belief that the increased financialization of markets have led to greater problems than benefits. This might seem contrary to the very ethos of decentralization (which is what the Blockchain is all about), but in light of the financial scandals and outright criminal shenanigans that we have witnessed over the past three decades, it would seem that personal profit maximization

---

[18]Website address: https://99bitcoins.com/bitcoinobituaries/

will always create circles of misaligned social interests and opportunistic, unscrupulous players. The unfolding events with respect to the Wells Fargo fake account and credit/debit card issuance scandal[19] is just one more example of how those who are responsible for our financial care have betrayed their charge for making a quick buck.

Money is not like other products, as it offers immediate purchasing power upon its issuance. Regulators may be working at a slower pace, but the importance of their work is not to be disregarded based on impatience and personally opinionated conspiracy theories. What is required is clarity, and the Blockchain provides this. On this basis, when thinking about money, I am inclined to side with a democratic system of currency issuance based on trust in the state rather than adopt multiple echelons of trust for private issuers of coinage. This is, however, a personal opinion and not one I advocate to the readers. My goal is to provide information that will instigate a change in the direction of the conversation currently being had about the way monetary systems work, and any conversation is bound to begin with differences in opinions. If the future were to provide evidence to prove me wrong, I would gladly adapt my belief system (and maybe even write a book about it).

In summary, the evidence reviewed seems to side with the conclusion that the role of currency issuance is a function best led by the state. As stated by the English essayist Walter Bagehot over a century ago (1873) in the context of free banking,

> *"We are so accustomed to a system of banking, dependent for its cardinal function on a single bank, that we can hardly conceive of any other. But the natural system—that which would have sprung up if Government had let banking alone—is that of many banks of equal or not altogether unequal size. ... I shall be at once asked, Do you propose a revolution? Do you propose to abandon the one-reserve system, and create anew a many-reserve system? My plain answer is, that I do not propose it: I know it would be childish. ... [A]n immense system of credit, founded on the Bank of England as its pivot and its basis, now exists. The English people and foreigners, too, trust it implicitly. ...The whole rests on an instinctive confidence generated by use and years. ... [I]f some calamity swept it away, generations must elapse before at all the same trust would be placed in any other equivalent. A many-reserve system, if some miracle should put it down in Lombard Street, would seem monstrous there. Nobody would understand it, or confide in it. Credit is a power which may grow, but cannot be constructed."* (Friedman and Schwartz, 1987)

Ultimately, when thinking about changing currency issuance and using different monies, it is not a question of how value is transferred. It is a question of how trust is replaced.

---

[19]Wells Fargo had been engaged in a multi-year scam. A clutch of employees (5300 exactly) at different branches opened over 2 million fake deposit & credit card accounts and used phony emails to enrol consumers in online- banking services without customer authorization. Clients were hit with fees for services they never asked for.

One digital money to rule them all—Fiscal Policy instead of Monetary Policy?

The Blockchain highlights the fact that the existing structures of money creation and policy making parameters were built for a pre-Internet world. As the world moves into a cashless environment, it requires policies that are adapted to it. But the changes to be made are not just with regards to the technical underpinnings of monetary design. In light of prolonged low interest rates, soaring debt levels, high deficits, and weak economic growth, what is also required is a rethinking of how we understand money and macroeconomic policies, and if moving to a completely cashless economy can help us address these issues. Without this line of questioning, the Blockchain is just a shiny new tool in an old, dilapidated shed.

Let's first look at why we need to go cashless and what would be the biggest consequences of doing so. The evidence provided earlier in this chapter (refer to "Fiat currency on a Blockchain") enumerates a number of advantages of moving to a cashless system from a monetary policy perspective. But the main point to be considered is negative interest rates.

If central bank liabilities were digital, paying a negative interest on reserves (essentially charging a fee) would be a fairly simple affair. But as long as money can be converted from electronic deposits to zero-interest bearing cash, it becomes very difficult to reduce rates below -0.25 to -0.50% (for example), and even harder to sustain that for long periods of time. Paper currency thus makes it difficult for central banks to take policy interest rates much below zero and, combined with the zero lower bound, this means that central banks cannot control interest rates nearly as much as they would like to in times of need.

The concept of paying a negative interest rate might seem incongruent to the function of monetary policy to some readers. But it is arguably not much different from inflation, which similarly reduces the purchasing power of a currency (Rogoff, 2014). If inflation were to become unstable, then paying negative interest rates would be a better approach to adopt.

The reason why negative interest rates have been in the news over the past year is mainly because of the persistently ultra-low inflation and near-zero interest rates (in most developed countries) over the past few years. When inflation becomes too low, it becomes harder for governments to deal with it, especially as interest rates drift toward the zero lower bound (also known as the "liquidity trap"). Second, since the crisis, world markets have seen a greater amount of economic volatility. The greater the volatility, the more likely it is that economies will be face severe downturns requiring central bank interest rate cuts (Rogoff, 2016), and therefore the more likely that we will need to indulge in negative interest rates. Third, an increasing tendency to save in emerging economies coupled with ageing populations in developed economies have had a net effect of reduced investment, and hence further perpetuate low interest rates. This was what Ben Bernanke alluded to when he hypothesised about a *"global savings glut."* It is for these reasons that central bankers have been indulging in negative interest rates and debating upon their use.

Owing to the rarity of the long-term use of this policy instrument, it remains to be seen whether negative interest rates will be an effective solution to the problems of low inflation and near-zero interest rates. Negative interest rates are still an experimental policy, and they may be effective in theory, but no one can be sure what issues could arise if rates become significantly negative. Governments technically could circumvent negative interest rates and make citizens pay small episodic taxes on the cash they hold. Even if we phase out cash and apply negative interest rates, other complications such as tax issues or legal obstacles could arise and threaten stability. But in light of the current situation of low inflation and interest rates, policy makers might need to make use of this lever, and a cashless system would be the most effective way to do so if we are to scale at the level of an entire economy.

The move towards a cashless system would also call into question our orthodox view of monetary theory. According to the orthodox view, government spending is to be constrained by the amount of revenue it earns via taxation and borrowing. If governments were allowed to issue more fiat money than the output of the economy, there would be too much money chasing too few goods, and this would ultimately lead to inflation. They should thus not be allowed to "print" money at their whim. Instead, to complement their spending, orthodox theory decrees that governments should borrow money, but only to a certain extent; for if they were to borrow too much, then they would compete with the private sector for funds which in turn would push up interest rates and curtail private loans and investment. The orthodox view thus looks at fiat money as an exogenous entity whose supply, relative to output, affects the price of goods. For this reason, the supply of money needs to be contained and is central to controlling inflation (Wray and Nesisyan, 2016).

But as we have seen in Chapter 1, with the fractional banking system, this is not how fiat money supply is determined and central bankers are not in the driver's seat when it comes to creating money. Money is created whenever a commercial bank offers a loan to a consumer. It is therefore the demand for loans that determines the money supply. Fiat money is thus endogenous to the economy and not exogenous, as described in the orthodox theory (Wray and Nesisyan, 2016). This endogenous perspective of money supply is referred to as the modern money theory.

It is important to understand the difference between the exogenous and endogenous function of money, as it will help us comprehend that governments do not have to depend on commercial banks for creating money and are not handcuffed to the fractional banking system. To explain this statement, we need to revert the conversation back to taxation. While the orthodox theory suggests that a government can only spend based on the revenue it receives from taxes and debt, the modern money theory states that a government does not need tax revenue before it can spend. In fact, if taxpayers need to pay their taxes in government fiat, then the government first has to spend before taxes are paid. In other words, the ability of governments to impose taxes in sovereign fiat gives them an advantage in terms of determining the money supply. Tax payments and bond sales (government loans) only come after the government has spent.

This concept of the endogenous and exogenous role of money and the comparison of the orthodox and modern money theories has been explained in detail and in the context of government balances by Randall Wray and Yeva Nesisyan in "Understanding Money and Macroeconomic Policy[20]" (2016). In their research, the authors come to three conclusions:

---

[20]Chapter 3 in the newly released (and similarly titled) book, *Rethinking Capitalism: Economics and Policy for Sustainable and Inclusive Growth*, edited by Michael Jacobs and Mariana Mazzucato (August 2016).

First, a sovereign state that issues its own currency in *not* financially constrained and its spending is *not* financed by tax and loan revenue, as government spending must precede tax collection and bond sales. Governments thus do not suffer from *financial* constraints. Instead they suffer from *resource* constraints. If a government were to spend more than the output, then inflation would occur. But inflation results from too much spending and not too much money per se. How the spending is financed thus does not determine inflation. Hence the question becomes *how* should governments spend? There could be suitable reasons for why a government should curb spending, but citing that they are running out of money should not be one of them.

Second, as the quantity of money to be produced is based on the aggregate demand for money, the orthodox view that central banks can control the economy with interest rates and reserve quantities is false. As per modern money theory, it is only interest rate control that is at the central banks disposal. Finally, the authors state that as the supply of money is essentially a government decision, monetary policy is in effect fiscal policy. As fiscal policy can directly stimulate aggregate demand, governments in effect have a strong ability to control spending. In their words,

> *"... fiscal expansion can raise demand without worsening private sector balance sheets; indeed, government deficit spending actually improves private sector finances by providing income and safe government liabilities to accumulate in portfolios.... governments with monetary sovereignty are not financially constrained: they spend as they issue their own IOU's [currency]. They can use this capacity to buy real resources, and in doing so to promote full employment."*

We began this chapter by asking ourselves what is the definition of capitalism in the context of markets, regulation, and policy. As we have seen, these three pillars of capitalism are in a state of change and the current definitions and ideologies on which they function are being challenged. Moreover, it is increasingly evident that, as the pace and impact of technological change continues to accelerate, any new definition will have to be one that is adaptable to the future ramifications.

What we need is a rethinking of capitalism. Since the crisis, policy makers have been rethinking this concept. Had they not, we would not have had initiatives such as QE and QQE that helped us avoid a global depression. However, now that the dust has settled, we need to review these actions and gauge their effectiveness.

Let us take the case of quantitative easing (QE). QE works because low, long-term bond yields push up prices asset prices. This stimulates asset holders to consume or invest more and is therefore bound to increase inequality (Turner, 2015). We can also look at sustained low interest rates. While the goal of ultralow rates is to stimulate spending, there is a greater possibility that they will encourage risky and leveraged speculation before they stimulate demand in the economy. And they can only encourage demand by encouraging private credit growth, which is the bane of our problems.

Increasing private credit leads to financialization and the transformation of credit from being a means of achieving future prosperity to a commodity that can be exchanged for value. At the heart of this transformation is a conflict of categorization. Money and credit are in a different product category, as they are different from commodities, goods, and services. The creation of money and credit results in purchasing power, which in turn has macroeconomic consequences. This is not the same with creating a new product or services based on technological advances. Thus, applying the free market principles that govern the creation of goods and services to credit and money supply is fundamentally flawed and highlights how dicey and limited in scope monetary policy is. It is for these reasons that we need to turn our gaze to fiscal policy.

What policy makers need to understand is that today they have the capability of using technology to gain a more decisive position in markets, and that by the proper use of fiscal policy and regulation, they can create a monetary system that is more democratic and transparent. Ideas such as the Chicago Plan have existed for a long time, but with technology such as the Blockchain, we are in a position to utilize it at a societal level. This is not to say that we should immediately move to a 100% reserve system. As per the plan outlined by Benes and Kumhof, moving to a 100% reserve system would also entail writing off substantial quantities of debt. There are bound to be winners and losers in this case. What should therefore be envisioned is a way in which existing debt can be reduced gradually over time, while new bank businesses were conducted on the principles of the Chicago Plan. One option could be a modified use of CoCo bonds (see notes: "CoCo bonds and the Blockchain"), which allows for the conversion of debt into equity.

Making reforms that reflect these principles is crucial today because of our excessive debt levels. We must recognize that free market forces do not issue the optimal amount of credit or for the appropriate purposes. We need to reject the concept that credit creation can be left to the market and that the fractional banking system can be continue to operate in its present from.

Intervention is needed not in the issuance of credit, but in the quantity that is created. Less credit, however, does not mean less growth. As we have seen in previous chapters, a large amount of credit today is not used for economic growth, but is instead invested in housing/real estate. As a result, it does not proportionally increase demand, and leads to debt-overhang and recession. The main objective of policy makers should thus be to create a less credit-concentrated economy. Without such measures, capitalism is a ticking time-bomb propped up by inefficient regulations and policies.

As stated by Stephanie Kelton in "The Failure of Austerity: Rethinking Fiscal Policy" (2016),

> "Along with aggressively deregulating financial (and other) markets, nearly every OECD country has substantially cut taxes over the past thirty years. The average marginal income tax rate on top earners dropped from 66% in 1981 to 43% by 2013. Average corporate income tax rates were also cut sharply, plunging from 47% to 25%, and taxes on dividend income declined from 75% to 42% over the same period. Instead of unleashing the job creators and extending prosperity to all, these supply-side maneuvers were closely associated with widening inequality and greater financial instability. In other words, these experiments have failed. Capitalism has become more unstable, the distribution of wealth and income has become more unequal and it takes the system longer and longer to claw back the jobs that are lost each time we suffer a recession," (Jacobs and Mazzucato, 2016).

Moving to a sovereign, cashless, Blockchain-based monetary infrastructure based on the principles of the Chicago Plan is one way for governments to not just reduce debt levels, but also to rewrite the rule book on macroeconomics and governance. The role of policy is not just to correct and penalize the transgressions of free market players. It is also to shape markets in order to obtain the right allocation of resources, long-term value creation, social well-being, and lower inequality, and to ensure environment sustainability. Short-term GDP[21] growth can no longer be the primary objective of governments.

Thus, as the definition of capitalism begins to involve the democratic state to a greater degree, we should also use this opportunity to see how we can address the problems of technological unemployment, education, productivity changes, inequality, and ageism. One solution pathway could lie with helicopter money and universal basic income.

Helicopter Drops and Universal Basic Income

Refresh your memory and think about the last time you heard these "keywords": technological unemployment, income inequality, stagnant wages, poverty, regulatory gridlock. If you are a regular follower of the news, then the chances are that you may have heard these terms almost on a weekly basis.

But these terms are large-scaling in nature and talk about multiple socioeconomic or political issues. It's easy to get lost when thinking about these issues, as the barrage of data and opinions (mostly tangential) do not provide a steady anchor to everyday events and make us lose sight of the fundamental issue. The issue.... is the issue. So let's look at one particular entity that is connected to all of these keywords and see how recent developments of this singular entity is linked to all the jargon being flung about today. The entity we will choose is *Chatbots*.

A Chatbot is essentially a service, powered by rules and artificial intelligence (AI), that a user can interact with via a chat interface. The service could be anything ranging from functional to fun, and it could exist in any chat product (Facebook Messenger, Slack, telegram, text messages, etc.). Recent advancements in Natural Language Processing (NLP) and Automatic Speech Recognition (ASR), coupled with crowdsourced data inputs and machine learning techniques, now allow AI's to not just understand groups of words but also submit a corresponding natural response to a grouping of words. That's essentially the base definition of a conversation, except this conversation is with a "bot."

Does this mean that we'll soon have technology that can pass the Turing test? Maybe not yet, but Chatbots seem to be making progress towards that objective. The most advanced Chatbot today is Xiaoice (pronounced Shao-ice) developed by Microsoft, and

---

[21]GDP appears constantly in the news, business, and politics. Yet in recent times, its ability to appropriately represent the true productivity of a country is increasingly criticized. While writing a critique on this topic is beyond the scope of this book, readers are invited to look at other indicators such as the Social Progress Index and the OECD Better Life Index. Another excellent resource is Diane Coyle's, *GDP: A Brief but Affectionate History*, which shows why this statistic was invented, how it has changed, what are its pros and cons and why it is inappropriate for a 21st century economy driven by innovation, services, and intangible goods.

which can respond with human-like answers, questions, and "thoughts." If a user sends a picture of a broken ankle, Xiaoice will reply with a question asking about how much pain the injury caused, for example (Slater-Robins, 2016).

Unsurprisingly Chatbots are increasingly attracting investors. According to Tracxn (a Sequoia and Accel alumni-founded market research firm that globally tracks venture capital investment, corporate investment, and startup activity), over $140 million has been invested in Chatbots since 2010, with the majority, approximately $85 million, being invested between the 2015 to 2016 period (Tracxn, 2016). This interest is not just seen in finance, but almost any industry today: hospitality, journalism, medical, insurance, travel, retail, automotive, entertainment, etc. (CB Insights, 2016), and is creating a new wave of companies, such as X.AI. (AI scheduling assistant), Clara Labs, Julie Desk, Kono, Overlap, Babylon Health, Ozlo, Maluuba, GoButler, Your.MD, Arya (a research assistant), and so on. As stated in a recent report by *Business Insider*,

> *"Chatbots also have the potential to help businesses significantly cut labor costs. While complete automation of the customer service workforce is not feasible, automating customer management and sales positions in the US where possible through Chatbots and other automation technologies would result in considerable savings." ("The Chatbot Explainer," BI Intelligence, July 2016).*

A conversation used to be a uniquely human activity but with the rise of Chatbots, this precept is being put to the test. The developments with Chatbots is just one single example of how technology is replacing human labor in what were essentially human-centric jobs. So let's revisit those keywords from the beginning of this section, but from the context of Chatbots. What happens to the employment of existing call center workers with Chatbots? By 2020, Gartner predicts that this type of conversation automation will manage 85% of businesses' customer relationships (Busby, 2016). How many people will this potentially effect? Just in the US alone, 5 million people are employed in call centers, while in countries like India and the Philippines, call centers provide employment to millions of people. So what impact will this one technology have on income inequality, wages, and poverty levels when it replaces labor?

Finding an answer to that question is not the reason for citing it. It is more to help us see that if we were to pull apart the fabric of a single technology, it reveals a tapestry of spillover effects which our current definition of capitalism is unable to envision, let alone provide contingency plans. If we were to repeat this exercise with other technologies, similar revelations would ensue. It would also show us how addicted we are to the concept of gain and unconcerned with spill over effects. Think about it. When was the last time you heard a manager say out loud, *"What can I do to increase the number of employees?"*

This brings us back full circle to the topics that were discussed in the beginning of this chapter (refer to Sidebar 3-1). While initially we were looking at technology from the vantage point of markets, regulations, and policy—the pillars of capitalism—looking at the minutiae of a single strand of technology brings us to same conclusion. Technology's impact on jobs is the big yellow elephant in the room. Moreover, as technology continues to grow and evolve, it provides benefits to a few (who extort rent controls from it) and eliminates labor in the process. The charts in Figure 3-5 are from the Federal Reserve Bank of St. Louis. They help us see this paradigmatic shift in process. Notice the way employment and profits have taken distinctly opposing trajectories since the crisis.

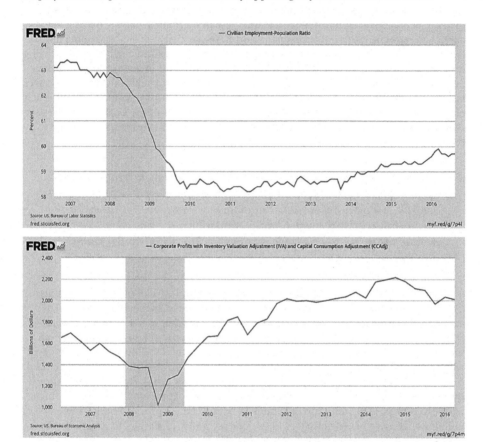

Figure 3-5. *Comparative charts of employment and corporate profit over the last 10 years*

This trend is to be expected. Labor is the biggest expenditure of a corporation and if you can get rid of labor and replace it with technology, profits will go up *ceteris paribus*. But the effect this has is not limited to profits margins. When people in one sector are replaced by technology on a massive scale, it evidently causes unemployment in that sector, but also leads to underemployment[22] in similar or related sectors. This creates a ripple effect, for as higher-skilled workers are forced to apply for the jobs of lower-skilled workers, it creates a self-sustaining circle of poverty for marginalized groups, pushes down wages across sectors, puts more burdens on the state, and impacts monetary and

---

[22]The concept of technological underemployment and unemployment has been explored in detail by Guy Standing in his very excellent book, *The Precariat: The New Dangerous Class*, (2011).

fiscal policy. Thus the question becomes: how does capitalism respond to the juggernaut of technological evolution?

Technology is embryonically linked to innovation, and innovation is often cited as the cure-all to problems in any sector. But the link between markets and governments in the context of innovation is often sidelined. It is for this reason that when we talk about innovation, especially innovation which is going to replace cognitive and manual repetitive work, we also need to talk about the effect it has on capitalism (see Sidebar 3-1). What needs to be remembered is that as labor size gets reduced, it also lowers/stagnates wages. While this makes it almost impossible for the working class to insure itself, it is also a concern for central bankers, for as people are displaced from jobs, it will reduce aggregate demand, exasperate income inequality, and augment the disparity between savings and investment, which in turn will force down the price of borrowing money, i.e., the interest rate. In net sum, technological innovation, while being the force that is pushing society forward, is also pushing us towards the zero lower bound.

It is for this reason that we need to overturn the current dominant paradigm with respect to the narrative of life under capitalism. The dominant paradigm today is that the private production of wealth is appropriated by the state for social purposes. But this is a fallacy for, in reality, wealth production is social and collective, which is then appropriated privately. To explain this statement, let us conduct a simple experiment. Look around you and select a piece of technology. It could be the lights around you, the tablet on which you read this book, or your smartphone that is attached to you at all times. Now that you have selected a technology, dissect it completely and trace back the origin of every piece of technology that it embeds. You will find that in every case, the technology you are analyzing could not have existed had it not been for a government grant. This is true even of the Blockchain. While the Blockchain was first created by a single person/group (Satoshi Nakamoto), what it represents is decades' worth of research and development in cryptography, encryption, economics, and game theory—all subjects that have been funded massively by governments. Had it not been for the ARPANet, Vint Cerf and Bob Khan would have never received the necessary funding to develop packet-switching data and you would not be reading this book had that happened.

The development of technology is hence a collective production of wealth and it is for this reason that we need to turn the narrative of capitalism and show that there is no separation between free markets and the state. There would be no markets without states and there would be no capitalism if there was no state. But there would be no state if there were no private entrepreneurs. Hence, the relationship between markets and states is symbiotic and it is wrong to believe that they are separate entities.

By following this train of thought, we can thus see that if technology is developed by the collective efforts of the state and leads to the production of wealth, then it would only be logical for the contributors (the citizens) to receive a dividend for the investment they have made. It is this dividend that I refer to as the Universal Basic Income (UBI).

A UBI is an income that is granted unconditionally to every member of a political community. As per the Basic Income Earth Network (BIEN) there are criteria to be adhered to when talking about UBI:

1. It is an income that is given to secure existence and allow social participation.

2. It is an individual right's claim and is paid to individuals rather than households.

3. It is payable without means-tested verification.

4. There is no obligation to work. It is paid irrespective of any income from other sources.

5. It is paid without requiring the performance of any work or the willingness to accept a job if offered.

While the concept of Universal Basic Income was not devised with technological unemployment in mind, it is increasingly bearing relevance to the current economic diaspora. It is essentially a guaranteed salary that is given to every person, every month, irrespective of what they do and how they live. It is an unconditional pact between the citizens and the state that ensures that everyone receives an income just for being part of the community. There are various ways in how such a goal can be implemented and the following parts of this section detail the history of UBI, the experiments that were conducted, the results of these experiments, and how we can create a framework for the UBI with the Blockchain.

The first major proponent of UBI was Thomas Paine, who stated in *Agrarian Justice* (1795) the philosophy behind a basic income. According to Paine, every owner of land owed a rent to the community for the land he held, as it was with this land that he was able to improve his prosperity. Paine thus suggested that this rent ought to be given back to the community in the form of a UBI,

> *"In advocating the case of the persons thus dispossessed, it is a right, and not a charity, that I am pleading for. But it is that kind of right which, being neglected at first, could not be brought forward afterwards till heaven had opened the way by a revolution in the system of government. Let us then do honour to revolutions by justice, and give currency to their principles by blessings....*
>
> *Having thus in a few words, opened the merits of the case, I shall now proceed to the plan I have to propose, which is ... To create a national fund, out of which there shall be paid to every person, when arrived at the age of twenty-one years, the sum of fifteen pounds sterling, as a compensation in part, for the loss of his or her natural inheritance, by the introduction of the system of landed property: And also, the sum of ten pounds per annum, during life, to every person now living, of the age of fifty years, and to all others as they shall arrive at that age."* (Paine, 1795)

Paine, whose other works influenced the drafting of the US Constitution, was not the only person in history to propose UBI. Over the years, philosophers, politicians, economists, and social scientists such as Bertrand Russell, Dennis Milner, C.H. Douglas, James Meade, Milton Freidman, F.A. Hayek, and Ben Bernanke have all been advocates of UBI in one from or another.

Freidman had an alternative approach when thinking about UBI. As per his theory, if an economy was undergoing a fall in demand (which can result with technological unemployment and underemployment), he suggested that the government print some money and throw it from a helicopter. As people would pick up the scattered bills and spend them, there would be an increase in demand for goods and services, and nominal GDP would rise and result in some increase in inflation. This increase in inflation would of course depend on whether people spent or saved the money, but the net result would be tied to the quantity that was scattered from a helicopter. As per Friedman, a government was never out of options when it came to increasing demand, as we could drop cash into the state. Too much and we get inflation. But if it was small enough, then it could produce desirable results.

While Friedman's idea might seem a bit dramatic and farfetched, today it is in fact technically feasible with or without a Blockchain. A state could route, say, a €1000 to every citizen's bank account via their commercial bank accounts. Alternatively, he suggested a negative income tax or a cut in tax rates or a tax credit (paid in cash). The end result according to Freidman would be the same: nominal demand would go up and the extent to which it would go up would be proportional to the amount of cash injected. As it is effectively putting more purchasing power in the hands of consumers, it would avoid higher asset prices, curb credit expansion, remove the need for ultralow interest rates and thus be more beneficial than traditional fiscal or monetary policy instruments.

Incredible as this idea is, when we look at it in reference to all the material we have reviewed with regards to fractional banking, there is a chink in its armor. If the government were to apply a UBI via the existing system, it would be creating additional commercial bank reserves at the central bank. This would thus help commercial banks create additional private credit and debt-based cash. Hence, the initial stimulative effects on demand would soon be overcome by the multiplying effect it would have on private credit issuance and bring us back to where we are today in terms of rising debt levels and runaway credit.

The only way that such a system could feasibly work is if the banking system was based on the Chicago Plan. In such a system, the base money would be the only money in circulation. As a result, an increase in supply would stimulate demand but not increase private credit growth. Governments would thus be able to control the economy through pure fiscal policy. An extract from Adair Turner's *Between Debt and the Devil* neatly summarizes how the concept of helicopter drops and the Chicago Plan could work,

> *"Fractional reserve banks thus complicate the implementation of money finance[23] but the model of 100% reserve banks suggests the obvious solution: any dangers of excessive long-term demand stimulus can be offset if central banks impose reserve asset requirements. These requirements would force banks to hold a stipulated percentage of their total liabilities at the central bank and thus would constrain the banks' ability to create additional private credit and money. Those ratios could be imposed on a discretionary basis over time, with the central bank increasing them if inflation threatened to move above target. But they could also in theory be deployed in an immediate and rule-driven*

---

[23]Overt Money finance is the act of creating new money and giving it to people via spending or tax cuts.

fashion, increasing the required reserves of commercial banks at the same time as the electronic money drop and by precisely the same amount.

This would essentially impose a 100% reserve requirement on the new fiat money creation. We can in effect treat the banking system as if it were in part a 100% reserve system and in part a fractional reserve: we do not have to take an absolute either/or choice" (Chapter 14, Pg. 221, Between Debt and the Devil, Turner, 2015).

If you have got to this part of the book after reading all that was written before, then connecting the dots will be evident to you. A cashless society in which the government is responsible for the issuance of fiat money on a sovereign Blockchain can not only address the problems of debt, tax evasion, and excessive financialization, but can also be a tool by which governments can apply radical society-changing initiatives such as UBI. This is a concept that policy makers need to seriously consider, especially when faced with challenges such as technological unemployment and increasing income inequality. If we are to find an antidote to the current socioeconomic malaise, then we cannot depend on existing theories and practices, for they have been tried, tested, measured, and still found lacking. UBI is a program worth exploring and, while it is beyond the objective of this book to focus on this subject in depth, it has been included it in the text to show that it is indeed technically feasible. But it is by far only one example of what can be done with such a framework. What else can be done will be explored in the next chapter.

There are policy makers who are seriously considering the application of UBI, and some recent statements by Yanis Varoufakis show the level of thinking regarding this subject,

"To put it simply, in the 20th century, we had the stabilization and civilization of capitalism through the rise of social democracy, the New Deal in the United States and the social market developments in Europe. Unfortunately, this deal is finished and it can't be revived. .... Basic Income is (thus) a necessity...it is not a question of whether we like it or not...it will be a major part of any attempt to civilize capitalism as capitalism is going through a spasm caused by its own generation of technologies that undermine itself." (Varoufakis, 2016)

Those readers interested in learning more about UBI can refer the list of resources that were referenced in the notes section of this chapter (see Notes: UBI Reading).

Examples of UBI

We will conclude this note on UBI by seeing examples of its deployment, the impact they had, and how we can envision the deployment of a similar program.

Alaska

In the 1970s, during the construction of the Trans-Alaska pipeline, the state of Alaska received a massive inflow of money as companies acquired leases for oil drilling rights. The Alaskan government thus created the Alaska Permanent Fund, which paid every resident (650,000 Alaskans) a UBI of $2000 per person. The program is still in place and has been responsible for helping residents in the rural areas deal with unemployment and is cited as making Alaska one of the most egalitarian states.

Mincome, Canada

In March 1973, the government of Manitoba reserved a sum of $83 million USD for a project that was labeled as Mincome. The project was executed in the small town of Dauphin, just northwest of Winnipeg, which has a population of 13,000. Everybody in the town was guaranteed a UBI with the goal being that no one fell below the poverty line. 30% of the town's inhabitants—around a 1,000 families—got a check in the mail each month and a family of four received what would now be around $19,000 a year, irrespective of their social or economic class.

Initially, there were political fears that giving people a UBI would reduce work participation and encourage the development of large families. But in reality, the opposite occurred. Young adults got married later, birth rates dropped and school participation increased. Men worked the same hours as before (on aggregate) and women used the money to take time off work to care for their children or pursue their studies. Mental health complaints reduced, domestic violence took a fall, and even hospitalizations decreased by 8.5% (Bregman, 2016). The project ran for four years and was scrapped with a change in government. But Mincome was a success.

Otjivero, Namibia

The effect of how a UBI can drastically reduce poverty levels can best be seen in this village of Otjivero. In 2009, the small poor desert town was selected for an experiment. The 930 inhabitants would each receive $100 Namibian, or about €7, a month unconditionally. When the experiment began, almost all residents lived in cardboard or plastic houses. A year into the experiment, there was a marked rise in the kind of houses the residents lived in. Entrepreneurship went up and the average income grew 39% over the UBI (Stern, 2016). Women became more independent and those residents suffering from HIV were able to get the treatment required. School dropout rates fell by 40% as parents no longer had the save the money that was reserved for fees, and malnutrition went down from 42% to 10%. UBI didn't just make them prosperous and independent, it also made them heathier.

There have been other experiments of UBI with almost similar results. That is not to say that UBI is a solution to all problems related to poverty and societal well-being. If it is set too low and accompanied with irradiation of all social benefits or tied to certain conditions, UBI can also be misused and create more harm than good. There is also the question of immigration that needs to be considered. Will a new entrant to a country's citizenry receive the same benefits or will they be able to do so only after a certain period of time? These are questions that merit debate and rightly so.

Funding the Deployment

But the evidence of all the experiments that have been conducted in America, Canada, Europe, and Africa all show positive effects. When you give money to people with no conditions, work participation goes up as individuals now realize that they do not have to do a job just to gain an income. They are capable of pursing an interest that matters to them and, in most cases, individuals say that they work even more than before as they are now pursuing a career of their choosing. In almost all cases, women get more independent, overall education levels rise (especially adult education levels), and poverty levels drop. The general consensus is a reduction in stress and an increase in happiness—something that GDP, our yardstick for growth, is incapable of measuring.

So how would one go about getting the funds for deploying UBI at the level of a developed country? There are a number of approaches that have been proposed. Willem Buiter's paper, "The Simple Analytics of Helicopter Money," offers us a mathematical method which can help in the creation of such a system. But for the purpose of avoiding mathematical formulae, we can refer to some recent work done by Andy Stern, the former president of the Service Employees International Union and senior fellow at Columbia University, who details funding possibilities for a UBI in his recent book, *Raising the Floor* (2016).

As per Stern's estimates, it would cost the US government between $1.75 to $2.5 trillion to give a UBI of $12,000 per year to all 18–64-year-olds. Stern proposes that we find these resources by eliminating food stamps ($76 billion per annum), housing assistance ($49 Billion per annum) and earned income tax credit ($82 billion per annum). He also proposes that revenue can be raised by eliminating the government's $1.2 trillion tax expenditures[24] and by imposing a financial transaction tax that taxes stock sales at 0.1% at issuance and 0.04% on transfer. As per his estimates, doing the latter would raise revenue by $150 billion a year. His other funding possibilities come from imposing a wealth tax on personal assets (as proposed by Piketty) and reducing the military budget and farm subsidies, and increasing levies on oil and gas companies.

Apart from the above stated funding sources, we have also seen how the implementation of the Blockchain can lead to lesser tax evasion from companies and how moving to a financial system that is more in line with the Chicago Plan can reduce existing public debt levels. All of these means coupled with the savings and cost reductions that will be attained from the move to a cashless economy not only provide us with the means to apply initiatives such as UBI, but demand why we are not applying them already.

Making policies based on probabilities

When I was a young recruit in the French Foreign Legion, my platoon commander always had a saying that I have found increasingly relevant in everyday life. Irrespective of where we were deployed, be it Africa or Afghanistan, he would always say, *"ç'est le terrain qui command,"* which, loosely translated, means that it's the land on which you are that

---

[24]Tax expenditures: when the government spends revenue via the tax system by giving a deduction on taxable income. These expenditures normally benefit higher earners.

commands your actions. No matter how well-trained a soldier can be, it is always his ability to gauge his environment that will give him clarity about his situation and enable him to adapt to the surroundings in which he is immersed. That's why training is so important. Not just to become competent in performing an action, but being capable of executing an action that you were not trained for. It is this formula of resourcefulness that can mean life or death in the battlefield and which coincidentally also determines how to plan a successful business strategy.

Capitalism today is in the throes of an environment that is constantly changing. We are attempting to adapt to this change, but we are using a scaffolding that was devised at a different time. Is it a wonder then that in spite of all our technological progress, we still have increasing levels of income inequality? Is it a surprise that we still use telephones and fax machines to settle trades that are conducted on a nanosecond basis? Is it really a shock when we realize that our first reaction to an idea like the Chicago Plan is to shun it and find reasons why it would not work, rather than challenge our existing belief system? And is it really a surprise that the ones who understand how the system works extoll a rent that is scandalous and vulgar by any measure of humanity?

The Blockchain is not a solution to these problems. As stated at multiple intervals in this book, is not a panacea. It is a tool which, if deployed correctly, can allow policy makers to create a capitalistic system that is not dependent on the fractional banking system, which is more transparent, more ordered and less financialized, and has lower levels of debt. But it cannot reach the zeniths of its capabilities if it is used just to make transactions faster and help financial institutions save on some costs. It has to be deployed in tandem with wide-arching societal programs that address the current economic malaise.

Undertaking such an endeavor is bound to be fraught with doubt and will require that we rigorously test our theories before deploying a project that can have wide-ranging social benefits. It is in this context that I introduce the subject of complexity economics, which we will explore in relative detail in the next chapter.

If we are to redefine capitalism, then what we require for the future is not just a new theory that is holistic in nature and modern in its outlook, but a buffet of theories. The reason for this multipronged approach is simple. As we have seen, economies are complex structures with multiple actors playing multiple roles, who are constantly changing the form and shape of the market with multiple spillover effects. This essentially means that the market is not in a state of equilibrium, as stated in traditional economics, but in a state of entropy. Information is exchanged and creates pockets of organized data structures which show some guise of steadiness. But as technological evolutions occur in bursts of concentric circles, it disrupts the false sense of serenity that is presented as a façade and forces the actors to adapt to the new environment they are immersed in. This is why innovation has become the chant of corporations and the curriculum of universities.

If we are to accept this based on the evidence that has been provided, then we come to a stark realization. Are we to continue governing ourselves on the efficient market hypothesis or adapt to the entropy of information that makes up to market place? With the Blockchain becoming mainstream, this question gains more gravitas, as we now have access to even more information that can be shared across multiple parties. Would it not make sense in that case to accept the entropy for what it is and develop theories and frameworks that would help us adapt to this state of constant flux? This is the promise of complexity economics and, in the next chapter, we will get an educated understanding of what this is and the models that can be used via this branch of science.

It must be remembered that, as information changes hands, it creates ripples of decisions which can create multiple scenarios. A government might think that by putting money in the hands of its citizenry via a UBI, it would spark demand. But what if that does not happen? What if the citizens prefer to save their money instead, or use it for other purposes such as saving it or taking holidays *en masse*? Is there any model that the government has that can offer a contingency plan to any reaction at either extreme or at different levels of granularity?

This is what complexity economics will help us to. By using a defined set of variables (and there is the possibility of using a great number of multiple variables as input data in complexity science models), we can create different simulations that will help policy makers not necessarily predict the future, but determine how to react in case a certain scenario begins to take form in reality. This scenario creation possibility, along with the advantages of the Blockchain, is what will be required if we are to safeguard ourselves from future crises.

For these objectives to be reached requires not just a comprehension of where we are going, but also where we come from, and it is the reason that this chapter refers to projects and proposals that have been stored in the annals of economic history. By juxtaposing the past, the present, and potentialities for the future of economics with the scientific methods of complexity science, we can develop theories, simulate economies, and test them rigorously to decide what course of action needs to be taken. Doing so will make economic policy proactive rather than reactive.

When we look at a capitalistic nation, how do we use the very force that is changing us to help address the jobs that it is removing? How do we define innovation in the context of capitalism? How do we raise the innovativeness of an entire capitalistic state so as to put ourselves on a trajectory of growth and find solutions to the problems that befall us today? Would it be irrational to ponder that the answers to these questions require that we need to innovate the theories of capitalism as they are defined and executed? If technology is practically changing the paradigms of employment and growth, then ought we not to meet it halfway by changing the paradigm of economic theory?

The answer to these questions, as stated in the beginning of this chapter, lies in culture, for capitalism is both an economic as well as a cultural construct. As technology reshapes our lives, we need to develop a culture which can be traditional in nature, but has to emphatically be modern in its outlook. A culture in which citizens are comfortable with change, in which entrepreneurs and businesses think in terms of probabilities to find opportunities, where experimentation is based on the scientific method, and where theories are put to the test on a constant basis. Without such a culture, we will not be able to have a change in our economics mindsets, no matter how hard we scream about innovation.

Coming up with the right theories will be almost as important as having the right leadership in order to instigate this change in mindset. Theory is important, as it gives us direction. But theories also need to be tested to be proved valid. While current macroeconomic theories have been rigid, the future theories that we need to develop need to be more flexible. But when we talk about capitalism, testing a theory ends up involving citizens who are engaged in economic activities. Evidently, this is a risky practice to be adopted and might not go down too well if it causes adverse impacts on swathes of a population. This is why simulating the theories and testing their viability is of the upmost importance if we are to develop a buffet of theories.

While technology destroys old frameworks, it is also creating new ones. The technological framework of the Blockchain allows us to gain information about the entire financial system and create theories that incubate the financial system. But to test our theories we will also need to use new tools and methods. It is for this reason that we need to turn our gaze to complexity science models, as they are attuned for these kinds of analyses.

Notes

The following sections provide additional information on some relatively technical concepts.

CoCo bonds and the Blockchain

Source: "The future of financial infrastructure," Section 5.5 - Capital Raising: Contingent Convertible ("CoCo") Bonds, World Economic Forum, 2016.

Unlike traditional bonds, contingent convertible (CoCo) bonds are financial instruments which can be converted into equity. Banks use CoCo bonds to increase their capital ratios in case they fall below a predefined threshold (e.g., bank capital falls below 7.5%). Regulators also use CoCo bonds if a discretionary circumstance is determined about a bank during a stress test.

The main use of CoCo bonds are to absorb losses when the capital of the issuing bank falls below a certain level. Private investors are usually reluctant to provide additional capital to banks in times of stress. To address this, governments can inject capital to prevent insolvency but such public sector support costs taxpayers and distorts the incentives of bankers (Avdjiev et al., 2013). CoCo's address this problem and absorb losses by converting debt into equity when the capital of the issuing bank falls below a threshold level. As debt is reduced, bank capitalization increases and regulatory capital requirements are met.

The issuing banks determine CoCo bonds attributes (trigger options and maturity dates) through market value calculation. The bonds are then sold on the market (mostly to other banks, hedge funds, and insurance firms) and triggered according to market performance or regulator intervention. However, as regulators can only gain insight into the capital ratios during stress tests (say, once every quarter), CoCo bonds currently suffer from delayed activation times and cannot be converted immediately into equity when the conditions are met. As a result, no CoCo bonds have been converted into equity, and as markets have become uninterested, CoCo bond issuance has flatlined over the last few years. High market volatility has also reduced yields and not helped CoCo bond sales.

But a solution could lie with the Blockchain and Smart Contracts. Banks could issue tokenized CoCo's with the key attributes (trigger parameters, coupon rate, maturity date, etc.) encoded via Smart Contracts. The bank then analyzes its capital ratios and adds this information to the tokenized CoCo. This would provide transparency to the investors and, in case the conditions are met, the CoCo would be activated with notifications sent immediately to the regulators and the bank's leadership.

Such an operating methodology could increase confidence in CoCo's and allow for real-time reporting to regulators. Banks would also need to do less stress tests, as regulators would have real-time access to the banks' capital ratio. This would enable CoCo's to become a key tool in strengthening banks' capital levels and prevent taxpayer bailouts.

Scalability

Source: "Centrally Banked Cryptocurrencies," George Danezis and Sarah Meiklejohn, Dec. 2015.

Most critics of the Blockchain cite the scalability issue as an argument for why it cannot be deployed at a large scale. There is evidence to support this claim. The Bitcoin network can currently handle 7 transactions per second whereas PayPal handles over 100 and Visa handles on average anywhere from 2,000 to 7,000. This lack of scalability is due to the following:

1. the significant computational energy that is expended in the proofs-of-work process (which helps manage the ledger and makes double-spending attacks excessively expensive), as it has to broadcast results on the network

2. the fixed supply: this provides little or no flexibility for policy aimed at controlling its volatility

As the Bank of England asked *"whether central banks should themselves make use of such technology to issue digital currencies,"* researchers from University College London responded by creating RSCoin, a cryptocurrency framework that separates the generation of the money supply from the maintenance of the transaction ledger. This framework is different from other cryptocurrencies in that the supply is centralized. Thus, the model is ideal for adoption by central banks and in line with the proposals that have been made in this chapter.

Some of the stated benefits of RSCoin include:

- Unlike traditional fiat money, RSCoin provides the government with a transparent transaction ledger, a distributed system for maintaining it, and a globally visible monetary supply. This makes monetary policy transparent, allows direct access to payments and value transfers, supports pseudonymity, and benefits from innovative uses of blockchains and digital money.

- The transaction validation responsibility can be given to trusted third parties. In this way, RSCoin works on the basis of permission and is similar to Ripple's validation model.

- RSCoin supports a simple and fast mechanism for double-spending detection. By adapting a variant of the Two-Phase Commit protocol (a specialized consensus protocol that coordinates "commit" or "abort" processes in a distributed transaction), the researchers were able to achieve a higher level of scalability—2,000 transactions per second with 30 miners (or minettes as named by the authors—minettes could be institutions with an existing relationship to the central bank, such as commercial banks, and thus to have some existing incentives to perform this service).

- Most transactions were cleared within a second and the performance was found to scale linearly as the number of minettes was increased.

As the article is rather technical and goes beyond the purpose of this chapter, I have avoided integrating the full mathematical workings of RSCoin. Interested readers can find the article for free at: http://arxiv.org/pdf/1505.06895v2.pdf

Sarbanes-Oxley Act

Source: Chapter 16, The Philosophy, Politics and Economics of Finance in the 21st Century: From Hubris to Disgrace, "Regulation and Fraud," by Andrea Cilloni and Marco A. Marinoni (2015).

The Sarbanes-Oxley Act of 2002 (SOX) is a US federal law that has strengthened both qualitative and quantitative regulatory control systems standards for all companies listed on the US stock market. In the global context, such legislation impacts powerfully on other economic systems. The main novelties of the SOX in terms of a company's audit system are:

- Establishment of the Public Company Accounting Oversight Board (PCAOB), an organization coordinated by the Securities and Exchange Commission in order to establish a regulatory standard for the assessment of internal control systems.

- Standards of independence of the auditing companies were established to limit conflicts of interest. This mainly consists of the prohibition for an auditing firm to provide any non-audit services to the same clients as those to which it provides audit services certifying the financial statements. The PCAOB may allow exceptions on a case-by-case basis, where services represent less than 5% of the total fees paid for the audit of accounts.

- The individual responsibility of the directors and senior executives for the accuracy and the completeness of the financial statements and of integrated notes is preserved.

- Adequate information based on evidence for all relevant off-financial statement transactions and other relationships, so called "special purpose entities," must be provided.

- The Corporate and Criminal Fraud Accountability Act of 2002 describes the penalties for manipulation, destruction, or alteration of the certified business performance or any interference with investigation thereof.

Multiple Currency Mechanisms

Source: "A 'Social Bitcoin' could sustain a democratic digital world," Kaj-Kolja Kleineberg and Dirk Helbing, April 2016.

Kleineberg and Helbing state the current monetary system is ill-suited in design to control highly interconnected and complex systems like today's economic and financial systems. The reason for this, they state, is because currency monetary systems only have one control variable (they cite interest rates). As a result, these systems are difficult to control and nearly impossible to predict. However, they find that, in spite of this limitation, these systems still exhibit the tendency to self-organize.

Based on these concepts, they state that in a hyperconnected multidimensional financial system, top-down control is destined to fail. Instead, a bottom-up system would help in creating value and unleashing creativity and innovation. Such a system would need to function on multiple currency mechanisms, as the economy would become a complex, dynamic system where self-organization based on varying incentives would be key to developing resilience and sustainability. Rather than simply creating multiple currencies, the authors state a currency (like bitcoin) needs to have multiple incentive dimensions to represent sociodigital capital. Implementing these incentives in a bottom-up way would then allow economic systems to self-organize and promote creativity, innovation, and diversity.

To develop this multidimensional incentive system, the authors introduce the "Social Bitcoin," which is similar in most respects to any virtual currency, except that it has a reputation element intrinsic to its use. The money can earn its own reputation based on its use. To devise this reputation-gaining element, the social bitcoin is said to have two dimensions: one dimension allows for the investment of this currency in financial products, while the second dimension does not. Instead, the second dimension of the currency allows it to be invested only in real ventures that would be sustain development of the economy (such as infrastructure, for example). The two dimensions are also exchangeable based on a conversion rate. The authors also state that we do not need to stop at two dimension. Anything that is deemed socially useful can be represented as a dimension in the currency vector. Thus, it's almost as if we could encode social responsibility into the currency.

The authors then describe an example of how this would work. They describe a hypothetical situation in which information exchange is managed in a bottom-up way rather than the currency system of central monopolies. Individuals would thus route information using their social and technological connections on multiple networks simultaneously, rather than relying on service providers. The Social Bitcoin would act as the incentive to perform the routing exercise and could be earned (mined) by performing search and navigation tasks. The value of the social bitcoin would be based on the trust in the system (as with regular cash) and how it was being used. The way it would be used would determine its exchange rate from one dimension to another.

The rest of the paper deals with a mathematical model that illustrates the potential effects of a Social Bitcoin. It is seen that increasing diversity (in terms of the use of multiple networks) is key to the functioning of this self-governing system and that achieving this is based on increasing the diversity of the system. The paper does not provide any "set in stone" conclusions. Rather, it is an experiment that looks at how multiple-currency can not only be varied in number, but also be multidimensional in nature—an interesting concept that is in its infancy and which merits further research.

CHAPTER 4

Complexity Economics: A New Way to Witness Capitalism

If we assume equilibrium, we place a very strong filter on what we can see in the economy. Under equilibrium by definition there is no scope for improvement or further adjustment, no scope for exploration, no scope for creation, no scope for transitory phenomenon, so anything in the economy that takes adjustment - adaptation, innovation, structural change, history itself - must be bypassed or dropped form theory. The result is a beautiful structure, but it is one that lacks authenticity, aliveness and creation. -W.B. Arthur, 'Complexity and the Economy,' (2014).

Towards the end of 2008, Queen Elizabeth paid a visit to the Economics Department of the London School of Economics. During her visit, she asked a few simple and straight-forward questions to the economist's present: *"Why did no one see it [the crisis] coming?"*; *"If these things were so large how come everyone missed it?"* (Pierce, 2008). While the responses varied in depth and breadth, two facts were clear: Firstly, an unflinching false sense of rectitude with regards to the doctrine that markets are the best handlers of the financial system had led to increased financialization and an unsupportable amount of debt build-up. Secondly, this belief in the ability of markets was based on the intransigent orthodoxies of academic economics and policy making. Not only had these theories failed to see the coming crisis, it had also weakened the financial system to the point that governments were forced to bail out the banks that were the cause of the problem in the first place. Sadly, although some steps are being taken to address these flaws, the underlying theories being taught and practised at institutions have yet to be thoroughly questioned, let alone be completely modified.

© Kariappa Bheemaiah 2017
K. Bheemaiah, *The Blockchain Alternative*, DOI 10.1007/978-1-4842-2674-2_4

Emulating the directness of the Queen's questions, the previous three chapters reveal three straight- forward facts - Firstly, increasing debt and financialisation of economies causes systemic risk and is currently one of the biggest challenges that national economies face. Secondly, financial markets are constantly in a state of flux and the accelerating profusion of new technologies is poised to increase the turbulence of this changing state. Thirdly, the current framework that governs markets, regulations and policies is maladroit to identify the symptoms of bubbles and crashes. In essence, the dominant strains in economic thinking, namely the Efficient Markets Hypothesis (EMH) and the Rational Expectations Theory (RET), are becoming increasingly ill-suited to gauging and understanding financial and macroeconomic stability.

As technology continues to make the financial system more complex, these problems are poised to become more frequent. Hence, rather than focus on ways to maintain the status quo, what is required is a fundamental rethinking of how we study economics and how we understand and measure capitalism. Without adopting a new mindset, we will be forced to acknowledge the threat of a never-ending series of booms, busts and crises. Simply put, we cannot expect to solve the problems of today, let alone tomorrow, with an intransigent belief in the tools and theories of yesteryear.

Ironically, it is by studying the history of technology and its sequential metamorphic impact on capitalism that solutions can be found, as every time we are faced with new technological trends, we come face to face with a reoccurring ironic dilemma. On one hand technology makes industries and services more efficient and more capable of addressing our needs. But on the other, it forces us to reframe the kind of jobs and tasks that need to be performed and how the education and skillset of the workforce needs to be adapted to function in the new, updated economy. It would seem that the task of rethinking economics is analogous to a macabre quandary - not only does technology force us to change our capitalistic mindsets, but we are also required to be very expedient in our efforts if we are to keep up with the speed of technological change. Thus, to begin the final chapter on the redefinition of capitalism, we need to understand the galloping tendencies of technological changes in the context of static economic theories.

Technology and Invention: A Combinatorial Process

Ray Kurzweil, the noted inventor and futurist, once said that the exponential growth curves exhibited by current technological trends is based on the tendency of technology to 'feed off' technology. In light of the pace of change that we currently witness, this can be accepted as a fair statement if we are to accept that every technology that has been invented, is being invented and will be invented follows the very same formula - they are combinations of technologies that already existed and do not come out of sheer inspiration alone.

This might seem like a common-sense statement to some and in the past, philosophers, historians, sociologists and economists, such as Lewis Mumford, George Basalla, Joel Mokyr and Paul Romer, have come up with anecdotal theories that state this as a concept. But if we are to respect the Popperian scientific method to making a claim, then we need to consult the research that pertains to this subject to prove our hypothesis. More importantly, if we are to state that technology is created by combining bits and pieces of previous technological inventions, then we also need to extend this hypothesis to the process of invention as it is invention that generates new technologies.

Studies done by researchers from the Santa Fe Institute and the Oxford Martin School have found that invention, and thus almost any technology by proxy, exhibits this combinatory phenomenon. In a 2015 paper published by the Royal Society,[1] titled, '*Invention as a combinatorial process: evidence from US patents*,' the researchers studied US patent records from 1790 to 2010 in an attempt to conceptualize invention, which is how we get new technologies. Patents were considered as the 'carriers' of technology or as the 'footprints' of invention, as they leave behind a documentary trail in the way technologies evolve. By executing this study, the researchers were able to show that invention was the manner in which technologies (either very new or previously in use), were brought together and combined in ways not previously seen (Youn *et.al*, 2015). As per this study, and others[2] that have begun investigating the concept of combinatorial evolution[3] of technology, invention can be conceptualised as combinatorial possibilities. In other words, invention is simply the novel combination of existing technological capabilities and is evolutionary[4] in nature.

This tendency of technology to build itself on previous or existing technologies is very similar to biological evolution. Kevin Kelly makes the analogy between biological evolution and technological evolution in a more succinct manner. As per his research, the long-term co-evolutionary trends seen in natural and technological paradigms share five common salient features: ***Specialisation, Diversity, Ubiquity, Socialization and Complexity.*** These five features are exhibited by any technology. As FinTech is one of the protagonists in this book and in modern capitalism, let's analyse the evolution of this technology:

Financial technology finds its roots in the history of computing (refer Notes: A brief history of computing). Initially computers were made for very specific or *specialised* operations. For example, early computers such as the Differential Analyser, invented by Vannevar Bush in the mid 1930's, were analog computation machines[5] that were created to solve ordinary differential equations to help calculate the trajectories of shells. As World War Two broke out, these advances in computing were adopted and developed by

---

[1]The Royal Society is a Fellowship of many of the world's most eminent scientists and is the oldest scientific academy in continuous existence.

[2]See '*Technological novelty profile and invention's future impact*', Kim et al., (2016), EPJ Data Science.

[3]The term 'combinatorial evolution', was coined by the scientific theorist W. Brian Arthur, who is also one of the founders of complexity economics. In a streak that is similar to Thomas Kuhn's '*The Structure of Scientific Revolutions*', Arthur's book, '*The Nature of Technology: What It Is and How It Evolves*', explains that technologies are based on interactions and composed into modular systems of components that can grow. Being modular, they combine with each other and when a technology reaches a critical mass of components and interfaces, it evolves to enter new domains, and changes based on the new natural phenomena it interacts with. In sum, Arthur's combinatorial evolution, encompasses the concepts of invention, biological evolution, behavioural models, social sciences, technological change, innovation and sociology.

[4]Even evolution is not free from the combinatorial approach. Charles Darwin best known for the science of evolution, build his classification system on the work of Carl Linnaeus (1707-1778), the father of Taxonomy.

[5]The Differential Analyser consisted of multiple rotating disks and cylinders driven by electric motors linked together with metal rods that were manually set up (sometime taking up to two days) to solve any differential equation problem.

various militaries to communicate sensitive information by integrating the techniques of cryptography - a kind of natural selection. To combat this, pioneers such as Alan Turing and his mentor Max Newman, set about designing and building automated machines (Turing Machines) that could decrypt these camouflaged communiqués. This effectively changed the use of the computer and increased the *diversity* of the kinds of computers.

After the war, advances by notable inventors such as John Mauchly, Presper Eckert and John von Neumann (a veritable polymath) led to the creation of the EDVAC (Electronic Discrete Variable Automatic Computer), the first binary computer. With binary computers coming of age, there was an increasing need to develop software to give instructions to computers. Punch cards were soon replaced by logic gates (from Boolean algebra) and languages such as COBOL and FORTRAN (FORmula TRANslation), helped in the creation of early operating systems. As software design began to evolve so did the functionality of computers. Programming languages and such as BASIC, LISP, SIMULA, C, C++, UML, Unix, Linux, etc., helped in the construction of distributed communication networks, the internet and ultimately the worldwide web. As the cost of transistors began to drop (Moore's Law), more tasks got computerized leading to the *ubiquity* of computers in almost all functions of business and life.

This ubiquitousness gradually entered the sector of trade and thus finance. As trade is a fundamental social interaction, the *socialization* of computers for communication and value exchange was a natural evolutionary technological development. Increased socialization via digital channels over the past two decades has led to more interconnections between different nodes and led to a *complex* interwoven structure, where there is no central point that holds the entire edifice in place. As the developmental process of computing continues to become increasingly distributed, the future of computing (and Fintech by extension), is bound to increase in *complexity*. Selection, diversity, incremental variation and temporal progression (Wagner & Rosen, 2014) will be the hallmarks of tomorrow's technology and captialism.

It is the final stage of *complexity* that poses the greatest intellectual challenge to our understanding of modern day capitalism. As the previous chapters have shown, the increased complexity that has arisen with the socialization and financialisation of banking and commerce has created a system that is opaque and difficult to regulate. The entry of new technologies in the financial system, such as the Blockchain, will help us gain more transparency but will also further add complexity to the system, as every participating node will become a point of both communication and value exchange. If regulators face difficulties identifying points of systemic risk and malicious players in an economy today, the problem is bound to get increasingly complicated in a more inclusive and complex cashless system.

Secondly, we also need to consider the accelerating consilience of technology. The concept of accelerating consilience of technology needs to be highlighted as it sets the stage for understanding the reason why there is a disconnect between the way economics and technology is studied and analysed. This disconnect is especially important as the pace of technological evolution and the disruptive impact it has on the economy is getting shorter and quicker as seen in Figure 4-1.

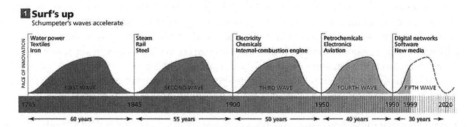

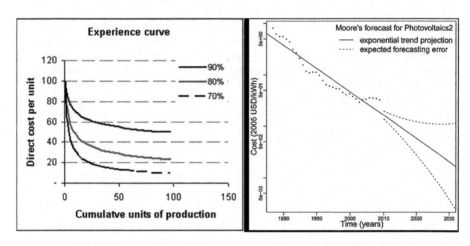

Figure 4-1. *The quickening pace of Konratiev waves*
Source: The Economist, 'Innovation in Industry - Catch the Wave,' 1999.[6]

As technology continues to accelerate, it has a profound impact on the economy as technological performance results in reduction of production costs. Wright's law (1936) and Moore's Law (1965) shows that as technological performance increases, it is accompanied with a reduction in the cost of production (Figure 4-2). Theodore Wright (who created Wright's Law) predicted in 1936 that as technologies improve exponentially with time, costs would decrease as a power law of cumulative production. Some recent research from MIT and the Santa Fe institute shows that a combination of an exponential decrease in cost and an exponential increase in production would make Moore's law and Wright's law indistinguishable (as originally pointed out by Sahal) (Nagy et al., 2013).

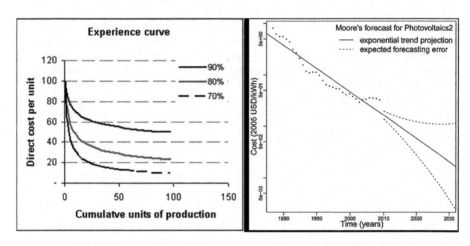

Figure 4-2. *Technology curves and their economic effect on the cost of production.*
Left image: Wright's Law (1936); Right image: Moore's Law (1965)
Sources: Left image - Wikipedia; Right image - `http://dx.doi.org/10.1371/`
`journal.pone.0052669`

---

[6]In economics Kondratiev waves (named after The Soviet economist Nikolai Kondratiev), are cyclic phenomenon that link the cycle of a technology's invention, expansion and ultimate replacement to their economic effects. Although Nikolai Kondratiev was the first to study the economic effects of technology on prices, wages, interest rates, industrial production and consumption in 1925, Joseph Schumpeter was responsible for their entry into academia.

This link between the combinatorial evolution of technology and the effect it has on a networked economy is key to understanding not just the economic impact of technological progress, but also in understanding a key tenet of modern day capitalism - technology and the economy follow the same patterns of evolution as seen in ecological systems, and in doing so, increase the complexity of the system.

The Blockchain (which itself is a combination of cryptography, computer science, game theory and monetary economics), is just one element that is increasing the complexity of economics. Other technologies, which have also been discussed in this book, show that most new businesses being created today do not depend on a single technology to propose value to clients. It is because of this accelerating consilience that new businesses are able to scale faster than in comparison to the path that was followed by older incumbents.

If the economy were to be looked at as a network of production agents where each node is an industry, then owing to the consilience of technology, the goods produced by one industry are used as inputs to another industry. As technology from one industry begins to combine with that of another, innovations occur which lead to production cost reductions and the emergence of new technologies. As the inputs get cheaper or better in terms of efficiency, it leads to the creation of new goods. As new products become ubiquitous, improved social connections (including management styles), lead to better distribution of the technology and the associated economies of scale. The greater the connection between the industries, i.e.: the more networked the structure of the economy, the faster this phenomenon repeats itself leading to exponential changes in technological evolution and production cost reductions (Also refer, Farmer and Lafond, 2015).

We can infer from the above statement, that technology and investment decisions are in a constant state of change and are rarely static. But while the endogenous role of technology in the economy has gained increased traction in academic circles, the study of economics has yet to make the transition towards treating change in the economy as an entropic system immersed in an ecological environment. Even one of the most highly cited papers on this subject, '*Endogenous Technological Change*' (1990), by Paul M. Romer, the current Chief Economist of the World Bank, is modelled around finding the state of equilibrium in light of technological change.[7]

As these physical flows of technology are accompanied by monetary flows, the economic impact of technological change are two sides of the same coin. As technological complexity continues to increase, the networked economy of modern day capitalism is bound to get more complex as well. But in spite of this increasing complexity and the accompanying entropy that is tied to it, the economic models that are used today are still based on states of equilibrium.

Therefore, if we are to fix the disconnected views we have about technology and economics, we need to rethink economic theory. As a system gets more complex, new bonds are formed, old bonds are destroyed and the repercussions of these creative - destructive movements create a state of constant change or entropy. So why is it that when we learn about economics, we are taught theories of equilibrium and rational expectations, when the changes occurring are entropic and mostly unforeseen, i.e. not rationally expected? If technology creates complexity, why is that the theories of

---

[7]In this paper, the model is driven by technological change that arises from intentional investment decisions made by profit-maximizing agents.

economics are based on states of equilibrium in spite of the fact that changing nature of technology is highly endogenous to economics and capitalism? A primary reason for this mode of thinking is based on how we cognitively interpret the world and why we are constantly trying to predict the future. Sidebar 4-1 offers some neuroscience insights.

SIDEBAR 4-1: A RATIONALE FOR RATIONAL EXPECTATIONS:

Sources: 'How to Create a Mind: The Secret of Human Thought Revealed', Ray Kurzweil (2014); 'Neuroscience for Organizational Change', Hilary Scarlett, (2016); 'Social Cognitive Neuroscience of Leading Organizational Change', Robert A. Snyder, (2016).

Rational Expectations is based on the innate working methodology of the human brain. We must remember that the human brain did not evolve in the current cosmopolitan and urban environment. It was designed in the treacherous environment of the Savannah thousands of years ago, and evolved to achieve two primary objectives: How to survive and how to predict.

Survival is the brain's natural state and is based on a trade-off between Risk and Reward. As there were more risks in the early environments of humans, it was more important to identify risk to survive. As a result, the brain is more attuned to this state. When presented with any situation, the brain analyses any potential risks to survival and this primary instinct is faster to kick in, has stronger impulses and sensations and lasts longer as a memory. When certain stimuli trigger the reward network of the brain, studies show that the brain reacts slower (as it is not our natural state). The sensation is also milder and relatively short-lived (you forget praise after a few days, but not abuse).

To be able to survive in the face of constant risk, the brain had to be able to predict. In fact, the brain can be seen as a constant prediction machine that is continuously trying to find safety and avoid risk. Our brain's neocortex constantly predicts what it expects to encounter. It is an ingenious tool that recognises, remembers and predicts patterns *sans arrêt* and develops hypothesises of what we will experience. As Ray Kurzweil puts it, predicting the future is actually the primary reason that we have a brain. The statement below exemplifies how the brain is constantly predicting, even when there is no sign of apparent danger:

"I cnduo't bvleiee taht I culod aulaclty uesdtannrd waht I was rdnaieg. Unisg the icndeblire pweor of the hmuan mnid, aocdcrnig to rseecrah at Cmabrigde Uinervtisy, it dseno't mttaer in waht oderr the lterets in a wrod are, the olny irpoamtnt tihng is taht the frsit and lsat ltteer be in the rhgit pclae. The rset can be a taotl mses and you can sitll raed it whoutit a pboerlm".

But the exercise of prediction is a fatiguing one. The brain constitutes only 2% of our body mass but consumes 20% of our energy. As a result, the brain tries to save energy by taking cognitive shortcuts. It attempts to make predictions using abstract concepts and even if we are exposed to events with multidimensional aspects, the brain represents the pattern of events in a one-dimensional sequence of lower-level patterns. In other words, the innate built-in predictors of our brain try to save energy by thinking in terms of linearity. Our brains are most comfortable making predictions that possess a linear function.

Consider this simple example: a bat and ball cost €1.10. The bat costs €1 more than the ball. So how much does the ball cost? In most cases, the first answer that our minds instinctively predict is 10 cents. But if we were to work out this simple calculation, we would find that the actual cost of the ball is 5 cents. ((Bat + Ball = 1.10); As (Bat = 1+Ball); This means ((Bat + Ball) = (2 Ball + 1) = 1.10); Therefore, 2 Ball = 0.10; Ball = 0.05).

The historic tendency of the brain to prefer linear predictability could be why we have struggled in our modifying our method of economic thinking in the context of technological change. Both these subjects may have displayed linear growth trends in the past. But as we have discussed in the introduction to this chapter, technology is based on consilience the integration of older technologies.

As technology gets increasingly digitized, the consilience of technology is accelerating and evolving at an exponential rate. The logarithmic curve seen in Figure 4-3 is representative of this fact

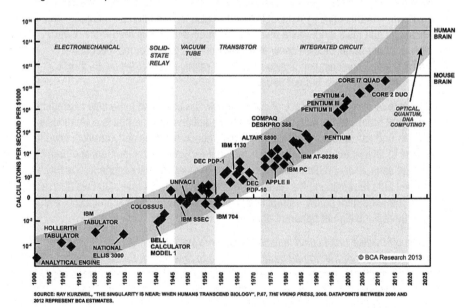

Figure 4-3. *Moore's Law: Over 199 Years And Going Strong*
Image Source: BCA Research Special Report, 'Human Intelligence and Economic Growth - From 50,000 B.C. to the Singularity' (2013).

As the graph shows, these exponential curves are relatively recent in the history of economics. When Adam Smith published the 'Wealth of Nations', in 1776, the subject of economics represented linear scales. Technology evolved at a much slower pace (refer to Figure 4-1) and this made the social science of economics develop models that were well suited to linear technological growth curves and our linear way of predictive thinking. For a long time, this was the status quo and the Rational Expectations theory (RET) was not an error but a natural representation of simpler economies.

But as technology evolves and begins to grow at exponential rates, the increasing complexity that it is creating is challenging this theory. RET is based on the theory of perfect competition in economics which postulates perfect knowledge. But as interactions grow increasingly, the view the participants have of the economic system is always partial and distorted due to information asymmetries. So how can we 'rationally' expect anything when we do not have 'perfect' knowledge?

The information provided by the Blockchain will help us address this issue to a certain extent, as will new data analysis techniques. But the exercise of knowing everything about the economy seems like an asymptotic pursuit of perfection. It for this reason that when looking at the economy, we need to predict in terms of probability of the outcomes rather than creating exact linear models. The task of rethinking economics via this lens will be a daunting challenge, but remains feasible in my opinion. One of the most surprising results of recent research in neuroscience is the *neuroplasticity* (see notes) of the brain. The brain is constantly updating its cognitive map, or belief system, based on new information. As new ideas take hold, older beliefs are upgraded or discarded. Economics maybe an old discipline of study, but science shows us that we can still teach an old dog new tricks.

Economic Entropy versus Economic Equilibrium

Technology is generally studied as per the scientific method since science is the creative engine of technology. The scientific method was best described by the philosopher Karl Popper, who stated that any science should be scrutinized by decisive experimentation to determine a scientific law. As per this method, also known as Popperian falsifiability, the empirical truth of any scientific law cannot be verified beyond a shadow of a doubt and cannot be known with absolute certainty. They can only be falsified by testing - Even a single failed test is enough to falsify and no number of conforming instances is sufficient to verify. Scientific laws, and thus the study of technology, are hypothetical in character and their validity remains subject to testing.

While the scientific method largely applies to the natural sciences, its rigors ensure the establishment of facts. But while we hold the natural sciences to such exacting standards, we do not extend the same discipline of analysis to the social sciences, especially to economics. Indeed, for the past several decades, mainstream economics has been less concerned with describing reality and has preferred to base its theories on an idealised version of the world. The reason for this could possibly be traced backed to the neuroscience findings we have discussed in Sidebar 4-1. Conventional economics, after all, is searching for an answer to a difficult question that is very centric to human society - it wishes to know how agents in the economy (banks, firms, investors and consumers) might react to the general pattern of the economy they are creating together. Linear models that are easier to digest offer a delicious simplicity.

As a result, to answer this question, contemporary economics has preferred to dogmatically adhere to theories based on what it considers are reasonable axioms. The most eminent of these theories is the Efficient Market Hypothesis (EMH) which sees the economy as a perfect, rational, mechanistic entity, where asset prices fully reflect all available information. Agents thus logically behave (perform actions, create strategies, make forecasts) in aggregate patterns that would represent all the information at their disposal. As a result, as per RET, all agents have a single optimum view of the future and over time all market participants converge around that view. If one agent were to execute an action that was contrary to this view, another agent would behave in a way to leverage that action to his or her interest and offset the discrepant action. The result is an economy that is static in origin and always trying to achieve equilibrium.

This theory of economics, although very eloquent, is quite absurd. It is completely divorced from actual data and any kind of scientific method. While EMH states that agents are 'utility maximising' and make decisions based on RET, almost no agent has the time nor the resources to go through the optimisation process and calculate the best course of action. Even if agents had all the information, the complexity of the decision-making process at hand (especially in light of the information overload provided by today's technologies), means that computation of such a task is bound to be restricted to 'good enough' rather than the 'best one under all circumstances'. Moreover, agents can make choices for moral or superstitious values that might have nothing to do with rationality. But neither the EMH, the RET or any mathematical framework of economics take these conditions into consideration. Not only are they devoid of good scientific practices, they are detached from human interests and societal reality.

Economics is a social science because it involves people and social interactions that are demonstrated in acts of trade and social allegiances. Although every participant is working towards his or her individual benefit, their view of the world is always incomplete and their actions are always biased. Owing to this, they will not take the appropriate action as stipulated by EMH and RET. George Soros defines this incomplete view of the world as the '*principle of fallibility*' and the biased decision making process as the '*principle of reflexivity*' in his '*Theory of Reflexivity*'.

Soros first published his theory of Reflexivity in his book, 'The Alchemy of Finance', in 1987. The book was a big success as fund managers and investors clamoured to discover what his investment secrets were. But very little attention was paid to his philosophy of Reflexivity. In a lecture[8] he gave following the publication of his book, Soros himself said, *"the philosophical arguments [in his book] did not make much of an impression. They were largely dismissed as the conceit of a man who has been successful in business and fancied himself as a philosopher"*. However, the theory is interesting because of the principle role uncertainty plays in it.

Uncertainty is something that is normally reserved to risk assessment. EMH and RET do not stipulate exacting codes of conduct or modes of operation to encompass the concept of uncertainty. However, uncertainty needs to addressed at a fundamental level as the economic decisions made by agents bask in uncertainty. Agents making decisions (be it buying, selling, producing, strategizing, or forecasting), also have to anticipate the future decisions that other agents are going to make. Market prices, after all, are the agents weighted-average view of what is going to happen in the future. As the future is contingent on accurately anticipated decisions of others, uncertainty poses a central role in logical economic decision making.

RET circumvents this problem by postulating that in every market, there is a single optimal set of expectations and agent's views will converge around it. But this hypothesis bears no resemblance to reality. In practice, every agent has different interests and since these interests cannot be known, agents have to make their decisions in conditions of uncertainty as there is no other choice. Their decisions are bound to be based on information asymmetries and personal biases. This is seen in the form of asset price distortions, fluctuating stock prices and currency volatility. Soros called this phenomenon of volatility and distortion owing to personal decision making the '*human uncertainty principle*'.

The human uncertainty principle and the volatility that is brings along with it, are the fundamental reasons why the economy is never in a state of equilibrium. Individual decisions made by agent's cause price distortions which set in motion boom-bust phenomena, leading to the creation of bubbles, crises and recessions. The past four decades have seen 8 major crises,[9] or a crisis every five years on average. If there is anything that is constant in the economy, it the fact that it is in a constant state of entropy.

Thus, the first point to consider when deciding how to rethink the study of the economics is to acknowledge that agents in an economy react to the outcomes that have been created by others as well as themselves. As these decisions lead to volatility, an economy should not be looked at as a machine-like system operating at equilibrium, but more like an ecology where actions, strategies, and beliefs compete simultaneously creating new behaviours in the process. In other words, an economy is always forming and evolving, and not necessarily in equilibrium.

---

[8]See "A Failed Philosopher Tries Again."

[9](i) LatAm sovereign debt crisis - 1982, (ii) Savings and loans crisis - 1980s, (iii) Stock market crash - 1987, (iv) Junk bond crash - 1989, (v) Tequila crisis - 1994, (vi) Asia crisis - 1997 to 1998, (vii) Dotcom bubble - 1999 to 2000, (viii) Global financial crisis - 2007 to 2008.

Secondly, we need to consider the relationship between technology and the economy, for while the economy creates technology, it is also created by technology, as has been explained earlier. The impact of technolgy on the economy has also been discussed in a number of recent works such as Brynjolfsson's and McAfee's *Race Against the Machine* (2011). The economy is therefore not just a container of technology but also an expression of them (Arthur, 2014). As technology changes, markets, regulations and policies need to change as well. In essence, technological change restructures the economy.

Owing to the constant change that is predicated by uncertain agent decisions and technological evolution, the economy is in fact usually in disequilibrium and behaves more like an organic entity in a vibrant ecology, where structures are constructed and reconstructed, and where openness to change is emphasised. Just as technology is endogenous to the economy, so is disequilibrium. Equilibrium could exist, but it is a temporary state of existence. Non-equilibrium is the natural state of affairs.

If the economy is seen in this light, then the reactions of technology with agents and the following assemblages and adaptations that are seen in an economy are reflective of the study of complex systems, an academic discipline that observes the deep laws of complexity and emergence in any system. Complexity theory was born in the 1970's (Wilson, 1998) and was originally inspired by 19th century physics, specifically the fields of classical mechanics, statistical non-equilibrium physics and thermodynamics (Helbing and Kirman, 2014). The main tenets of complexity theory borrow their conceptions from chaos theory, self-criticality and adaptive landscapes, to bring into focus the way complex systems grow, persist and collapse.

The first scholars of complexity theory began their formulations at the Santa Fe institute, and based their study of complex systems on abstract non-linear transformative computer simulations. They attempted to recreate the same phenomenon seen in complex systems, be it rain forests or collisions of protons in the large hadron collider (LHC[10]), in massive computer-aided simulations. By adopting this approach, they attempted to achieve a higher level of understanding comprehensive systems consistent in the real world. In the past, this group of scientists were largely ignored by mainstream academia as traditional academics found their conclusions too vague and metaphoric.

This was partly due to two reasons - the lack of data and slow computing power provided insufficient evidence to support their theories. But over the past two decades this has changed. Increasing amounts of data and exponential rises in computing power, now allow practitioners of this discipline to recreate and study complex operations, such as, simulating the remnants left behind after proton bombardments. As the study of complexity gained traction, a few of the members of the Santa Fe institute began

---

[10]LHC: The Large Hadron Collider is the world's largest and most powerful particle accelerator located at the CERN, the European Organization for Nuclear Research (Conseil Européen pour la Recherche Nucléaire). The LHC is a 27- kilometre ring of superconducting magnets that accelerates particles such as protons to the speed of light before colliding them to study the quantum particles that are inside the protons. On the 4th of July 2012, the ATLAS and CMS experiments at CERN's Large Hadron Collider discovered the Higgs boson, the elementary particle that explains why particles have mass. It was, and will be, one of the most important scientific discoveries of the century.

to ponder if the methods and tools at their disposal would allow them to study the interactions that were occurring in a complex economic system? A result of this thought experiment led to the creation of complexity economics in the early 1990's.[11]

Complexity economics does not attempt to sidestep the complexity and entropy of a dynamic, vibrant and ever changing economic ecosystem. On the contrary, the very basis of complexity economics is to use tools and methods that inculcate non-equilibrium phenomenon. The mathematics of complexity science is based on non-linearly interacting components (agents), where the system spends long periods of time far from equilibrium. The system may exhibit multiple states of equilibria, but these states are unstable and temporary as feedback and emergent properties (such as new technology), produce counter-intuitive behavioural traits. The system is studied as a highly connected network with no top-bottom control parameters, and where agents are unable to behave as they prefer since they cannot act independently.

All these features are observed in our current economic and financial markets, especially when considering the emergence and growing popularity of distributed value exchange networks. But in spite of this, owing to our dependence and attachment to out-dated dogmas of economic thought, we continue to delude ourselves in thinking that the economy functions in a state of equilibrium, and study the subject based on this convenient view.

It is surprising that this mode of thinking is the dominant view not only in academia, but also in economic governance. One might think that if commercial banks were investing millions of dollars in Blockchain technology, then policy makers would also be updating their methods and models of analysis according to the capabilities of the new systems. Would it not be sensible to prepare for a Blockchain future by developing tools and methods that are capable of leveraging the real-time transactional data between multiple economic agents who are making Knightian decisions[12] on a transparent cashless Blockchain? The answer of course, is no.

In spite of the similarities between complex economic systems and our current (and future) economic system, we continue to use models based on the general equilibrium economic theory, the most popular of which, is the Dynamic Stochastic General Equilibrium Model (DSGE). DSGE based models have been dominant tools in macroeconomic modelling, economic forecasting and policy construction since the early 1980's and continues to play this role today - For example, in 2009 the Reserve Bank of New Zealand developed and adopted the **KITT** (Kiwi Inflation Targeting Technology) DSGE model as their main forecasting and scenario tool (Beneš *et al.,* 2009). Hence, to fully understand why we need to consider the use of complexity based models, in the context of the Blockchain, it is essential for us to first review equilibrium economic models.

---

[11]Some of the early trailblazers who combined the study of complexity theory with economics include, Kenneth Arrow (economist), Philip Anderson (physicist), Larry Summers (economist), John Holland (physicist), Tom Sargent (economist), Stuart Kauffman (physicist), David Pines (physicist), José Scheinkman (economist), William Brock (economist) and of course, W. B. Arthur (economist), who coined the term complexity economics and has been largely responsible for its initial growth and exposure to mainstream academia.

[12]Knightian uncertainty is an economic term that refers to risk. It states that risk is immeasurable and not possible to calculate. *"Uncertainty must be taken in a sense radically distinct from the familiar notion of Risk, from which it has never been properly separated"*, Frank Knight, economist from the University of Chicago.

The Mathematical Wizardry of Equilibrium Economic Models

Today, most central banks use DSGE models for monetary policy analysis and business cycle forecasting. As we have seen in Chapter 3, it is monetary and fiscal policy that play a determining role in guiding the state of markets and the prosperity of a nation. Thus, owing to their fundamental role in monetary policy decision making, it is important to understand the history, abilities and limitations of these models.

Currently, most central banks, such as the Federal Reserve and the ECB,[13] use two kinds of models to study and build forecasts about the economy (Axtell and Farmer, 2015). The first, statistical models, fit current aggregate data of variables such as GDP, interest rates, and unemployment to empirical data in order to predict/suggest what the near future holds. The second type of models (which are more widely used), are known as "Dynamic Stochastic General Equilibrium" (DSGE) models. These models are constructed on the basis that the economy would be at rest (i.e.: static equilibrium) if it wasn't being randomly perturbed by events from outside the economy.

Although DSGE models are dynamic macroeconomic models of business cycle behaviour, their foundations are derived from microeconomics as they assume that the economy is based on optimising agents who make decisions based on rational expectations to maximize their objectives based on constraints[14] (Slobodyan and Wouters, 2012). The agents in the models are represented as households and firms - households consume goods, provide labour, invest and trade in bonds and accumulate capital in the form of real estate or liquidity. On the flipside, firms manufacture goods, provide employment and try to maximize profits based on their constraints. The interactions between firms and households result in guiding the economy through various stages of the business cycle and the central bank changes the nominal interest rate in response to changes in inflation, output, or other economic conditions. The central bank thus acts as a reactionary entity (in the context of the Taylor rule[15]) in DSGE models. To account for fiscal shocks, the models contain some portion of 'non-optimizing' households which deplete all their earnings. In the language of political correctness, these households are referred to as hand-to- mouth households. Notice the emphasis on business cycles, assumptions and rational expectations.

---

[13]The European Central Bank (ECB) has developed a DSGE model, called the Smets-Wouters model, which it uses to analyse the economy of the Eurozone as a whole. (See: Smets and Wouters, *'An estimated dynamic stochastic general equilibrium model of the euro area'*, Journal of the European Economic Association, Volume 1, Issue 5, September 2003, Pages 1123-1175).
[14]These constraints include: budget constraints, labor demand constraints, wage constraints (Calvo constraint on the frequency of wage adjustment), capital constraints, etc... (Slanicay, 2014).
[15]The Taylor rule is a set of guidelines for how central banks should alter interest rates in response to changes in economic conditions. The rule, introduced by economist John Taylor, was established to adjust and set prudent rates for the short-term stabilization of the economy, while still maintaining long-term growth. The rule is based on three factors: (i) Targeted versus actual inflation levels; (ii) Full employment versus actual employment levels; (iii) The short-term interest rate appropriately consistent with full employment (Investopedia). Its mathematical interpretation is: **r = p + 0.5y + 0.5(p - 2) + 2**. Where, *r = the federal funds rate, p = the rate of inflation, y = the percent deviation of real GDP from a target* (Bernanke, 2015).

The origins of these models can be traced back to the 1940's, following the publication of Keynes' *General Theory* (1936). Following the publication of this seminal work, governmental and academic bodies began the construction of large-scale macroeconomic models based on this style. Specific or ad-hoc rules were postulated, converted into variables and equations were created based on Keynesian macroeconomic theory. For close to three decades, these *neo-Keynesian models* were the mainstay of macroeconomic decision making.

But as the 1960's ended and the 1970's rolled in, advances in technology challenged the assumptions on which these models were built. As these models depended on a direct trade-off between inflation and unemployment, they were unable to appropriately consider the labour replacement function of technology. Secondly, they were incapable of integrating variables that represented microeconomic changes such as the elastic substitution of goods, the elasticity of labour supply (especially as technology replaced physical labour making economies more service oriented rather than manufacturing intensive), etc. Finally, they did not recognize that the decision-making rules of economic agents would vary systematically with changes in monetary policy. This final flaw is often referred to as the *Lucas Critique*.

The Lucas Critique and the introduction of Rational Expectations (following a seminal paper by Muth in 1961), led to demise of neo-Keynesian models. In its stead, DSGE models came into being. The first DSGE models were known as *Real Business Cycle (RBC) models* were introduced in the early 1980's and were based on the concepts detailed by Finn E. Kydland and Edward C. Prescott in 1982. RBC models were based on the assumptions of perfect competition on the goods and labor markets and flexible prices and wages, and increasingly gained traction thanks to their success in matching some business cycle patterns (Slanicay, 2014). These models saw business cycle fluctuations as the efficient response to exogenous changes which implied that business cycles were created by 'real' forces and that productivity shocks were created by technological progress.

But in spite of the theoretical underpinning that technology was the main source of business fluctuations, after a period of use, the RBC model began to lose favour with academics and policy makers. A host of empirical studies found that the contribution of technology shocks to the business cycle fluctuations was relatively small and the predictions made by RBC models with regards to labour and productivity in response to technology shocks began to be rejected. A second reason for their rejection was their view on monetary policy - In most RBC models, monetary policy was taken to have no effect on real variables even in the short run. This was at odds with the longstanding belief of that monetary policy had the power to influence productivity output and unemployment in the short term (Christiano et al., 1998)(Also see 'The Trouble With Macroeconomics', Romer (2016) .

Owing to these differences, the RBC models began to undergo a phase of evolution which led to the creation of another class of DSGE models also known as *New Keynesian models (NK models)*. These models were build on top of the existing framework of RBC models but their construction was also influenced by a new theory that had begun to gain increasing traction in the field of economics at that time - *contract theory*. This theory might be familiar to most readers, as two of the three[16] economists who developed the theory received the Nobel Memorial Prize in Economic Sciences in October 2016.

---

[16]Contract theory was first developed in the late 1960's by Kenneth Arrow (winner of the 1972 Nobel prize in economics), Oliver Hart and Bengt R. Holmström. The latter two shared the Nobel prize in economics in 2016.

Contract theory introduced the concepts of price and wage rigidities (See Sidebar 4-2 and 'Theories of Wage Rigidity,' Stiglitz, 1984) in NK models. The older RBC models were thus enhanced with some Keynesian assumptions, namely competition on goods, labour and rigidities. By including nominal price and wage rigidities into the model, changes in short-term nominal interest rate were not offset by identical changes in the inflation, which caused real interest rate to vary over time. As a shift in the real interest rate affects consumption and investment, productivity outputs and employment levels adjusted in relation to the new level of aggregate demand. Monetary policy was thus no longer neutral in the short term, as it was in the older RBC models.

The evolution of DSGE models however, is still far from complete. Although contract theory allows for the introduction of rigidities and allows monetary policy to be an effective tool in the short-term, empirical facts have shown that there are gaps with the models prognostications. Recently, economists such as Gregory Mankiw, Ricardo Reis and Laurence Ball have shown that the sticky price effects in these models don't explain observed persistent inflation (See Mankiw & Reis, 2001, 2002). This has led to the introduction on a new kind of rigidity - sticky information. As per sticky information, knowledge about macroeconomic conditions disseminate slowly through the economy which effects the decision-making process of household and firms, and thus effects wages and prices (Reis, 2006). This insight has also led to the creation of SIGE (Sticky Information General Equilibrium) models, a new variant of DSGE models.

All DSGE models share the core assumptions on the behaviour of households and firms and were constructed to represent the self-regulating spirit of markets and economies. However, they are still predicated on a state of equilibrium. While firms adjust to new demand levels and changing interest rates, in the long run, all prices and wages are said to adjust and return the economy to 'its natural equilibrium' (Slanicay, 2014). As per these models, in the case of an unanticipated shock, the economy would deviate from its equilibrium, but after a certain amount of time it would revert back to the equilibrium. The length of the adjustment process is influenced by the degree of nominal and real rigidities (Goodfriend and King, 1997) and the graduality of the adjustment process would make room for potential welfare enhancing economic (monetary) policy which would minimize the distortions, and thus stabilize the economy around its equilibrium (Slanicay, 2014).

SIDEBAR 4-2: A BRIEF NOTE ON CONTRACT THEORY AND THE RIGIDITIES OF THE MARKET

Source: 'Some Notes on Historical, Theoretical, and Empirical Background of DSGE Models', Martin Slanicay, 2014; 'Challenges for New Keynesian Models with Sticky Wages', Susanto Basu and Christopher L. House, 2015.

As employees, we have employment contracts. As debtors, we have credit contracts. As owners of property, we have insurance contracts. Although both counterparties in a contract would like to cooperate, there are competing incentives for the principal (the employer/firm) and the agent (the employee). Contract theory deals with these conflicting incentives that operate between individuals, workers, employers and governments.

What contract theory does is to provide us with a way to understanding the design of a contract and how to draw up better contracts, to address the issues described above. The power of the theory is not to give us steps to follow when making a contract but rather providing us with the faculty to think clearly about the issues involved.

This is especially important for two reasons - Firstly, there is the issue of risk. Risk sharing is an important part of a relationship, since employees would prefer not have to bear all the uncertainties firms experience with variable revenue and profits. Firms, on the other hand, would rather pass on some of these risks to workers, so that their costs can be aligned with their revenue.

Secondly, there is the issue of contact incompleteness. Since all elements of a contract cannot be specified (there are always unforeseen circumstances), there is always the question of what should happen if an unexpected event occurs which has not been specified in the contract. If such an impasse were to be reached who would decide what needed to be done? This is a key issue as the person with the right to make a decision on the unspecified elements of the contract has more bargaining power, which would lead to decision making imbalances.

To respond to these contractual issues, and other such problems, the developers of contract theory created an intellectual framework that allowed for agents and principals to design contracts for various policies and institutions. Both developers played unique roles. Holmström developed the Informativeness principle, which set out how optimum pay should be linked to performance, while Hart's contribution made substantial progress on incomplete contracts. Their work has been applied widely and on a range of issues, from how to address the competing interests of company shareholders and managers, to the rights of investors in bankruptcy, to how to construct political constitutions.

In the context of New Keynesian and DSGE models, Contract theory played a role in *Labor Market Flexibility*, which is the firm's ability to make changes to their workforce in terms of the number of employees they hire and the number of hours worked by the employees, and *Price Stickiness,* which is the resistance of the price of a product/service to change (despite changes in the broad economy) owing to imperfect information in the markets, or non-rational decision-making by company executives.

This 'rigidity' of wage and price change are important to DSGE models as monetary business-cycle models lean heavily on price and wage rigidity, and as real wage and labor market dynamics are intrinsic to the inflation process. Thus, understanding the types of contracts in contract theory provides context to understanding the finer workings of DSGE models. Some of the rigidities are:

Explicit Contracts

Explicit Contracts are used in formal business agreements such as sales of property or high-value assets, and financial transactions where significant value or obligations apply. For DSGE models, nominal rigidities are focused on long-term wage contracts and the effects of long-term agreements about prices and wages on the potential of monetary policy. The reasons for this are - (i) wage negotiations are costly in time for both workers and firms; the longer the period of the contract, the less frequently are these transaction costs incurred; (ii) negotiations may fail and workers may resort to strike action in order to improve their bargaining position; and (iii) if the firm lowers wage paid to its employees following a negative demand shock and other firms do not, it reduces its relative wage, thus possibly increasing labor turnover, which is costly to the firm. The impact of long-term contracts also depends on whether the contract renegotiations are synchronized (like the shunto system for negotiating wages in Japan), or whether the economy has the non-synchronized system of overlapping (staggered) contracts. In the latter case, nominal prices (wages) exhibit more inertia in the face of shocks than in the former case. Staggered price setting can arise as a rational response of firms to an imperfect information environment.

Implicit Contracts

These contracts refer to voluntary and self-enforcing long term agreements made between two parties regarding the future exchange of goods or services. In such circumstances, sellers have certain monopoly power even though there may be many firms in the market that sell a similar product. As customers make repetitive purchases, it is of an interest of a firm to discourage customers from searching the market for a better price. Frequent price changes provide incentives for customers to look elsewhere. While customers notice a price increase immediately, a price decrease produces smaller response among customers because it takes time for such information to be noticed by customers of other firms. Together with efforts of a firm to maintain its regular customers, this asymmetry in responses of customers results in relative price stickiness. DSGE models are concerned with implicit contracts as it helps explain why the real wage frequently diverges from the marginal productivity of labor.

Efficiency Wages

Efficiency wages are wages that are higher than the market equilibrium. Some reasons that managers might choose to pay efficiency wages are to reduce turnover and attract productive employees. Also, if working efforts of workers are positively related to the real wage rate, employers may be motivated to set wages above the equilibrium wage in order to increase productivity of their employees.

Menu Costs

A menu cost is the cost to a firm resulting from changing its prices. Menu costs can prevent firms from setting their prices optimally, thus causing private profit losses which are, however, lower than these menu costs. By engaging in "near-rational behaviour" these firms deviate from the optimal price (wage) setting. and reduce their transaction costs associated with searching information about demand (labor supply) changes. In such case, profit losses caused by deviations of prices (wages) from their optimal value can be offset by reductions of their transaction costs. Such behaviour cab be optimal from the firm's perspective but causes significant losses of aggregate output and employment.

The extensive use of DSGE models in the past few decades have not been without strife. As the economy has gotten increasing interconnected, greater amounts of data are available to agents. Consequently, the rational expectations of agents have begun to fluctuate with greater intensity than before. As the expectations of firms and households are unobservable older DSGE models cannot distinguish whether changes in activity are a function of altered expectations today or lagged responses to past plans. For example, they cannot determine whether a rise in business capital investment is attributable to revised expectations about sales or is part of a sequence of gradual capital acquisitions related to earlier investment plans (Brayton *et al.,* 1997).

As a result of this, the Federal Reserve began developing and using a new tool for macroeconomic policy analysis in 1996 (it has undergone periodic revisions) and is referred to today as the FRB/US model. As per the description given on the Board of Governors of the Federal Reserve System, '*One distinctive feature compared to dynamic stochastic general equilibrium (DSGE) models is the ability to switch between alternative assumptions about expectations formation of economic agents. Another is the model's level of detail: FRB/US contains all major components of the product and income sides of the U.S. national accounts.*' (Text in italics taken from an article published on the Board of Governors of the Federal Reserve website in April 2014. See website link below[17]).

Owing to the scope and scale of the model, the FRB/US model can be considered the most advanced macroeconomic policy tool in use today (although there are various critiques of this model dating back to the 1970s when the conceptualisation of this model first began). But the FRB/US model is still '*a large- scale estimated general equilibrium model of the U.S. economy*' (Federal Reserve Board, 2014). The key words to be underlined in the previous phrase are 'estimated' and 'equilibrium'. Almost every model that has existed since the 1960's till today are based on these two terms. Whether we use Traditional structural models, Rational expectations structural models, Equilibrium business-cycle models, or Vector Auto Regression (VAR) models (See Notes 'Types of Macroeconomic Models'), the base parameters on which these models are build are assumptions, estimations and equilibrium.

---

[17]https://www.federalreserve.gov/econresdata/frbus/us-models-about.htm

Secondly there is not real inclusion of the financial market. The family of DSGE macroeconomic models, which we have rapidly covered, emerged as a synthesis between the Chicago school of thought and the new Keynesian approach over the period of the Great Moderation (1983-2008). This was a period during which the relative stability of the economy allowed for policy approaches that could only rely in the use of monetary policy (i.e.: the rate of interest). This was because the Chicago led thought considered that all that was needed to face business cycles and/or recessive trends was an active monetary policy. Some thought that not even that was needed since they believed that free market adjustment will always find the way out (Garcia, 2011). This belief was also shared by the new-neo-Keynesians, who believed that fiscal policy was not needed to deal with business cycle or recessive trends. Hence both schools of thought converged in the idea that all that was needed to avert the risks of business cycles or recessive trends was a clever monetary policy guided by a monetary rule (García,2010). The result was the gradual crowding out of fiscal policy and even less attention to fiscal policy alternatives. However, the crisis has shown us how ineffective economic policy can be if it guided only by fiscal policy. It is also one the main reasons for proposing a Blockchain based fiscal policy system. (Also see: '*The Case for Monetary Finance*[18]*- An Essentially Political Issue,'* Turner, 2015).

This wide-spread accepted assumption that financial markets would function as the best determinants of price based on agents making logical decisions, and hence there was no need to factor in models of financial markets was directly related to the EMH. If markets effectively reflect the prices of assets, then why bother modelling the financial sector? This rationale was based on two assumptions - firstly, that the financial sector always tends to be in equilibrium, and secondly, that financial markets are complete, i.e.: unbalances (defaults, insolvencies, illiquidity, etc.) are balanced over time. But as we have seen in the previous chapters, this is not reflective of reality. Thus, it is unsurprising to learn that DSGE models are unable to capture the full view of international financial linkages (Tovar, 2008).

The RET premise is another pitfall of DSGE models. There is sufficient scientific evidence, notably from Douglass C. North, winner of the 1993 Nobel Prize for Economics, that under uncertainty, there is no certitude of rational behaviour. In his own words,

> *"Frank Knight (1933) made a fundamental distinction between risk and uncertainty. In the case of the former, probability distributions of outcomes could be derived with sufficient information and therefore choices [are] made on the basis of that probability distribution (the basis of insurance). But in the case of uncertainty no such probability distribution is possible and in consequence, to quote two of economics most eminent practitioners "no theory can be formulated in this case" (Arrow, 1951 p. 417) and again "In cases of uncertainty, economic reasoning will be of little value" (Lucas, 1981, P 224). But human beings do construct theories all the time in conditions of pure uncertainty-- and*

---

[18]As per Turner, Monetary finance is defined as a fiscal deficit which is not financed by the issue of interest-bearing debt, but by an increase in the monetary base - i.e. of the irredeemable fiat non-interest-bearing monetary liabilities of the government/central bank. Eg: Helicopter Money.

indeed act on them ... It is the widespread existence of myths, taboos, prejudices and simply half-baked ideas that serve as the basis of decision making. Indeed, most of the fundamental economic and political decisions that shape the direction of polities and economies are made in the face of uncertainty." (Douglass C. North, 'Economics and Cognitive Science,' Procedia - Journal of Social and Behavioural Sciences, 2010).

Another Nobel prize winner, Daniel Kahneman,[19] stated a similar point in his Prospect Theory. Kahneman was able to prove empirically that decisions under uncertainty did not point towards a 'rational behaviour of agents' and that it was risk aversion that dominated behaviour. Albert Bandura, Professor Emeritus of Social Science in Psychology at Stanford University, makes a similar claim in his Social Cognitive Theory, in which he states that,

"Rationality depends on reasoning skills which are not always well developed or used effectively. Even if people know how to reason they make faulty judgments when they base their reasoning on incomplete or erroneous information, or they fail to consider the full consequences of different choices. They often misread events through cognitive biases in ways that give rise to faulty beliefs about themselves and the world around them. When they act on their misconceptions, which appear subjectively rational to them, they are viewed by others as behaving in an unreasonable or foolish manner. Moreover, people often know what they ought to do but are swayed by compelling circumstances or emotional factors to behave otherwise." (Bandura, 'Social Cognitive Theory,' 1998).

It is important to emphasis the role of RET in the context of DSGE models as they act as an input variable in these models. As it was seen in both the DSGE and the FRB/US model, agent expectations are the main channel through which policy affects the economy (Sbordone *et al.,* 2010). But if the structural parameters are based on wrongly assumed microfoundations, the model is bound to make bad predictions and have errors even though it is technically Lucas-robust.

Finally, it is their attachment to equilibrium that is the bane of these models. DSGE models are based on the absolute belief that the market adjustment will always tend to equilibrium. This belief is based in four principles: (i) Under budget constraints, consumers always maximize their individual utility; (ii) Under resource constraints, producers always maximize their profits; (iii) Markets may become turbulent owing to exogenous shocks. But this always returns to a state of equilibrium after a few quarters; and (iv) Agents make decisions based on rational expectations. Hence, even if a shock were to move the economy from steady state growth, within a few quarters the market would make a dynamic adjustment process and return to its previous state.

---

[19]Daniel Kahneman is known for his work on the psychology of judgment and decision-making, as well as behavioural economics, for which he was awarded the 2002 Nobel Memorial Prize in Economic Sciences.

DSGE models are therefore based on an assumption of a steady state equilibrium of the economy. They allow for real amounts of time being taken to move towards that steady state and also allow for dynamic interaction between three integrated blocks supply, demand and monetary policy. Hence, the "dynamic" aspect of the DSGE label - in the sense that expectations about the future are a crucial determinant of today's outcomes (Sbordone *et al.*, 2010). They also allows for a random (i.e. stochastic) element in the path being taken towards that steady state. But the underlying premise is the existence of an omni-present state of equilibrium. Figure 4-4 offers a graphical interpretation:

The Basic Structure of DSGE Models

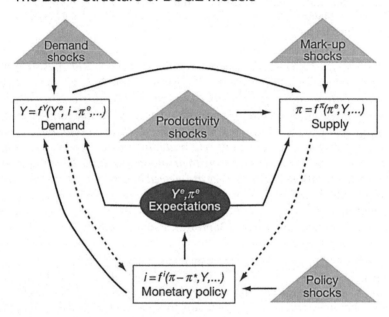

Figure 4-4. *The Basic Structure of DSGE Models*
Image source: 'Policy Analysis Using DSGE Models: An Introduction,' Federal Reserve Bank of New York

The reason these models always tend to equilibrium, it is because they are built to perform in this way and not because they are accurately interpreting the real economy. Willem Buiter, Chief Economist of Citigroup, points that one of the main reasons for this mode of construction is because policy decisions tend to create non-linear behaviours. As the interactions of this non-linearity with agent uncertainty creates complex mathematical problems, DSGE modellers removed the non-linearity elements and reduced the complex evolution of random variables into a linear system with additive stochastic variations. In an article titled, '*DSGE models and central banks*,' Camilo E. Tovar, a senior economist at the IMF also supports this argument by stating that, '*there are important concerns related to the degree of misspecification of current DSGE models.... DSGE models are too stylized to be truly able to describe in a useful manner the dynamics of the data'* (Tovar, 2008). In the same article, published by the Bank of International Settlements, he also states that, '*Possibly the main weaknesses in current DSGEs is the absence of an appropriate way of modelling financial markets.'*

The premises on which these models are constructed are however representative of a bigger problem. In a short article titled, '*The unfortunate uselessness of most 'state of the art' academic monetary economics,'* posted on the website of the Centre for Economic Policy Research (CEPR), Willem Buiter explains what are the consequences of using DSGE models based on linearity an equilibrium,

> '*When you linearize a model, and shock it with additive random disturbances, an unfortunate by-product is that the resulting linearized model behaves either in a very strongly stabilising fashion or in a relentlessly explosive manner. There is no 'bounded instability' in such models. The dynamic stochastic general equilibrium (DSGE) crowd saw that the economy had not exploded without bound in the past, and concluded from this that it made sense to rule out, in the linearized model, the explosive solution trajectories. What they were left with was something that, following an exogenous random disturbance, would return to the deterministic steady state pretty smartly. No L-shaped recessions. No processes of cumulative causation and bounded but persistent decline or expansion. Just nice V-shaped recessions....*
>
> ... '*The practice of removing all non-linearities and most of the interesting aspects of uncertainty from the models that were then let loose on actual numerical policy analysis was a major step backwards. I trust it has been relegated to the dustbin of history by now in those central banks that matter.'...*
>
> ... '*Most mainstream macroeconomic theoretical innovations since the 1970s ... have turned out to be self- referential, inward-looking distractions at best. Research tended to be motivated by the internal logic, intellectual sunk capital and aesthetic puzzles of established research programmes rather than by a powerful desire to understand how the economy works - let alone how the economy works during times of stress and financial instability.'...*
>
> *(Buiter, 2009)*

These statements reflect not just a bad ideation of economic theory but also a reflection of mathematical ignorance and arrogance that is turning economics into a posterchild for the bad application of science. Paul Romer, the current Chief Economist at the World Bank, explored the growth of this tendency over the past seven decades' in his paper, 'Mathiness in the Theory of Economic Growth' (2015). Mathiness, Romer defines, '*is [what] lets academic politics masquerade as science. Like mathematical theory, Mathiness uses a mixture of words and symbols, but instead of making tight links, it leaves ample room for slippage between statements in natural versus formal language and between statements with theoretical as opposed to empirical content.'* (Romer, 2015) (Also see '*The Trouble With Macroeconomics,'* Romer, 2016).

Romer's analysis tests the mathematical foundations of a number of seminal articles in the field of economics including - Solow's 1956 mathematical theory of growth, Gary Becker's 1962 mathematical theory of wages, McGrattan and Prescott's 2010 paper on price-taking models of growth and Boldrin and Levine's 2008 paper on Perfectly Competitive Innovation. He also analyses the work of other prominent economists such as Robert Lucas (Nobel Prize in Economics in 1995) and Thomas Piketty (who wrote Capital in the Twenty-First Century) among others. His analysis shows how Mathiness has been used repeatedly to bend data to fit a model. More disturbingly, these practices have been accepted by the academic community which makes the discipline of economics divergent from Popper's scientific method of testing. A few extracts from his paper illustrate these statements,

'In addition to using words that do not align with their formal model, Boldrin and Levine (2008) make broad verbal claims that are disconnected from any formal analysis. For example, they claim that the argument based on Euler's theorem does not apply because price equals marginal cost only in the absence of capacity constraints. Robert Lucas uses the same kind of untethered verbal claim to dismiss any role for books or blueprints in a model of ideas: "Some knowledge can be 'embodied' in books, blueprints, machines, and other kinds of physical capital, and we know how to introduce capital into a growth model, but we also know that doing so does not by itself provide an engine of sustained growth." (Lucas 2009, p.6) ....'

'...the fact that oversight was not picked up at the working paper stage or in the process leading up to publication may tell us something about the new equilibrium in economics. Neither colleagues who read working papers, nor reviewers, nor journal editors, are paying attention to the math.... Perhaps our norms will soon be like those in professional magic; it will be impolite, perhaps even an ethical breach, to reveal how someone's trick works' (Romer, 2015).

Romer's paper was inspired by a paper published in 2014 by Paul Pfleiderer, a professor of finance at Stanford University. In his paper, titled, 'Chameleons: The Misuse of Theoretical Models in Finance and Economics', Pfleiderer discusses how theoretical models in finance and economics are used in ways that make them "chameleons" when they are built on assumptions with doubtful connections to the real world but whose conclusions that are **uncritically** (emphasis added) applied to understanding our economy. Pfleiderer shows that most economic models 'cherry pick' the data they want to use to support a desired result. Any data that does not perform this function is excluded, and as a result, the conclusions depend not only based on what is included but also by what is excluded. In his view, this occurs because models, and specifically their assumptions, are not always subjected to the critical evaluation necessary to see whether and how they apply to the real world (Pfleiderer, 2014).

Pfleiderer provides a few examples of chameleon models in his paper. However, there is one that bears citing and emphasis as it is directly related to the subject of debt which is one of the principal topics in this book. Sidebar 4-3 presents an extract from his paper and provides a fitting conclusion to this critique of equilibrium economic models.

SIDEBAR 4-3: A CHAMELEON MODEL OF DEBT:

Source: 'Chameleons: The Misuse of Theoretical Models in Finance and Economics',
Pfleiderer (2014).

In April 2012 Harry DeAngelo and René Stulz circulated a paper entitled "Why High Leverage is Optimal for Banks." The title of the paper is important here: it strongly suggests that the authors are claiming something about actual banks in the real world. In the introduction to this paper the authors explain what their model is designed to do:

"To establish that **high bank leverage** is the natural (distortion-free) result of intermediation focused on liquid-claim production, the model rules out agency problems, deposit insurance, taxes, and all other distortionary factors. By positing these idealized conditions, the model obviously ignores some important determinants of bank capital structure in the real world. However, in contrast to the MM framework - and generalizations that include only leverage-related distortions - it allows a meaningful role for banks as **producers of liquidity** and **shows clearly** that, if one extends the MM model to take that role into account, it is **optimal for banks to have high leverage**".

[emphasis added by Pfleiderer]

Their model, in other words, is designed to show that if we rule out many important things and just focus on one factor alone, we obtain the particular result that banks should be highly leveraged. This argument is for all intents and purpose analogous to the argument made in another paper entitled "Why High Alcohol Consumption is Optimal for Humans" by Bacardi and Mondavi *[a fictional paper]*. In the introduction to their paper Bacardi and Mondavi explain what their model does:

"To establish that **high intake of alcohol** is the natural (distortion free) result of human liquid-drink consumption, the model rules out liver disease, DUIs, health benefits, spousal abuse, job loss and all other distortionary factors. By positing these idealized conditions, the model obviously ignores some important determinants of human alcohol consumption in the real world. However, in contrast to the alcohol neutral framework - and generalizations that include only over consumption related distortions - it allows a meaningful role for humans as **producers of that pleasant "buzz" one gets by consuming alcohol,** and shows clearly that if one extends the alcohol neutral model to take that role into account, it is optimal for **humans to be drinking all of their waking hours**".

[emphasis added by Pfleiderer]

The Deangelo and Stulz model is clearly a bookshelf theoretical model that would not pass through any reasonable filter if we want to take its results and apply them directly to the real world. In addition to ignoring much of what is important (agency problems, taxes, systemic risk, government guarantees, and other distortionary factors), the results of their main model are predicated on the assets of the bank being riskless and are based on a posited objective function that is linear in the percentage of assets funded with deposits. Given this the authors naturally obtain a corner solution with assets 100% funded by deposits. (They have no explicit model addressing what happens when bank assets are risky, but they contend that bank leverage should still be "high" when risk is present.)

The DeAngelo and Stulz paper is a good illustration of my claim that one can generally develop a theoretical model to produce any result within a wide range. Do you want a model that produces the result that banks should be 100% funded by deposits? Here is a set of assumptions and an argument that will give you that result. That such a model exists tells us very little. By claiming relevance without running it through the filter it becomes a chameleon.

One might ask, "So what if the DeAngelo/Stulz model is presented in a way that makes it a chameleon? What's the harm?" Won't people who read the paper realize its limitations? Some will, but not all. For example, in an article entitled "Capital punishment: Forcing banks to hold more capital may not always be wise" in the September 14, 2013 issue of The Economist, it was written:

In a new paper Harry DeAngelo of the University of Southern California and René Stulz of Ohio State University show that this premium means that banks, unlike other firms, are not indifferent to leverage, as the Modigliani-Merton theorem suggests. Mr DeAngelo and Mr Stulz show that it is better for banks to be highly levered even without frictions like deposit insurance and implicit guarantees.
[See, 'Capital Punishment', The Economist print edition, Sep 14th, 2013]

At the very least chameleons add noise and contribute to public misunderstanding and confusion about important issues

The analysis provided by Pfleiderer shows us why a new approach to understanding the economy is required urgently. DSGE models were unable to predict the crisis because they are based on unrealistic assumptions, just like infinite credit, and are incredibly simple caricatures of the real world which fail to consider that economy is never in equilibrium, but is rather in a continual state of adaptive change.

What we require today is an approach to economic modelling that is based on the complex interactions that take place in real economies which create a state of entropy rather than equilibrium. Fortunately, there is a way to perform this feat using the methods and tools of complexity science and via agent-based modelling (ABM). Using these methods, we can simulate the actions of millions of artificial households, firms, and people in a computer and watch what happens when they are allowed to interact.

By adopting such new techniques not only will we make the study of economics more scientific, but we will also be introducing a new way to think about economics. The critique of DSGE models shows us how the study of economics has evolved over the years. However, most of the effort has been directed towards altering bits and pieces of existing theories in relatively minor ways to explain empirical facts. Economists cling to past theories and attempt to rectify them to better understand the changing economy. But this approach has provided little insight to understanding the structural changes that emerge as an economy evolves. For example, the idea that an economic system could develop towards a distributed value exchange system with bottom-up participation and with new patterns of competition, efficiency and growth has received little attention because the concept of participatory decentralised organisation has been regarded as incompatible with efficient economic outcomes (Helbing and Kirman, 2014).

Research in economics today consists of working with modest amounts of data on a personal computer to create and solve abstract simple models that bear little resemblance to reality (Axtell and Farmer, 2015). Current models distil millions of individuals into one household and thousands of firms into just one firm, and then rationally optimize their risk-adjusted discounted expected returns over an infinite future. And they do all of this with a laptop and some maths. It is surprising to note this since we create and run models that use the largest computers to crunch petabytes of data to predict global climate change, for oil/gas exploration, for molecular modelling and for weather forecasting. But when it comes to modelling the economy, apparently a laptop and some cherry-picked data will suffice.[20] The fact that financial firms on Wall Street use teams of meteorologists running a bank of supercomputers to gain a small edge over others in identifying emerging weather patterns, but don't use or find DSGE models quite useless, speaks volumes about their worth. If economists' DSGE models offered any insight into how economies work, they would be used in the same way (BloombergView, 2014).

The main problem with current mainstream economics is its methodology. The addiction on building models that show the certainty of logical entailment has been detrimental to the development of a relevant and realist economics. Insisting on formalistic (mathematical) modelling forces the economist to give upon on realism and substitute axiomatic for real world relevance (Syll, 2016). However, reality refuses to bend to the desire for theoretical elegance that an economist demands from his model. Modelling itself on mathematics, mainstream economics is primarily deductive and based on axiomatic foundations (Sinha, 2012).

Complexity economics offers us a chance to rethink the way we study economics and leverage the transparency offered by the Blockchain. As we begin to learn about complexity economics, we must remember two points: First, the economy is never in equilibrium, but is rather in a continual state of adaptive change. Second, we shall embrace the complex interactions that take place in real economies through a relatively new computational technology called agent-based modelling (ABM). Let's see how we can teach an old dog new tricks.

---

[20]Case in point - US investment in developing a better theoretical understanding of the economy is very small -around $50 million in annual funding from the National Science Foundation - or just 0.0005 percent of a $10 trillion crisis. (Axtell and Farmer, 2015).

An introduction to Complexity Economics and Agent Based Modelling

"Science is the poetry of reality", Richard Dawkins

If we are to provide a new perspective on how to look and measure the economy, then we need to begin by asking why has economics adopted this ontological notion that the economy is an equilibrium system and borrowed the mathematical toolkit that goes with that? The answer to this question lies in the beginnings of economics as a formal branch of study.

In the 1870s, Léon Walras a French mathematical economist, came across a book titled, *'The Elements of Statistics'* (Eléments de statique), by Louis Poinsot, a French mathematician and physicist. The book represented what was at that time the cutting edge in the fields of mathematics and physics, and explored concepts such as the analysis of static equilibrium systems and simultaneous and interdependent equations (Beinhocker, 2007) (Also see Mirowski, *'More Heat than Light,'* 1991). Walras borrowed heavily from this book in coming up with his own theories which resulted in the formulation of the marginal theory of value and the development of general equilibrium theory. He was not alone in adopting this approach and another economist of the time, William Stanley Jevons, performed the same exercise by borrowing from another renowned physics textbook, the *'Treatise on Natural Philosophy,'* by Lord Kelvin and Peter Guthrie Tait[21] and independently developed the marginal utility theory of value.[22]

These economists opened a new period in the history of economic thought by making the case that economics is a mathematical science concerned with quantities. Indeed, Walras went so far with Poinsot's ideas that he reduced economic agents to atoms who functioned on physical laws and which were devoid of learning or adapting new behaviours (Walker, 1996).

What followed from these early days was the gradual progression of treating economics as a mathematical subject based on equilibrium equations and where agents behave as per the aggregate tendencies of the market (Refer the previous note on 'Mathiness' by Romer). This legacy can even still be seen today in the form of maximization principles (eg: utility) that mirrors the framing of physics in terms of minimization principles (eg: principle of least action) (Sinha *et al.,* 2010), and in the form of the 'flow of money,' which was created by Bill Philips (of the Philips Curve fame), based on his construction of the MONIAC[23] (Figure 4-5). The mapping of macroeconoic movements to the flow of fluids was representative that these thinkers looked at the economy as a subject of physical inquiry.

---

[21]Tait (1831 - 1901) was a Scottish mathematical physicist, best known for knot theory, Topology, Graph Theory and Tait's conjecture.
[22]William Stanley Jevons, Léon Walras and Carl Menger simultaneously built and advanced the marginal revolution while working in complete independence of one another. Each scholar developed the theory of marginal utility to understand and explain consumer behaviour.
[23]The MONIAC (Monetary National Income Analogue Computer) was a hydraulic simulator that used coloured water to show the flow of cash.

However, the introduction of mathematical game theory in the 1950s by John von Neumann, threw a monkey wrench into this link between economic and physics. When game theory was introduced (See '*Theory of Games and Economic Behaviour*,' von Neumann and Morgenstern), economics immediately realised that the maths of this field could be used to study the behaviour of selfish agents to get the better of other agents in an economy. But in experiments conducted with actual subjects, the agents showed irrational cooperative action was the norm (Sinha *et al.*, 2010). Economists thus reduced and embraced the abstract idea that an economy converges to equilibrium where the negative actions of one agent are offset by the postive actions of another. It is this fallacy that complexity economics attempts to solve.

Figure 4-5. *Professor A.W.H (Bill) Phillips with the Phillips Machine (MONIAC)*
Source: The Phillips Machine Project' by Nicholas Bar, LSE Magazine, June 1988, No 75.

What we have seen until now is that while we conduct economic study using deterministic and axiomatized models, economic phenomena are not derived from deterministic, axiomatic, foreseeable or mechanical precepts. The reductionist approach that was adopted by Classical and Neo-Classical economists in the past, ignored the dependencies and interconnections between different agents, their influence on each other and the macroeconomic consequences of these interactions. Instead of analysing these interactions, economists reduced the general behaviour of a system to a set of essential rules and then attempted to study these parts individually, in an attempt to gain a picture of the whole. This provides them with an aggregated view of specific economic phenomenon, which are then generalized and applied as the rational rules of conduct for the economy. This reductionist excludes the study of unfolding patterns created by agents and simplifies their individual consequence, creating a separation between reality and its formal representation (Bruno *et al.*, 2016).

Complexity economics challenges the fundamental orthodox assumptions of equilibrium, archetypal agents and rational behaviour. It attempts to change the narrative of the study of economics by emphasising the importance of network effects, feedback loops and the heterogeneity of agents. Axiomatisation, linearization and generalization are replaced by a study of the interconnections and the relevance of relationships among agents, and the effect they have on their economic environment and vice versa. Heterogenous interacting agents who make new decisions based on new information they receive from their environment and other agents replace the tradition 'rationally' minded independent agents who make decisions whilst standing still in time (Gallegati and Kirman, 2013).

Time and Information play key roles in this new paradigm of economic thought as they highlight the importance of the meso-layer, which is the connective tissue between the micro and macro structures of an economy. In complexity economics, abstract and dogmatic theories are replaced by a study of the patterns that are formed when interacting agents are exposed to new information and make decisions that influence others around them and change the structure of the economic environment in doing so. As the economy and the decisions that are made by agents' changes over time, new structures are formed. Complexity economics is thus about formation - the formation of new structures within an economy, based on exogenous and endogenous changes, and how these formations affect the agents who are causing it (Arthur, 2013).

Information as well plays a key role as changes in decisions and the introduction of new technologies affects the concentration and dispersion of knowledge and knowhow. As information is constantly changing, agents are bound to interact to increase their knowledge of these changes. As interaction is ever-present, it adds to the non-linearity and the development of shocks which reduces the direct proportionality between cause and effect: a small shock can lead to a large effect based on the interpretation of the shock by the agents. This also means that the standard tools of physics cannot be used *sic et simpliciter*, due to the agent's cognitive abilities to process information and make consequential decisions based on new information.

The aspect of information merits highlighting, not just because it is ubiquitous in today's digital economy, but also because it is directly related to the prosperity of an economy. In his book, '*Why Information Grows*' (2015), César Hidalgo[24] shows that information is a growing entity that has the ability to manifest itself in new products which are essentially cauldrons of information. The production of new products is based on the accumulation of knowledge and expertise in networks of agents. The higher the number of links between agents, the larger the network and the greater the accumulation of knowledge. This concept is important to understand as the growth of economics is based on the growth of information. Hidalgo shows that more prosperous countries are those that are better are making information grow, while those regions which produce networks with less porous boundaries hinder the growth of information and are limited in their long-term adaptability to economic changes.

Thus, a crucial part of complexity economics is the flow of information and how this information affects agents. The network of the economy can still produce aggregate patterns, but what is important to note is that firstly, these patterns are evolutive, and secondly, it is the individual decisions of agents that cause a pattern to emerge. The agent is effected by this pattern and interprets it as new information. As new information is introduced, the decisions of the agent's change, and a new pattern begins to form. The two are not separated but intrinsically linked. Aggregation is not just the process of summing up market outcomes of individual agents to obtain an economy wide total. It is the two-way interdependency between agents and the aggregate properties of the system: interacting elements produce aggregate patterns that those elements in turn react to it (Gallegati and Kirman, 2013). The **meso-layer** thus plays a key role in this study of economics.

In contrast to the Walrasian approach, where agents do not interact at all, complexity economics looks at interactions as the base of economic development, since these interactions not only influence macro patterns, but also create progressively complex networks that allow them to compensate for having limited information. This approach of seeing the economy where actions and strategies constantly evolve, where time becomes important, where structures constantly form and re-form, where phenomena appear that are not visible to standard equilibrium analysis, and where a meso-layer between the micro and the macro becomes important (Arthur, 2013) are the key branches of complexity economics.

Complexity economics is thus the study of a history-dependent, living and always evolving system whose properties emerge as a result of the interaction between self-adapting individual agents, who in adapting to new information, change the system level behaviour and the overall state of the system. Breaking down the system to individual components thus destroys down the systems properties (Bruno *et al.*, 2016). Hence the main areas of the study of complexity economics include, self-organization, pattern development and pattern recognition, agent-decision making, network propagation, interdependence of interactions, emergence, learning and memory, endogenous innovation, institutional effects, unpredictable dynamics, heterogeneity, path dependence, topology, change and evolution, holism and synergy (Manson, 2001). This interdisciplinary branch of study combines elements of physics, mathematics, computer science, ecology, engineering and, of course, economics.

---

[24]Hidalgo is a statistical physicist, writer, and associate professor of media arts and sciences at MIT. He is also the director of the Macro Connections group at The MIT Media Lab and one of the creators of the Observatory of Economic Complexity - http://atlas.media.mit.edu/en/

It is not my intention to provide a complete education of complexity economics in this chapter. Firstly, I am not qualified to do so, and secondly, there is a growing body of researchers and academics who have done this admirably well in recent times. Table 4-1 lists some of the work I have referred to which could provide an anchor to your own investigative efforts.

Table 4-1. *Reference books for Complexity Economics and Agent Based Modeling*

Author(s)	Book
W. Brian Arthur	Complexity and the Economy (2014)
Dirk Helbing	Quantitative Sociodynamics (2010)
Dirk Helbing	Thinking Ahead - Essays on Big Data, Digital Revolution, and Participatory Market Society (2015)
César Hidalgo	Why Information Grows: The Evolution of Order, from Atoms to Economies (2015)
Sitabhra Sinha, Arnab Chatterjee, Anirban Chakraborti, Bikas K. Chakrabarti	Econophysics: An Introduction (2010)
Sitabhra Sinha, Arnab Chatterjee, Anirban Chakraborti, Bikas K. Chakrabarti	Econophysics of income and wealth distributions (2012)
Linda F Dennard, Kurt A Richardson and Göktuğ Morçöl	Complexity and Policy Analysis (2008)
Uri Wilensky and William R and David S. Wilson and Alan Kirman	An Introduction to Agent-Based Modelling: Modelling Natural, Social, and Engineered Complex Systems with NetLogo (2015) Complexity and Evolution: Toward a New Synthesis for Economics (2016)
Jean-Luc Gaffard and Mauro Napoletano	Agent-based models and economic policy (2012)

What I hope to provide in the remaining part of this chapter is a summary of the key areas of study that are associated with complexity economics, so that you may identify a branch of study that peaks your interest to continue your own research in this domain. The pleasure of studying complexity economics is that as you embark on this voyage, you will be exposed to a plethora of influences from other disciplines, giving you a holistic view of science. With that introduction, let's look at some of the key topics in this discipline:

- **Dynamics**
- **Non – Linearity**
- **Power Laws**
- **Networks**

- **Feedback loops**
- **Path Dependence**
- **Emergence**
- **Agents**

Dynamics

In complexity economics, agents are influenced by others and by the behaviour of the system as a whole leading to emergent behaviour at the aggregate level. While the Walrasian economy is closed, static, and linear in the sense that it can be understood using the tools of algebraic geometry and manifold theory, the complex economy is open, dynamic, nonlinear, and generally far from equilibrium (Beinhocker, 2007). The dynamic interactions are based on the specifications of the agents - agents try to act as rationally as they can but are influenced by other agents and the aggregate behaviours of the changing market place causing them to deviate from a previously optimal behaviour. Figure 4-6 graphically interprets this statement:

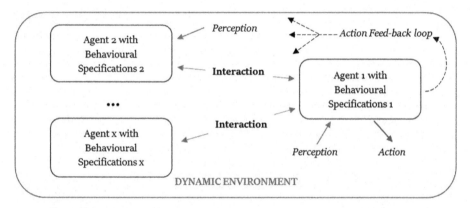

Figure 4-6. *Representation of a dynamic environment and agent's decision making influences Reference: Chapter 7, 'Computational Complexity,' Robert A. Meyers, (2012).*

Non - Linearity

An extension of the dynamics seen in a complex economy is non-linearity. A system is linear if one can add any two solutions to the equations that describe it and obtain another, and multiply any solution by any factor and obtain another (Ladyman, Lambert and Wiesner, 2012). This is referred to as superposition principle (Bruno *et al.,* 2016) as the whole is looked upon as the sum of its parts. As complex systems depend on the interactions between agents, superposition does not work as the whole is looked up as something more than its parts. Thus, small changes effected by one agent can have large effects on the environment and vice versa.

Non - linearity can thus be defined as disproportionality. As we have discussed in Box 9, our thinking is attuned to be linear and the tools we use in economics represent that facet. In regression analysis, for example, the scores that do not fit into our linear models are treated as errors or have extreme variations. Complexity economics treats such variations as the intrinsic characteristics of interrelated systems. Non - linearity thus plays a central role in complexity economics.

Power Laws

The effects of agents on a non-linear dynamic system follow rules of power laws. Power laws imply that small occurrences are very common, but large eco-system changes are rare. For example- patterns involving incomes, the growth of cities, firms, the stock market and fluctuations of returns, order flow, volume, liquidity and even natural calamities such as hurricanes and earthquakes, all follow power laws. A power law, can also be called a scaling law, as there is a direct relationship between two variables. Mathematically this can be interpreted as,

$$Y = aX^{\beta}$$

where 'Y' and 'X' are variables of interest,
"is called the power law exponent,
and 'a' is typically an unremarkable constant.

So, if X is multiplied by a factor of 10, then Y is multiplied by 10; i.e.: Y 'scales' as X to the power.

Power laws or scaling laws are seen in different disciplines of study, particularly physics. A commonly known power law is the Pareto principle (used in marketing studies for example) or the also known as the 80/20 rule, which states that, for many events, roughly 80% of the effects come from 20% of the causes. The study of power laws in markets has increasingly been a subject of interest to econophysicists[25] (a complimentary offshoot of complexity economics) as power laws signal the occurrence of scale independent behaviour that is closely related to phase transitions and critical phenomenon. Some reliable examples of power law distributions occur in financial markets (Sinha *et al.,* 2010) (Also see, '*Power Laws in Finance*', Chapter 5, 'Econophysics: An Introduction,' Sinha et al., (2010); '*Power Laws in Economics: An Introduction,*' Xavier Gabaix (2008)).

Complex systems are more commonly characterised by probability distributions that are better described by a power laws instead of normal distributions, as these gradually decreasing mathematical functions are better at probabilistically predicting the future states of even highly complex systems (Levy D. L., 2000).

---

[25]Econophysics is an interdisciplinary research field that applies theories and methods originally developed by physicists in order to solve problems in economics. Refer Table 2 to see sources of Econophysics textbooks.

Networks

The study of network science and its related disciplines is a pillar of complexity economics. Agents in a complex economy participate in interwoven overlapping networks that allow them to compensate for their limited access to information. In the Walrasian economy, agents do not interact at all. Rather, each agent faces an impersonal price structure (Beinhocker, 2007). However, in complexity economics, the study of networks is conducted with a high level of granularity, as economic exchanges between agents (be it credit-debt relations, change of ownership of assets, simple monetary transactions or exchanges between banks or nations) do not happen randomly. They are dependent on the position and the reputation of each individual node. A node which has a more important role to play (eg.: large banks) will have more interconnections to other nodes making it a hub. There can be correlations between links to a hub leading to assortativity, or assortative mixing, which is the preference of a node to attach itself to another node that is similar to it in some way. This can also lead to the clustering of connections between nodes that identify themselves as part of a particular sub-group leading to displays of cliquishness; i.e. nodes associating with each other based on belonging to an exclusive clique. Figure 4-7 provides a visual interpretation.

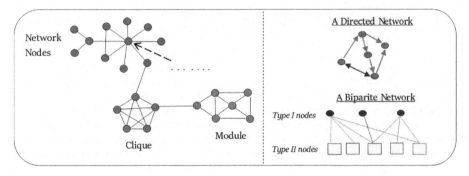

Figure 4-7. *Formation of sub-groups in networks*
Reference: 'Introduction to social network methods,' Hanneman and Riddle, 2005.

These condensating properties of networks are crucial to identifying the emergence of patterns and judging the centres of gravity of a network. More importantly how central points in a node affect the behaviour of other nodes. This can be observed in the manner the topology of the nodes changes over time and the information feedbacks that are propagated in dynamic interconnected systems means that some nodes will change alliances while others might leave the network altogether leading to a constant rearrangement of links between the existing nodes. Network topology is relevant for systemic risk as nodes can be affected randomly or according to some of their intrinsic properties. For example, if we are to look at credit claims or credit relationships, then nodes can be conceived as agents and links could represent credit claims and liabilities. By identifying the density of connected subsets of nodes within a network we can identify communities that are highly leveraged. Thus, instead of looking at communities ubiquitously as we do today, community detection in real economic networks provides an approach to identify the propagation and contagious of defaults.

As it can be seen from the Figure 4-7, Graph Theory is the natural framework for the mathematical study of networks, as a complex network can be represented by X nodes and Y edges (links), where every edge corresponds to a specific pair of nodes in the network. A network can be classified as directed or undirected based on the links - a *directed* network in one in which the nodes are directly associated in a certain direction. An *undirected* network in which there is no such orientation. The links between nodes can also have varying weights based on the capacity and intensity of the relationship. Most complex networks have a high amount of varying heterogeneity creating a complex network topology.

Based on this type of links, networks can also be sub-divided and classified according to the distinct relationships they have between nodes. For example, as seen in figure 4-6, a network can have nodes which possess a distinct type of linking between nodes of certain groups. This could be seen between shareholders and companies or between different peer groups, or seen between insurers and insureds.

Clustering is another important attribute of networks. If a pair of nodes *a, b* are connected to a pair of nodes *b, c;* then *a, c* can also be connected via *b.* In such situations, the nodes *a, b & c* are said to be clustered. The average clustering coefficient, which measures the compactness of the neighbour of node *a,* is a measure of the cliquishness of that section of the network. The average clustering coefficient of the network would thus be an average of the cliquishness of nodes such as *a* and would represent the compactness of the network. A network which is very compact would be referred to as Small World Network (SWN). In many real-world networks, this is something that is commonly seen (Sinha *et al.,* 2010).

At the meso - level, i.e.: between groups and clusters within the network, many networks exhibit modular structures. The presence of modular structures alters the way dynamical phenomenon, such as the spread of risk, contagion, harmonisation, breakdown of sub-groups, etc., occurs on the network. Unsurprisingly, there is a body of research now being conducted that is focused at observing the meso - linkages in networks (See: '*Network Approaches to Interbank Markets, Fricke, Alfarano, Lux and Raddant (2016); 'How likely is contagion in financial networks?,'* Glasserman, and Young (2015)).

Figure 4-8 shows how networks can be visualised even at the macro level of an economy. This work which is being conducted by César Hidalgo and a group of researchers, allows us to see the linkages of trade and commerce at the national and international level. (For more information on visualising economies based on their exports and the complexity of their economy, visit the Observatory of Economic Complexity.)

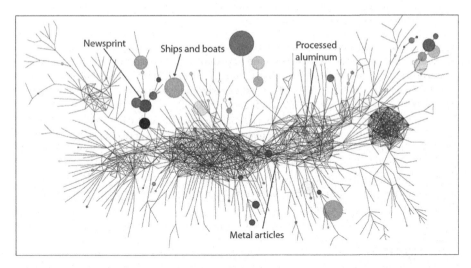

Figure 4-8. *Norway's exports from 1963-1969, shown on a complex network. (Note the sectorial linkages).*
Source: 'Linking Economic Complexity, Institutions and Income Inequality,' (D. Hartmann et al., 2015).

Feedback loops

As self-organizing systems interact, the system's agents exchange information leading to the emergence of complex patterns. This exchange is commonly referred to this as feedback (Refer figure 4-5). A node or a part of a network receives feedback when the way its neighbouring nodes or parts interact with it at a later time depends upon how it interacts with them at an earlier time (Bruno *et al.*, 2016). Owing to this mechanism, change in a certain variable can result in either the augmentation (positive feedback) or a reduction (negative feedback) of that change. When this change repeats itself, a loop is said to emerge.

A feedback loop means that the loop's behaviour is self-reinforcing: it will run on and on until something intervenes. An example of a positive feedback loop could be between income and consumption. The bigger the income per capita in an economy, the more people consume. This will produce a further increase in their per capita income, and so on. On the other hand, inequality also happens to be a kind of feedback loop found in self-organizing systems (DiMaggio and Cohen, 2003).

The interaction between the two feedbacks is an example of a self-perpetuating process seen in complex systems. A feedback loop is also the reason behind self-organisation. As agents adapt and inform themselves via feedback, they begin to form alliances based on internal constraints and preferences and subsequently establish themselves into autonomous organizational structures that do not need central co-ordination. Dissecting the emergence of this organizational process is akin to witnessing the physical embodiment of Adam Smith's invisible hand.

Path Dependence

In a word, path dependence can be summarized as history. Path dependence is the dependence of economic outcomes on the path of previous outcomes, rather than based on current conditions. For example, the statement "we saved and invested last year and therefore we have assets today" might be more fashionably expressed as, "the capital stock is path dependent'" (Margolis and Liebowitz, 1998).

The attachment of history to the present is one of the main attributes of complexity economics. In recent times, there have been a progressive neglect of observing the past to determine where we will go in the future. But as complex systems change and evolve with time, they have histories. The decisions made by agents in the past, and by the network by proxy, is responsible for their present behaviour. Any analysis of a complex system that ignores the dimension of time is incomplete, at most a synchronic snapshot of a diachronic process (Bruno et al., 2016).

Emergence

Just as the chemical composition of a complex molecule are a result of the nuclear and electronic interactions, in the complex economy, macroeconomic patterns emerge due to micro-level exchanges and behaviours. Markets are a well-known example of emergence. Markets function as long as buyers and sellers exist and conduct the exchange of assets, services and goods for money and vice versa. Markets are therefore related to the activity of purchasing and selling and can be neither explained by the properties of buyers or sellers, nor by the characteristics of trade (Noell, 2007) (Bruno *et al.*, 2016).

Emergence relates to the dynamic nature of interactions between components in a system (Gallegati and Kirman, 2012). The dynamic character of emergent phenomena is not a property of a pre-established, given whole - but arises and becomes apparent as a complex system evolves over time (Goldstein, 1999). Complexity in a system can arise, after all, from simple rules - this is seen in examples such as cellular automata, neural networks and genetic algorithms (Refer Notes). This is because of the non-linearity of the systems relations. As the system becomes complex, emergence manifests itself in the form of *self- organization*. In other words, no external forces are needed for the system to take on certain properties and traits and these systemic properties arise from far-from-equilibrium conditions (Morçöl, 2008).

Far-from-equilibrium conditions tend to be sensitive to external shocks - a small change can have large scale impacts (see (iii) Power Laws, above). Although we cannot analytically derive the properties of the macro system from those of its component parts, we can nevertheless apply novel mathematical techniques to model the behaviour of the emergent properties (Beinhocker, 2007). This is a vital addition to the toolkit of complexity economic models, as once a complex system's properties emerge, the systems properties are irreducible to the properties of its components, since the laws that govern complexity are different from the laws that govern its constituent parts (Kauffman, 1996). Tools based on Agent Based Modelling (discussed below) are thus essential and help us detect and study the development of patterns.

Studying the emergence of patterns based on the interactions between agents, allows us to study the evolutionary process of differentiation, selection, and amplification, from which arises novelty, order and complexity growth (see Kevin Kelly). This is important to note as in economics, goods and services exist in niches or cliques (see (iv) Networks above) which are created by other goods and services (combinatorial) and agents earn revenues based on which niche they exist in and which nodes they interact with (Kauffman, 1996).

While the Walrasian economy has no macro properties that can be derived from its micro properties (for instance, the First and Second Welfare Theorems[26]), there is no mechanism for studying the emergence of novelty or growth in complexity. In a complexity economics, these interactions can be modelled giving us the ability to see the evolution of an economy with a bottom-top approach. Modelling these higher-level constructs is not a simple task and can be done to a certain extent with agent-based modelling (ABM). We will explore ABM is detail shortly, after defining agents.

Agents

An agent is an autonomous computational individual or object with particular properties and actions (Wilensky and Rand, 2015). This autonomous entity has the ability to decide the actions it needs to carry out in the environment it is immersed in, and the interactions it needs to establish with other agents according to its perceptions and internal state (Bandini *et al.*, 2012).

In the complex economy, agents have limited information and face high costs of information processing. They compensate for this by feedback loops and sourcing information from their network groups of trust. However, there is no certitude that when faced with new information, or new technology, they will immediately and efficiently shift to new heuristics. Agents interpret the data presented to them in their own way and make their own non-optimal decisions based on that.

The decision-making process of an agents depends on its architecture, which refers to the internal structure that is responsible of effectively selecting the actions to be carried out, according to the perceptions and internal state of an agent. Different architectures have been proposed in order to obtain specific agent behaviours and they are generally classified into *deliberative* and *reactive* (Bandini *et al.,* 2012). Making an autonomous decision is based on a trade-off between 4 options - (i) the timing of the action; (ii) whether or not to fulfil a request; (iii) whether to act in the absence of a trigger event, i.e.: a proactive decision; (iv) basing the decision on personal experience or hard-wired knowledge (Russell and Norvig, 2009). Different agents will embody different nomenclatures of these trade-offs.

---

[26]**The First Welfare Theorem:** Every Walrasian equilibrium allocation is Pareto efficient. **The Second Welfare Theorem:** Every Pareto efficient allocation can be supported as a Walrasian equilibrium.
The First and Second Welfare Theorems are the fundamental theorems of Welfare Economics. The first theorem states that any competitive equilibrium, or Walrasian equilibrium, leads to a Pareto efficient allocation of resources. The second theorem states the converse, that any efficient allocation can be sustainable by a competitive equilibrium.

In the neoclassical economy agents are said to have perfect information and can cheaply decide what is the best (i.e.: rational) decision. This approach has been adopted because neo-classical economists assume that the choices of all diverse agents in one sector (consumers), can be considered as the choices of one 'representative' standard utility maximizing individual whose choices coincide with the aggregate choices of the heterogeneous individuals (Kirman, 1992).

Kirman[27] believes this reasoning is flawed for four reasons - Firstly, there is no justification that shows that the aggregate of individuals, represents the actions of an individual. Individual behaviour is not directly linked to collective behaviour. Secondly, no matter how maximizing an agent, there is no guarantee that the way an agent behaves to a change in the economy (eg: interest rates), is representative of the aggregate reaction of the individuals the agent 'represents'. This makes analysis of policy changes particularly flawed. Thirdly, if the representative agent has makes a decision for or against the aggregate decision, since he or she is a utility maximizer, there is no way to decide whether one decision is better than another. Lastly, trying to explain the behaviour of a group by one individual is constraining and having a single entity embody the decisions of a dynamic group can lead to the creation of an individual with unnatural characteristics. Thus, creating a model for empirical testing based on a representative agent creates disadvantages at it is not representative of the heterogeneity of agents and the microfoundations on which this school is thought is constructed.

The study of macroeconomics thus needs to be based not on the study of individuals in isolation, but on the heterogeneity of agents and the aggregate patterns that are created by the direct interaction between different individuals. Complexity economics allows us to address this issue by using computer programs to model and simulate the behaviour of each agent and the interaction that among agents. By using Agent Based Simulation, we can investigate the dynamics of complex economic systems with many heterogeneous and not necessarily fully rational agents (Levy, 2012).

The rationality behind decision making is a key aspect of creating representative agents in these simulations. As stated by Kirman, the assumption today is that rational behaviour will be exhibited in aggregate in the economy. This may be true for a small subset of agents, but there is no certainty that all agents are equally rational (as stated in conventional models). In reality, agents are '*bounded*' in terms of their rationality based on their past and present knowledge, and the consequences of their actions. The agent's beliefs are thus probability statements that are linked to the information they possess and the economy in which they are immersed in. Based on these probabilities, they develop adaptive, non-optimal heuristics for making decisions in a complex environment. But as Kirman points out, there is no assurance that, when faced with novel information, individuals will shift efficiently to new heuristics.

---

[27]Alan Kirman is professor emeritus of Economics at the University of Aix-Marseille III and at the Ecole des Hautes Etudes en Sciences Sociales. He is a heterodox economist and has published numerous papers and books on Complexity Economics, Game Theory and Non-Linear Dynamics among other subjects. His latest book 'Complexity and Evolution: Toward a New Synthesis for Economics was published in August 2016.

Complexity economics accepts these agent characteristics and considers agents to possess 'bounded rationality'. Bounded rational agents are limited in their ability to optimize. This limitation may be due to limited computational power, errors, or various psychological biases which have been experimentally documented. This manner of looking at rationality is definitely far more complicated than the version that is assumed in neo-classical economics - perfect, logical, optimal, lucid, deductive rationality. But there are various reasons to reject this version of rationality.

Firstly, there is the threshold of complexity. An agent can only make rational decisions up to a certain logical complexity. They are therefore rationally bounded by nature. Secondly, there is the issue of trust. Agents cannot rely on other agents to make rational decisions. They are obliged to guess the behaviour of other agents (via feedback loops) and in doing so, enter the maze of subjective beliefs based on subjective beliefs, based on subjective beliefs (Arthur, 1994). The question, therefore, is not how to perfect rationality, but what to put in its place. Arthur states that the replacement lies not in rationality but in reasoning, namely, inductive reasoning.

Inductive reasoning is based on our innate ability to recognize patterns. While humans are not very good at deductive logic (with the exception of Sherlock Holmes), evolution has enabled us to become very adept at recognizing patterns and we begin recognizing patterns even as infants. When faced with a complex situation, we search for patterns, develop hypotheses and make simple models in our mind based on the probability of an event occurring (for example in chess). This process is referred to as inductive reasoning. Economic agents perform this exercise and use feedback from the environment to test their hypotheses and find reasons for their decisions in this way.

Explaining the concept of inductive reasoning is one thing. But as ABM is based on simulation, the elephant in the room is how do we model inductive reasoning? It is here that the trade-off between the 4 options plays a role. Agents weigh the 4 options when faced with a hypothesis and form a belief of which is the optimal decision to be made. The belief is not the result of correctness (as there is no way of actually knowing this). Rather it is a subjective choice based on a previous track record of having worked in the past. A belief is only discarded when it repeatedly shows a record of failure (Arthur, 1994). Different agents have different subjectivities that evolve symbiotically owing to feedback loops. Hypotheses and decisions are thus in a constant state of evolution (Also see: '*Knowledge, expectations, and inductive reasoning within conceptual hierarchies*,' Coley, Hayes, Lawson, Moloney, (2004)).

Thus, when creating an Agent-based simulation, multiple interacting agents (also known as 'microscopic simulation) are given 'micro' rules (since they are programs) that represent different behaviours of agents, based on real world data. Complexity economists thus do not make particular assumptions on about the sources of agents' characteristics and their behavioural rules. The characteristics of an agent may be due the agent's bounded rationality (i.e.: their nature) and can be influenced by the social rules or norms of the system. Agents follow a system of inductive reasoning to form beliefs that adapt to the aggregate environment that that co-create and co-evolve, making the economy is a complex adaptive system.

Modelling and simulating these agents are therefore based on the concepts of network science, feedback loops, power laws and non-linear dynamics. The precipitate of this amalgamation is the field of Agent Based Computational Economics (ABCE from here on). While complexity economics provides us with the theoretical rebuttal to neo-classical economics, ABCE models provides us with alternatives to DSGE models.

Using ABCE model, complexity economists can investigate systems that cannot be studied using conventional methods. These economists are now exploring questions such as -

- How does heterogeneity and systematic deviations from rationality affect markets?

- Can these elements explain empirically observed phenomena which are considered 'anomalies' in the standard economics literature?

- How robust are the results obtained with the traditional analytical models?

By addressing these questions ABCE complements the traditional analytical analysis, and is gradually being adopted in economic analysis. Schools such as MIT and the Oxford Martin School have departments that are dedicated to this branch of analysis, and research hubs such as the Institute for New Economical Thinking (INET) and the Waterloo Institute for Complexity and Innovation (WICI) are uniting scientists and economists from various disciplines to advance the research and the development of these tools. It is still early days for this approach to economic study, but progress is already being made. In the next section, what are the steps to be followed to make an ABM simulation and cover a few use cases that showcase how these methods and models can be applied to understand current economic phenomena.

Complexity Economics Models and Agent Based Computational Economics

"We shape our tools, and thereafter they shape us", John Culkin

A model is an abstracted description of a process, event or entity. When a model is capable of taking in certain inputs and manipulate these input values in an algorithmic way to generate an output, it is said to be a computational model. In a computational model, an agent is an autonomous, individual element of a computer simulation which has specific properties, states and behaviours.

Agent Based Modelling (ABM) is a computational modelling paradigm that enables us to describe how an agent will behave in a pre-defined model. In ABM, the behaviour of an agent is encoded in the form of simple (or complex) rules, which governs the way it interacts with the model and other agents (Wilensky and Rand, 2015). These models can be used to study a wide range of processes and systems and are gradually being used in the study of economics today.

Previous models that have been used in the study of economics were generally in equation form. This form of modelling is known as Equation Based Modelling (EBM). EBMs typically make assumptions of homogeneity. ABM differs from EBM as it can be used to model heterogenous populations. In doing so, ABM is capable of visualising the interactions between agents and give us results that are discreet and non-continuous.

As we have discussed in earlier parts of this chapter, continuous models are non-representative of economic phenomenon as they do not allow us to count accurately. For example - in population studies, EBM treat populations as a continuous quantity when in reality, a population is made up of discreet individuals (you cannot have 1.5 men or 0.5 women). Hence, for EBM to work, they need to make assumptions of large quantities (eg-population size) and need to aggregate results for these large populations.

This aggregation aspect is a key difference between ABM and EBM - EBM requires a complete knowledge of the relationship between agents. If there are two populations of agents, 'A' & 'B', then to build a EBM, you need to have an understanding of the relationship between population 'A' and population 'B'. As populations are treated as continuous quantities, EBM requires that we know the aggregate behaviour of population A and the aggregate behaviour of population B. Encoding this aggregate knowledge requires the use of differential equations and complicates the process. Even after the doing this, there is still another disadvantage. An EBM modeler may recognize that these 2 populations have interrelationships, but they have no way of explicitly representing these behaviours in EBM.

ABMs on the other hand, do not attempt to model a global aggregate pattern. Instead of focusing on aggregate behaviours of populations, ABM focuses on writing rules for the discrete agents in each of these populations. This puts less strain on trying to model the interactions between agents. The model is focused on seeing how these agents will interact and what patterns will emerge.

Based on this, aggregate behavioural trends will be generated and observed, over varying cycles of time. As ABM models describe agents and not aggregates, the relationship between ABM and the real world is more closely matched. It is therefore easier to understand as it provides us with a frame of reference we are used to witnessing in the natural world, instead of depending on a set of algebraic equations that bear very little semblance to reality.

As ABMs model each agent, their decisions and their interactions, they can provide us with both individual and aggregate level outcomes at the same time. It is also possible to study the history of an agent, or a group of agents and the overall aggregate trends that evolve over a period of time. This bottom-up approach of ABMs provides us with more detailed information than EBMs, which only provide aggregate results and nothing about the agents and their interactions.

ABMs also allow us to include the elements of randomness and probability easily. EBMs require each decision in the model, to be a deterministic one. However, once again, this is not how the real world operates. Agents find themselves in an economic environment that is prone to shocks (randomness) and changing attitudes of other agents (feedback). Thus, over time, agents make a sequence of decisions based on the feedback and the changing contours of their environment. Their decisions are not deterministic and do not follow a straight path.

Building a model that is based on deterministic decisions outcomes means that we need to understand every fibre of the environment and every notion of thought of the agents. This could be done for a small group of agents in a controlled environment. But the real world is messy, extremely complex and far from this kind of sterile environment. Agents are subjected to random events and make probability based decisions in a sequential process of adaptation.

As ABMs focus on conceptualizing the individual agents, it does not have to take into account how each agent will react to the multitude of environmental factors. The environmental factors are inputs to the model and create the ambience of the ecosystem which are beyond the control of a single agent (much like in real life). But the real focus is the agent. Thus, the development of these models is faster as there no requirement to determine the exacting outcomes that are created by changes in the environment.

As agents react with changes in the environment and by interacting with other agent, patterns may emerge which can then be tested empirically to determine if it is a constant behavioural attribute. If this is the case, we will see deterministic behaviour and these deterministic decisions can then be added to the rule making notions of the agent. ABMs therefore allow for the incorporation of deterministic rules along with randomness and probability, provided the reasoning is scientifically and empirically justified.

This is not to say that EBMs should be thrown out with the bathwater. There are a number of areas where EBMs are essential. The argument being made here is that it is ill-suited for economics. The reason for this is heterogeneity of agents. EBMs are useful when agents are homogenous and where aggregates are sufficient to represent a population. But economics does not enter this category. When we look at the stock market for example, we are immediately struck by the complexity and the dynamism of the agents, their decisions and the pace of change in the market. Reducing these complex movements to algebra based equations is a non-representative gross over-simplification of the economy.

ABMs overcome this challenge by focusing on the agent. For example, if we use an ABM to model a stock market, the modeller focuses on understanding individual level agent behaviour. Different agents will have different risk thresholds and will make different decisions. ABM thus focuses on specifying the agent's properties and leverages their heterogeneity by creating rules on how they will interact with each other. Moreover, in ABM the agent has access to the interactions they have had with other agents.

Based on this point of reference, they can change their behaviours and their allegiances with other agents. The ability to introduce randomness into the system allows us to see how agents will change their behaviour and their interconnect - For the stock market example, we can imagine a broker decides to liquidate his holdings as he has to pay for his children's college fees at an expensive school, or because he has won the lottery and decides to leave the game and sip piña coladas for the rest of his days. This will create a rupture between him and other agents who were cooperating with him. As agents have access to historical data, the question then becomes how would these other agents change their behaviour the next time they are informed that one of the stock broking comrades they interact with has just won the lottery?

There is no way to ascertain if the new lottery winner will follow the piña colada route. He might instead decide to invest the winnings in his portfolio for long term gain. This will have ripple effects on other agents he co-operates with. The question thus becomes two-fold: (1) How will agents behave when they realise that one of them has won the lottery? Will they break ties owing to past experience or decide to strengthen their relation with the lucky winner based on a hunch/personal bias/sentimental allegiance? (2) What happens when the lottery winning agent executes an action that is different from another agent who was in the same position in the past? Why did he not follow the piña colada route (maybe the retirement plan was not conducive to the current economic climate?)? Was it the environment that led to this decision or the agents innate risk aversion level? ABMs allow us to see these changes as they occur and create scenarios that are resemblant of reality.

While ABMs aim at encoding the individual agent, simulating thousands or millions of agents does require significant computing power. This is a trade-off that is characteristic of any model or simulation. The more detail there is, the greater the number of modelling decisions and the higher the computing power required. This problem in part is overcome by 'black-boxing' parts of the model (Wilensky and Rand, 2015). Black-boxing is the strategic use of equations to control computationally intensive parts of the model. But when required, the black-box can be 'opened up'.

Black-boxing is carried out owing to the number of variables or free parameters that are used the construct a model. ABMs have a much large number of free parameters to help it represent the level of detail of the process or environment it is trying to depict. But incorporating these free parameters is important as it allows us to control the assumptions of the model. While EBMs 'cherry pick' their free parameters and make assumptions of how they work (as it is not always possible to incorporate them into an equation), ABMs expose these assumptions and calibrate free parameters to observed, real world data. This is a time consuming but nevertheless an important task as it provides us with rich individual level data.

As the governing actions of the agents are defined, so are their rules of interaction. To set or modify these parameters and modelling decisions, thus requires that the ABM modeller have a grasp of how individual agents operate. Gaining this insight is a pre-requisite for ABM but not for EBM. While we do not need to model micro behaviours in ABM, we do need to need to have an understanding of the micro behaviours and individual level mechanisms. This can require the modeller to increase his range of study, sometimes beyond his area of expertise. But it is also a blessing in disguise when we are studying social systems.

Consider our previous stock market example - it is easier to think about the behavioural traits of an individual stock broking agent rather than think about how news of that agent winning the lottery will affect throes of agents who are related to this agent. In fact, the modeler does not even have to go into excruciating detail regarding the individual agents' traits. Starting with some initial hypotheses, the modeller can generate a model that represents these hypotheses. As the dynamics of the system evolve over discrete time steps, the results can be tested for validity and if they are representative of real world phenomenon, a proof of concept is formed.

The advantage of this approach is that it can be employed to study general properties of a system which are not sensitive to the initial conditions, or to study the dynamics of a specific system with fairly well- known initial conditions, e. g. the impact of the baby boomers' retirement on the US stock market (Bandini *et al.*, 2012).

Designing an ABM Simulation

The main aim of an ABM is to construct a computerised counterpart of an existing system using agents (mini-programs) with specific properties and governing rules, and to then simulate the system in a computer till it resembles real world phenomenon. Having achieved this feat, we can then create multiple scenarios and understand the system in greater levels of detail and identify threats and conditions that are conducive and non-conducive to the system.

Creating an ABM depends on a variety of factors such as what is trying to be modelled and available data for the subject. ABMs are generally classified into two types of models: *phenomenon-based* modelling and *exploratory* modelling.

In the former, the model is developed on the basis of a known phenomenon which exhibits a characteristic pattern and which is used as a reference pattern - examples include: the spiral shapes of galaxies, demographic segregation in urban areas, the symmetry seen in flowers, etc... The goal is to recreate the reference pattern using rule-defined agents. Once this goal achieved, changes can be made to see how new patterns might emerge.

The latter is more deductive in nature. After giving rules to agents, the agents are let to interact and the patterns that emerge are explored to see if the they can be associated to real world phenomenon. The model is then modified to provide us with an explanation of what happened and how we got there.

The structure of the model can also be based on the way the approach that is taken to construct it. If the modeller has sufficient information about the types of agents and the essential features of the environment, he can adopt a top-bottom approach, and follow a structured conceptual blueprint to build the model.

If the modeller does not have this granular level of insight, then he can adopt a bottom - up approach, in which he would begin creating the model from the bottom by discovering what the main mechanistic properties are, what are the features of the agents and what research questions need to be answered. In doing so, the conceptual and construction phases of the model grow in unison. Most modellers use both styles of when creating a model.

Irrespective of what approach is used, every ABM has three essential components - *agents*, the *environment* in which these agents exist, and the *interactions* these agents have with the environment and between themselves. Let us detail these three components in greater detail.

Specifying Agent Behaviour

Specificity is of key importance when selecting the behavioural traits and states of an agent. Too much information packed into an agent can lead to unmanageable agents who perform illogical actions. Uniqueness is also key. An agent must be distinguishable from another agent if they are to interact in a logical fashion. Hence the two main aspects of agent behaviour are the properties that they have and the actions (based on their behaviour) that they execute (Wilensky and Rand, 2015).

Specifying the agent's behaviour is what allows it to know what actions it can take. These can include ways in which it can change the state of the environment, other agents or itself. Agent actions are normally of two types - *Reactive or Deliberative*. Reactive agents are simplistic agents who obey condition - action rules, who normally do not possess a memory and exist to perform a very specific role in the environment (if input =0; say 'hello world'; if anything else = do nothing). They perform their actions based on the input they receive from other agents or the environment. They cannot be pro-active.

Deliberative agents are a more complex and have an action - selection mechanism governed by certain knowledge about the environment and memories of past experiences. This allows them to have a mental state, which is why they are also known as cognitive agents, which they use to select a sequence of actions for every set of perceptions they receive. The sequence of actions selected is to achieve a pre-stated goal. Deliberative agents are thus following a certain set of Beliefs, Desires and Intentions (BDI architecture), where Beliefs represent agent information about its environment, Desires are the agent's objectives and Intentions represent the desires an agent has selected and committed (Bandini *et al.*, 2012).

Most ABMs can have a heterogonous mix of reactive and deliberative agents. All agents also need to know how they are to react to changes in the environment and what actions they need to take when other agents make specific actions. Based on the type of actions they can take; we can group agents into different types of agents. For example, one agent may be coded to act as an investor (deliberative), while another can be coded to function exclusively as a connector (reactive) who connects investors together or investors and businesses together, but does not make investments itself. From this kind of classification, we can have *breeds* of agents who perform specific roles in the simulation. By dividing agents into different kinds of groups or breeds, we can see which interactions and decisions led to the creation of a phenomena and who was responsible for it.

All actions that are to be taken can be represented as system commands that regulate and control the agent's behaviour. Hence, actions are complex tasks that the agent executes in order to fulfil given goals and that take into account the environment reactions and correctives to previous actions (Bandini *et al.*, 2012).

Creating the Environment

The environment acts as the control parameters on which the actions of the agents are based. The environment consists of the conditions and habitats surrounding the agents as they act and interact within the model. However, this relationship between the environment and the agents is not just one way - as agents interact with the environment, the environment is set the change based on their decisions. Different parts of the environment can also have different properties and have different impacts on the agents that are in that vicinity. The environment is thus responsible for:

- Defining and indirectly enforcing rules.

- Reflecting and managing the social arrangement of all agents.

- Managing agent access to specific parts of the system.

- Aiding in agent decision making process by providing the right kind of input data

- Maintain the internal dynamics (e. g. spontaneous growth of resources, dissipation signals emitted by agents) (Bandini et al., 2012).

An important component of the environment is the 'Time Step' which determines in what sequence the order of actions need to be taken. Agents have autonomy and control over their actions, based on their behavioural specification and their interpretation of the actions of the other agents. But time still plays a key role as the actions of the agents have to occur in a sequence. Thus, the environment aids in governing this attribute with the time step.

An environment can also be modelled based on real world scenarios - for example Netlogo,[28] one of the popular platforms used in ABM for modelling decentralized, interconnected phenomenon, allows us to create the environment using a Geographic Information Systems Toolkit or a Social Network Analysis toolkit that mimics a real-world environment.

Enacting Agent Interaction

The main goal of ABMs is to witness the interaction between agents and with the environment. In case of economic models, a mix between a top-bottom and bottom-up approach is used - the top-bottom components consist of environmental macroeconomic factors such as changes in production, in exchange, in employment, etc... The agents are heterogenous in breed as this leads to interactions which has a bigger effect on emergence.

There are different ways in which agents can interact:

- Direct Interaction - In such models, there is a direct exchange of information between agents. A point-to-point message exchange protocol regulates the exchange of information between agents. When developing these models, care needs to be taken with regards to the format of exchange.

- Indirect Interaction - In the indirect interaction models, an intermediate entity mediates agent interactions. This entity can even regulate the interactions (Akhbari and Grigg, 2013).

This differentiation in the way that agents interact provides interaction mechanisms that allow collaboration to occur at different levels. In the real-world collaboration is a distributed task as not all agents can make decisions owing to inconsistencies in knowledge, roles and competencies. Hence, having separate interaction mechanisms provides specific abstractions for agent interaction and provides separated computation and coordination contexts (Gelernter and Carriero, 1992).

For example, if the interaction effects are weak, as seen in auction markets, then the structural dimensions of the model (such as the costs and the number of buyers and sellers), will determine the market results. If interaction effects are strong, as seen in labour markets, then the outcomes of the market will be highly dependent on the nets of interactions that are seen within the market structure (Salzano, 2008).

---

[28]Some other known languages and tools used are Repast and SimSesam. Both these platforms are more advanced than Netlogo but require some previous coding experience in Java. Netlogo is a dialect of the Logo language and is A general-purpose framework. Repast and SimSeam allow for easier integration of external libraries and higher levels of statistical analysis, data visualisation and geographic information systems.

This interaction strength concept brings us to the final concept in ABM modelling, which is the size. If we are to model an economy, to what level of granularity are we to descend? Should we model individual people or should we model large groups (banks, financial firms) as single entities that are representative of large groups of people? Is it really necessary to simulate multiple micro-agents?

Having discussed this subject with a few experts in the field, including Doyne Farmer[29] and Jacky Mallett,[30] the consensus I received is that the more detail the model has, the better it will be. As stated by Mallett during a one-on-one interview,

"The simple rule with mathematical system modelling or simulation is that you have to simulate and model down to the lowest level of detail that you can show effects the behaviour of the system. We from physics, we don't need to include detailed atomic level modelling to reproduce the behaviour of the planets in a solar system, although it is important to know their individual mass. Physics in fact usually deals with systems where the micro level doesn't influence the macro level - and unfortunately this approach seems to have influenced macro-economic quite strongly, without anybody questioning the underlying assumption.

Conversely however, if it can be shown that a particular level of detail does impact the behaviour of the larger system then you do need to include it. This is true in all disciplines.... This is why it's possible to dismiss all economic models that don't include the banking system, because it's trivial to show that national variations in banking system structure or the financial instruments it uses, can influence the economy.

---

[29]Prof. Doyne Farmer is a professor of mathematics at the Oxford Martin School. He is also Co-Director of Complexity Economics at The Institute for New Economic Thinking and an External Professor at the Santa Fe Institute. His current research is on complexity economics, focusing on systemic risk in financial markets and technological progress. During his career, he has made important contributions to complex systems (See Appendix 1), chaos theory, artificial life, theoretical biology, time series forecasting and Econophysics. He is also an entrepreneur and co-founded the Prediction Company, one of the first companies to do fully automated quantitative trading.

[30]Jacky Mallett has a PhD in computer science from MIT. She is a research scientist at Reykjavik Universit, who works on the design and analysis of high performance, distributed computing systems and simulations of economic systems with a focus on Basel regulatory framework for banks, and its macro-economic implications. She is also the creator of 'Threadneedle', an experimental tool for simulating fractional reserve banking systems.

The question about [modelling] individual households raises a very significant issue: are there distinctions at that level that could affect the macro-economy? There are and these include wealth distribution, property ownership, inheritance and pension providing methods - the German pay as you go approach for example, is very different from the financialisation approach which has big implications for the rest of the economy, because it influences the amount of lending available to the economy." (Also see: 'An examination of the effect on the Icelandic Banking System of Verðtryggð Lán (Indexed-Linked Loans)', Mallett, 2014).

This concludes our brief introduction to the key topics and design parameters of Agent Based Computational Economics.

ABCE models in use

In section section, we will go over some pioneering studies and have a look at the work of some researchers who are making significant head way in this field.

Kim-Markowitz Portfolio Insurers Model

One of the first modern multi-agent models was done by H.M. Markowitz and G.W. Kim to simulate the crash of 1987. Markowitz is known for being the Nobel prize winner for his founding work on modern portfolio theory. But apart from this, he was also one of the pioneers of ABCE. The motivation behind their simulation study was the stock market crash in 1987, when the U.S. stock market decreased by more than twenty percent within a few days. Following the crash, researchers focused their efforts on the looking at external and internal market characteristics to find the reasons of the crash. Kim and Markowitz decided to make use of ABM to explore the relationship between the share of agents pursuing portfolio insurance strategies and the volatility of the market (Samanidou *et al.*, 2007).

The Kim Markowitz agent based model involves two groups of individual investors: rebalancers and portfolio insurers (CPPI investors[31]). The rebalancers aim to keep a constant composition of their portfolio - they intend to keep one half of their wealth in stocks and the other half in cash. Portfolio insurers on the other hand, follow a strategy intended to guarantee a minimal level of wealth at a specified insurance expiration date. The insurers follow this strategy to ensure that their final losses will not exceed a certain fraction of their investment over this time period.

---

[31]Constant Proportion Portfolio Insurance (CPPI)- CPPI is a method of portfolio insurance in which the investor sets a floor on the value of his portfolio and then structures asset allocation around that decision. The two asset classes are classified as a risky asset (usually equities or mutual funds), and a riskless asset of either cash or Treasury bonds. The percentage allocated to each depends on how aggressive the investment strategy is.

Every Rebalancer agents started in the simulation with the same value of their portfolio ($100,000), with half of it in stocks and half in cash. As the agents were programmed to maintain this portfolio structure, if the stock prices were to increase, the rebalancers would have to sell shares as stocks weight in their portfolio will increase with the stock price. Thus, the rebalancers would sell shares until the shares again constituted 50% of their portfolio. If the price were to decrease, then the rebalancers would do the opposite and buy shares, as the value of their stocks would decrease as well with the fall in price. Thus, the rebalancers had a stabilizing influence on the market by selling when the prices rose and buying when the prices fell.

The rules for the insurers were built along the same lines as well and the goal of the insurers was to not lose more than a certain percentage (say 10%) of their initial wealth over a quarter. Thus, the insurer aims to ensure that at each cycle, 90%of the initial wealth is out of risk. To achieve this, he assumes that the current value of the stock assets will not fall in one day by more than a certain factor of 2 (Levy, 2009). Based on this assumption, he always keeps in stock twice the difference between the present wealth and 90% of the initial wealth. This determines the amount the insurer is bidding or offering at each stage.

If prices fall, the insurer will want to reduce the amount he wants to keep in stocks, and sells stocks. Doing this can destabilise the markets as the insurers flood the market with the stock and push the price down even further than before. On the other hand, if the prices of a stock were to rise, then the amount the insurer wants to keep in shares will increase leading him to buy more shares. This action can push the price of the stocks even more and create a price bubble in the process.

What the simulations of these two agents showed was that a relatively small fraction of insurers were enough to destabilise the market and create crashes and booms. Kim and Markowitz were thus able to show that it was the policy that was followed by the insurers that was responsible for the crash (Also see: 'Agent Based Computational Economics, Levy, 2009; Agent-based Models of Financial Markets, Samanidou et al., 2007).

The Santa Fe Artificial Stock Market Model

This model, also known as the Arthur, Holland, Lebaron, Palmer and Taylor Stock Market Model, was made in 2002 to study the changes in prices of assets based on the expectations of endogenous agents. At the time, standard neo-classical stock-market models assumed identical investors who used identical forecasts to come up with investment strategies. While the theory was elegant the researchers cited above found the assumptions to be unrealistic as it ruled out the possibility of bubbles, crashes, price volatility and extreme trading volumes, which are seen in real markets. They therefore created an ABM where the investors would have to create their own forecasts and learn which worked and which didn't work over a period of time.

The premise of their model was that heterogeneous agents form their expectations based on their anticipations of other agent's expectations. Agents would thus have to continuously form individual, hypothetical, expectation models, use them to create theories and then test them to see if they worked or not. Bad hypotheses would be dropped and new ones introduced. These changes would change the expectations of agents and thus effect prices. Prices were thus influenced by endogenous factors and would co-evolve with the market being co-created by the agents (LeBaron, 2002).

As the heterogeneity of the agents plays an important role in the model's evolution, emphasis was also made by the authors on inductive reasoning. Each inductively rational agent was expected to generate multiple expectation models which would be accepted or rejected based on their predictive ability. As prices and dividends changed, the patterns of agent's aggregate actions were expected to change as well since the agents would make new strategies. The authors defined this market 'psychology' as "*the collection of market hypotheses, or expectational models or mental beliefs, that are being acted upon at a given time*" (Arthur, 2013).

To simplify the study of agent strategies, the researches grouped expected outcomes into two administrative regimes - a regime in which rational fundamentalist strategies would dominate and a regime in which investors start developing strategies based on technical trading.

A fundamental rule would require market conditions of the type (example):

$$\frac{\text{Dividend}}{\text{Current Price}} > 0.04$$

A technical rule would have different conditions such as:

6-period moving average of past prices

If the technical trading regime was in action, then those agents following fundamentalist strategies, would be punished rather than rewarded by the market. By grouping strategies under two regimes (fundamentals vs. technical), the researchers were also able to analyse the influence of volatility properties of the market (clustering, excess volatility, etc.).

At first the modellers simulated a single stock in the market and gave the agent three choices:

1. Place a bid to buy a single share

2. Make an offer to sell a single shar

3. Do nothing.

These three options were then combined with behavioural actions of the agents which prescribed how they needed to act in different market conditions in a probabilistic manner. If the market created conditions that were not covered by these rules, the agents would do nothing. But if the market created conditions where more than one rule applied, then the agents would have to make a probabilistic choice according to which rule was better supported in these conditions. The choice was also influenced by the past actions of the agent - if a rule had worked before, then it was more likely to be used again.

As agents began to buy and sell the stock, the price would variate based on the demand functions. The environment was given instructions on how to increase the stock's price based on these demand requests. A constant absolute risk aversion (CARA) utility function was then used to transform the price predictions made by the changes in demand to initiate a buy/sell response in the agents. The trade-off in the agent's strategy would then be influenced by what regime in action - fundamental rule or technical rule regime.

What the modellers found was that over a period of time, the rules and strategies began to undergo mutations and changes. Weaker rules were replaced by copies of the rules that had the best success in the past. This represented the learning capacity of agents as they examined new strategies and adopted the best. The findings of this model showed that when there are small group of agents with a small number of rules (with small changes in dividends):

- There were no crashes or bubbles or any anomalies.

- The trading volume was low.

- Agents followed almost identical rules.

- The price of the stock would converge towards an equilibrium price.

However, when there were a large number of agents with a large number of rules:

- Agents became heterogeneous.

- Agents would collectively execute self-fulfilling strategies leading to large price changes.

- Trading volumes would fluctuate and the large trading volumes would create bubbles and crashes.

- That the rules and strategies were changing and were time dependent - if a strategy worked in the past, there was no guarantee it would work again if it was reintroduced at a later time period.

The modellers then began to run multiple simulations with a various number of stocks and agents with different sets of rules. They concluded that agents displayed a reflexive nature (refer Soros above) and that prices in markets were formed on the expectations of agents. These expectations were based on the anticipation of other expectations and this showed that expectations were not deductive but inductive in nature. Such markets composed of inductively rational agents exist under two regimes - a simplistic regime which corresponded to the rational expectation equilibrium and a more realistic, complex, self- organising one which showed the emergence of bubbles and crashes. Based on empirical comparisons between the models simulations and real world market phenomenon, they were thus able to show that financial markets lie within the complex regime. Since the publication of the results, there have been various variations of this model that have been widely used in economics.

The El Farol Problem and Minority Games

The El Farol problem stems from a bar known as the El Farol bar, in Santa Fe, New Mexico. It is a decision-making problem that was first devised by Brain Arthur based on a personal experience. Once a week on Thursday, the El Farol bar had a live band play music. But this posed a problem to the bar's regulars, as it meant going to a crowded bar, which was quite unenjoyable.

This also led a classic expectations problem - if a number of agents all thought that there would be too much of a crowd, and decided to avoid the bar on Thursday night, then very few people would go. If a large number of agents believed that the bar would not be too crowded and came under the basis of this expectation, then there would be too many people. The question that Arthur asked was how do people decide if they should go to the bar or not?

Arthur conceptualized the question in a simple way - he imagined that there were a 100 people who enjoyed the music being played on Thursday's at the bar. If agents in this population thought that the bar was going to be crowed (more than 60 people) then they would stay at home. If they thought it was not, they would.

If the attendance information was available and each agent could remember the attendance of the previous few weeks (say 3 weeks), then the agents could be modelled to work on a set of strategies based on these rules. The agents could make a choice of strategies based on imperfect information rules such as - attendance was twice last weeks', or an average of the last 3 weeks' attendance, etc. Based on these inputs, the agents could then decide how many people would attend this week and come up with a choice of whether to go or not.

The model was thus made in the following way:

- Attendance for the past X weeks = 44, 56, 73, 23, 56, 89, 44......

- Hypothesis of agents - predict next week's attendance to be:

    - The same as last week (44 in this case)
    - An average of last week
    - The same as 2 weeks ago
    - An average of the last 4 weeks and so on....

- An agent has a certain number of predictors to make his decision

- His decision is based on the more accurate predictor in this set, although this will change from week to week.

Using this modus operandi, when Arthur ran his ABM, he found that the average attendance was around 60 irrespective of which strategy the agents used, and on average 40% of the agents were forecasting over 60 and 60% below 60. Moreover, the population kept this 40/60 ratio over a period of time even though the membership of the agents in the groups kept changing. These findings, which can be seen in Figure 4-9, led to the conclusion that even in the face of imperfect information and multiple strategies, the agents had managed to optimally utilize the bar as a resource.

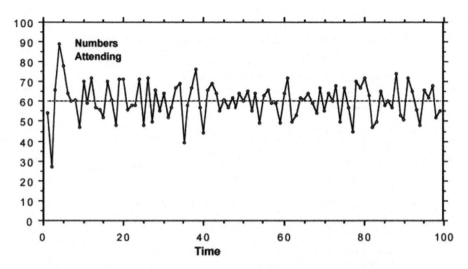

Figure 4-9. *Bar attendance in the first 100 weeks in the El Farol Problem*
Source: 'Inductive Reasoning and Bounded Rationality: The El Farol Problem', Arthur, 1994

The El Farol simulation is a cornerstone in complexity circles and has been cited in a range of papers and articles over the years. In 1997, it was generalized and put into game form by two physicists, Damien Challet and Y.-C. Zhang, to create something they called, 'The Minority Game'. The fact that the model has an economical origin and was developed by physicists, shows the interdisciplinary nature of the Minority Game.

In the original El Farol Bar problem, each individual of a population chooses whether to attend a bar on every Thursday evening. The bar has limited number of seats and can at most entertain x% of the population. If less than x% of the population go to the bar, the show in the bar is considered to be enjoyable. If not, all the people in the bar would have an unenjoyable show and staying at home is considered to be better choice than attending the bar. Arthur found the x% to be 60% and that agents used their past experience (which kept changing) to come up with a decision.

In the Minority Game, instead of using the history of past attendance, a string of binary bits which records the past few winning predictions or actions was employed as information. The predictions of the strategies were the winning choices in the next round, with no prediction about the actual size of attendance. Thus, binary information and predictions are implemented, and the winning choice is determined by the minority choice (instead of the parameter x in the Bar problem) at every round of the game. Hence the two choices are symmetric. Because of the minority rule, the population is restricted to be an odd integer in the original formulation (Yeung and Zhang, 2008).

The game goes as follows:

- A population of N agents competes in N repeated games, where N is an odd integer.

- At each round, each agent has to choose between one of the two actions, namely "0" and "1" which can also be interpreted as the 'sell' and 'buy' actions.

- The minority choices win the game at that round and all the winning agents are rewarded.

- As the game starts, every agent draws S strategies from a strategy pool which help them to make decisions throughout the game

- These strategies can be visualized in the form of tables where each strategy contains a "history column" (or "signal" column) and a "prediction column"

History	Prediction
000	1
001	0
010	0
011	1
101	0
111	1

- At every round of the game, agents make their decisions according to the strategy with the highest score at that particular moment. If there are more than one strategies with the highest score, one of these strategies is randomly employed.

The Minority Game (MG) is a simple model for the collective behaviour of agents in an idealized situation where they have to compete through adaptation for a finite resource. As the underlying strategy in this game is based on inductive reasoning and interaction between actors, there have been various updates and versions of this game. A lot of interest cumulated around the application of the game to interactions seen in financial markets as the MG refers to a simple adaptive multiagent model of financial markets.

Based on the possible interaction of investors in the financial market, some variants of the game show certain predictive abilities on real financial data. Though Minority Games are simple, they setup a framework of agent-based models from which sophisticated trading models can be built, and implementation on real trading may be possible. Although these sophisticated models are usually used for private trading and may not be open to public, Minority Games are increasingly becoming a useful tool to understand the dynamics in financial market.

Recent developments with ABCE models

The three ABCE models that have been discussed are 'classics' in the area of complexity economics. They are however just the tip of the iceberg. Following these seminal works, over the past few years, there has been an increasing amount of research being done in this area that is gradually attracting a more diverse set researchers from a number of fields to test, experiment and understand the economic changes that are occurring in complex financial systems. Table 4-2 offers a view of what the current areas of exploration are and the trajectories of insight that are in the process of being created. The issues being tackled are wide-ranging - from methods to identify systemic risk, to investigating the limits of fractional banking to governing policy making using ABCE insights.

Table 4-2. *A short selection of ABCE papers and research projects (in no particular order)*

Author(s)	Book/Research project/Articles
Gaffard & Napoletano	Agent-based models and economic policy, 2012
Kang Wei, Sun Cai-hong	Building the model of artificial stock market based on JASA, 2011
Jacky Mallett	Threadneedle: An Experimental Tool for the Simulation and Analysis of Fractional Reserve Banking Systems, 2015
Berman, Peters and Adamou	Far from Equilibrium: Wealth Reallocation in the United States
Hartmann, Guevara, Jara-Figueroa, Aristarán, Hidalgo	Linking Economic Complexity, Institutions and Income Inequality, 2015
Foxon, Köhler, Michie and Oughton	Towards a new complexity economics for sustainability, 2012
Alfarano, Fricke, Lux, Raddant	Network Approaches to Interbank Markets: Foreword, 2015
Arinaminpathy, Kapadia, May (Bank of England)	Size and complexity in model financial systems, 2012
Aymanns, Caccioli, Farmer, Tan	Taming the Basel leverage cycle, 2016
Baptista, Farmer, Hinterschweiger, Low, Tang, Uluc (Bank of England)	Macroprudential policy in an agent-based model of the UK housing market, 2016
Giovanni Dosi, Giorgio Fagiolo, Mauro Napoletano, Andrea Roventini, Tania Treibich	Fiscal and Monetary Policies in Complex Evolving Economies (2014)

The qualifications of the researchers named in the references show that a significant number of them are not economists by formal training. In fact, for most of them, their primary qualification is in the field of mathematics, physics and/or computer science. What this shows is that as complexity economics is advancing, the progress is being made a diverse set of researchers who come from a variety of scientific backgrounds. By applying the standards of scientific training to the subject of economics, these researchers are creating a new paradigm of economic thought.

This is the promise of complexity science. While economics has been in the hold with dogmatic ideologies and outdated DSGE models which have led to an inefficient understanding of economics in the past, the approaches that are being explored by complexity science offer a more inter-disciplinary approach as they base their approach from borrowing from the rich diversity of sciences. Figure 4-10 shows the contributions of various sciences and key people in their fields have allowed for this to occur.

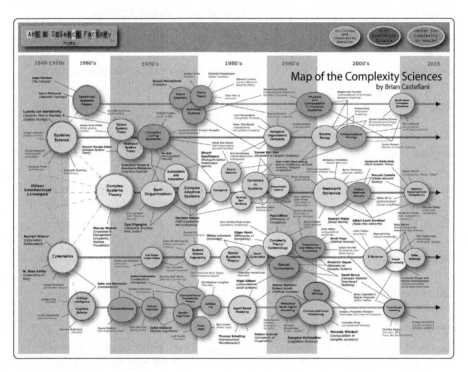

Figure 4-10. *Map of Complexity Sciences by Brian Castellani.*
Source: `http://www.art-sciencefactory.com/complexity%20map.pdf`

The previous three chapters have tried to showcase why the study of economics is in need of an upgrade. This is an essential point for as we have seen, it is based on these models and theories that policy makers make their decisions to govern our economy. This mode of thinking is what we can collectively describe as capitalism.

As we have seen, the mathematical study of economic theory was based on the models of theoretical physics. Using this *point de départ*, it has sought to establish itself as valid laws that can be used to explain, predict and govern economic behaviour and events. But instead of finding laws capable of being falsified through testing, economics has increasingly turned itself into an axiomatic discipline consisting of assumptions, and mathematical deductions, similar to Euclidean geometry.

But as we have seen, economics is anything but deductible and cannot be based on assumptions. As agents - be it consumers, banks, firms, or government agencies - perform different actions - be it buying, selling, trading, speculating, or investing - they are constantly innovating, forecasting and adapting to changes in the environment which is based on their interactions. This is turn creates an ever-evolving ecosystem which shows patterns that are temporary and never in a state of equilibrium. There will be a place for equilibrium in situations that are well-defined and static. But these will the exceptions to the rule of general entropy. The objective of economic theory therefore, should not be to formulate equations or to fit the agents to specific conditions. It should be to articulate insights from the changes taking place.

It is this shift in the way of looking at markets and policies that constitutes the re-definition of capitalism. A re-definition that is no longer a set of mathematical formulae but an ability to appreciate the changes occurring in an economy and to be comfortable when witnessing the creation of novel phenomenon. Economic theory in this case, would no longer be the formulation of theorems that can be applied generally, but the understanding of the forces of change that create patterns whilst acknowledging the consilience of science.

This shift is already occurring at a gradual pace and the role that complexity economics will play in this re-definition will be a central one. To highlight this point and to end this section on agent based modelling and agent based computational economics, I invite you to consider the following statements made by Jean-Claude Trichet, the president of the ECB, at an opening address at the ECB Central Banking Conference Frankfurt on 18 November 2010:

> *"When the crisis came, the serious limitations of existing economic and financial models immediately became apparent. Arbitrage broke down ... markets froze ... market participants were gripped by panic. Macro models failed to predict the crisis and ... [to explain] what was happening ...."*

> *"[In] the face of crisis, we felt abandoned by conventional tools. ... The key lesson ... is the danger of relying on a single tool, methodology or paradigm. The atomistic, optimising agents underlying existing models do not capture behaviour during a crisis period. Agent-based modelling ... allows for more complex interactions between agents. ... it dispenses with the optimisation assumption and allows for more complex interactions between agents. Such approaches are worthy of our attention we need to better integrate the crucial role played by the financial system into our macroscopic models."*

"I would very much welcome inspiration from other disciplines: physics, engineering, psychology, biology. Bringing experts from these fields together with economists and central bankers is potentially very ... valuable."

"A large number of aspects of the observed behaviour of financial markets is hard to reconcile with the efficient market hypothesis... But a determinedly empirical approach - which places a premium on inductive reasoning based on the data, rather than deductive reasoning grounded in abstract premises or assumptions - lies at the heart of these methods ... simulations will play a helpful role."

Putting it all together

"Economic theorists, like French chefs in regard to food, have developed stylized models whose ingredients are limited by some unwritten rules. Just as traditional French cooking does not use seaweed or raw fish, so neoclassical models do not make assumptions derived from psychology, anthropology, or sociology. I disagree with any rules that limit the nature of the ingredients in economic models", George Akerlof, An Economic Theorist's Book of Tales (1984)

It would seem that we have drifted from the topic of the Blockchain whilst endeavouring to grasp the basics of complexity economics. But actually, we were just setting the stage to the final point to be made in this book. The Blockchain is not a panacea. It is a tool and like any good tool, it is versatile and works better when it is part of a tool kit. Complexity economics is another tool that will need to be used to re- define capitalism, and to the precocious reader, the connection between the Blockchain and Complexity Economics must be evident already.

The Blockchain is many things - it is a shared ledger, a medium to issue money, a means of exchanging value in a decentralized way and a consensus mechanism that offers the possibility of achieving global financial inclusion. But what it is more than anything else is the digital embodiment of trust. A Blockchain is in essence, a codified truth-verification machine that has the ability to commoditize trust through a protocol on a decentralized network. The key word in that phrase is decentralized because markets are decentralized. An organization may be centralized with various hierarchies. But markets are decentralized and as we have seen in chapter 2 (refer the part on FinTech), and are getting increasingly so.

In decentralized markets with multiple agents, trust becomes a key factor as it has a cost associated to it. Owing to uncertainty, opportunism and limited information (bounded rationality), the lack of trust between agents limits the number of interactions and bonds that are formed in a network. This hesitation to form links based on lack of trust has been extensively studied in the field of transaction cost theory (also called new institutional economics) which was developed by Ronal Coase in 1937.

Transactional cost theory (TCT) is the branch of economics that deals with the costs of transactions and the institutions that are developed to govern them. It studies the cost of economic links and the ways in which agents organize themselves to deal with economic interactions. Coase realized that economic transactions are costly. In his seminal paper, 'The Nature of the Firm', Coase noted that while economies involve plenty of planning, a large part of this planning is not coordinated by the price system and takes place within the boundaries of the firm (Hidalgo, 2015). As firms have hierarchies, most interactions within a firm are political. This creates boundaries of power that influence transactions and interactions causing them to deviate from the clear-cut dynamics of market price mechanisms. This is seen in the form of contracts, inspections, disputes, negotiations, etc. These boundaries in turn rack up costs and the greater the cost associated with a transaction, the more friction associated with making the transaction.

But trust is an essential element in any network as it allows for the transfer of information, knowledge and knowhow. If there is a greater amount of trust in the network, links are formed more easily and transactions occur with a greater amount of fluidity thus increasing the network size. By reducing the cost of links and by providing porous boundaries that allow for greater exchanges of knowledge and knowhow high trust networks are able to adapt faster to changes in markets and technologies. This phenomenon has been discussed in great detail in the book '*Why Information Grows*' (2015), by César Hidalgo.

Using complexity models, Hidalgo develops TCT to show that in economic networks, the cheaper the link, the larger the network. Using Coase's work, he shows that trust is an essential element of social capital as it is the glue that is needed to maintain and form large networks which allows for the spread of knowledge and knowhow that are accumulated in these networks. Trust contributes to network size by reducing the cost of links.The links are therefore created more easily as the creation of new is not considered risky. Low trust networks on the other hand produce networks with less porous boundaries that limit their long-term adaptability. He concludes his book by stating that the growth of economies is based on the growth of information and those countries are that are better at making information grow are more prosperous. In sum, the greater the level of trust and the more complex the economy, the more prosperous it is.

As Blockchains are a mechanism that allow for the crypto-enforced execution of the agreed contracts through consensus and transparency, they offer a control mechanism that reduces the need of trust to a large degree (Davidson *et al.*, 2016). As the adoption of the Blockchain continues to rise, the potential that it offers to governments is not just in terms of increased transparency, but also as a way of increasing the trust in the economy. In a world beset by technological unemployment and inequality, the Blockchain offers governments a number of ways to rethink their functions and the institutions that make up their economy.

Moreover, they do not have to be passive witnesses to the transactional data that is flowing on these decentralized networks. By using the techniques of complexity economics, they can use this data to see how the significant elements of an economy are transacting within an economy and how their interactions are changing the ecosystem. Using this information, they can create simulations to see what reactions monetary and fiscal policies (i.e.: changes in the environment) will create and how the ripples of these environmental changes will affect smaller agents in the economy. Monetary and Fiscal policy will no longer have to be reactive in nature, but could be made perspective instead.

Of course, moving to such kind of a framework will not be an overnight process as it forces us to rethink market fundamentals and economic policy making from the ground up. But as we have seen in this chapter, this has already begun and there is a whole new field of scientific enquiry that is reformulating the way we think of the fundamentals of economic theory. The way this process can be enacted and the challenges it will create at the micro, meso and macro levels is a subject that will need to be addressed in detail in the years to come. It is beyond the scope of this book to provide such an encyclopaedic overview of all the issues that are related to this endeavour. As mentioned from the very beginning, the objective of this book has been to change the direction of the conversation that we have today with regards to capitalism. As we have seen in these four chapters, this conversation has already begun in some academic and policy circles. My objective has been to give these conversations a collective voice.

Conclusion

'I think the next century will be the century of complexity,' Stephen Hawking, January 2000

Economics and Ecology share a common etymological origin. They both derive themselves from the Greek word for household - 'Oikos'. 'Logy', derives itself from another Greek word, 'Logos' (from legein), which means to gather, count, or account. 'Nomos', on the other hand, derives itself from the Greek 'Nemein', which means to distribute or to manage. Thus, ecology at the root means the logic of the dwelling place, or the story of where we live. Economy is *eco* plus *nomos*, which means household management (oikonomia Greek).

It is surprising to realise that although these two words share the same origin, they have become completely separated over the course of time. This is not just from the perspective of how they are studied, but also in the way the they have been pitted against each other. As increased financialization, excessive consumerism and growing debt and inequality continue their upward curve, the problems of the climate change and the detriment of the ecology continue to rise as well. I have often pondered if our ecology would be in its present state had we begun the study of economics using the perspectives of the ecologist rather than the tools of the physicist (Walrasian approach).

The atavistic disciplinary chauvinism of economics also seems to ignore its Greek cousin, Democracy. Capitalism and Democracy are often seen to go hand in hand and that they are natural allies. Most capitalistic states are democracies are to a large extent capitalism and democracy are accepted in spite of all their shortcomings as there is no sound ideological alternative to replace them. But as the world gets increasingly complex with advances in technologies, such as the Blockchain, we need to take heed as to what the implications of these technologies are and how do we study the implications of these changes.

This feat cannot be achieved by solely focusing on the applications of technology. It requires that we also have a healthy understanding of economic history. As we have seen in this book, solution proposals to problems that face us today were made decades ago by economists who had a heathy appreciation of the limitations of economic theory and the definition of capitalism in the context of a liberal democracy. Adam Smith, David Ricardo, Karl Marx and all the way to Schumpeter tried to stay faithful to this approach. Yanis Varoufakis best summed up this dilemma at a speech he made at the New School in April 2016,

> *"Capitalism without the state is like Christianity without hell. It does not work ... The phenomenon of considering capitalism and democracy as natural bedfellows is a very recent phenomenon ...[But] unless we approach it [the study of capitalism] via ...a simultaneous study of economic history ... or the history of capitalism, the evolution of the conflict between social relations of production and technologies on one hand and the evolution of our ideas about the world that is being shaped by this historical evolutionary process [on the other hand]...unless we study the past, the present and the potentialities for the future through this prism, we have no chance of using a mathematized approach in order to secure any handle on the reality in which we find ourselves."*

Where capitalism is headed today is a step before it became communism - a bourgeois liberal democracy. It is our collective responsibility and vicarious liability to use technologies that are changing the definition of capitalism to create a more sensible, just and scientifically accurate version of it.

In a world of information where the answer to any question can be found, real value is derived from asking the right question. The Blockchain is a tool for transferring value and recording this information. Its time we started asking the right questions of what can we do with this tool.

Some Final Notes

The remaining sections provide further perspective to topics covered earlier in the chapter:

- Section "Technology and Invention: A Combinatorial Process"

- *Sidebar 4-1: "A rationale for rational expectations"*

- *Section* "The Mathematical Wizardry of Equilibrium Economic Models"

A brief history of computing

Sources: The Computing Universe: A Journey through a Revolution, Tony Hey and Gyuri Pápay, (2014); A History of Modern Computing (2nd Edition), Paul E. Ceruzzi, (1998).

The story of computing and computers goes back to the early 19th century when Charles Babbage, a mathematician who was trained at Cambridge, first had the idea to create a machine to calculate logarithmic tables. In 1819, shortly after leaving Cambridge, Babbage was working with the astronomer John Herschel and carrying out arithmetical calculations by hand. As the process was tedious and fraught with errors, Babbage hit upon the idea of making a machine that could perform routine calculations by following precise arithmetical procedures. This led Babbage to begin working on something later he called the Difference Engine - a machine that would calculate astronomical and navigational tables and record the results on metal plates (so that they could be used directly for printing). The project was later funded by the U.K. government and was developed by Babbage and Joseph Clement for well over a decade. It was cancelled in 1842, owing to differences between Babbage and Clement, and had cost the government over £ 17,000 - a princely sum in those days.

Babbage's Difference Engine was the first special-purpose calculator and the basis for his next idea, the Analytical Engine. Although he never secured the funds to develop the second project, the ideas in its design (documented in over 6000 pages of notes, hundreds of engineering drawings and operational charts) are the basis for today modern computers. These included a separated section for calculation (what we today refer to as a Central Processing Unit (CPU)), another section for storing data (or a memory) and a method of providing instructions to the machine (a programming language). Ada Lovelace, who corresponded with Babbage, also played an influential role in developing programming languages by emphasising that the Analytical Machine could manipulate symbols as well as numerical calculations. However, the real advances in programming languages came from George Boole who devised a language for describing and manipulating complex logical statements for determining the statements were true or false. Although Boole, who created Boolean Algebra, did not himself work in computing, his ideas of logical operations (AND, OR and NOT) were later used to improve the performance of later computers and in the creation of logic gates.

In the mid-1930s, Vannevar Bush an American engineer, inventor and head of the U.S. Office of Scientific Research and Development (OSRD) during the Second World War, had created an analog computer known as the Differential Analyser. This computer was used to solve ordinary differential equations which would help calculate the trajectories of shells. It consisted of multiple rotating disks and cylinders driven by electric motors linked together with metal rods that were manually set up (sometime taking up to two days) to solve any differential equation problem. Vannevar had recruited Claude Shannon (known today as the father of information theory), a young graduate who specialised symbolic logic.

Although the Differential Analyzer was a mechanical machine with moving parts, Shannon identified it as a complicated control circuit with relays. Shannon thus began creating the first generation of circuit designs and in the process, was able to transform information into a quantity that could be subjected to manipulation by a machine. Using Boolean algebra, logic gates and binary arithmetic (bits and bytes), Shannon was able to represent all types of information by numbers and in the process created the foundations for today's modern information theory. It is for this reason that he is referred to as the father of information technology.

As World War Two began in 1939, these advances in information technology had been adopted by various militaries to communicate sensitive information. Cryptography became a suitable way of camouflaging information and led to the creation of the Enigma machine. Luckily for the Allies, hope lay in the form of some work that had been done a few years earlier by another Cambridge mathematician, Alan Turing. Along with his mentor, Max Newman, Turing set about designing and building automated machines (Turing Machines) that could decrypt secret German military communications (as documented in the popular movie, 'The Imitation Game'). However, owing to an obsession for secrecy during the war years and for several years after that, the achievements made by Turing and the team at Bletchley Park in computer development was kept hidden from view.

Instead of Turing Machines, over the same time period, a machine called the ENIAC (Electronic Numerical Integrator And Computer) was being developed by John Mauchly and Presper Eckert across the Atlantic. Mauchly, a physicist, who was interested in meteorology tried to develop a weather prediction model. But he soon realized that this would not be possible without some kind of automatic calculating machine. As a result, he developed the concept of an electronic computer using vacuum tubes. It was during the time of developing ENIAC that he met the renowned polymath, John von Neumann, and with his help went on to design a stored-program computer, the EDVAC (Electronic Discrete Variable Automatic Computer), the first binary computer (ENIAC was decimal). See Figure 4-11.

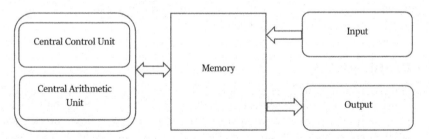

Figure 4-11. *General design of the Electronic Discrete Variable Automatic Computer. Reference Source: 'The von Neumann Architecture', The Computing Universe, 2014*

From an abstract architecture perspective, von Neumann's design is logically equivalent to Turing's Universal Turing Machine. In fact, von Neumann had read Turing's theoretical papers prior to designing his machine. Ultimately it was this simple design that was built upon by successive generations of computer scientists and led to the design of computers with multiple processors and the creation of parallel computing.

The period following the war saw great strides being made in the hardware of computers. From the early days of vacuum tubes and mercury delay-lines (a thin mercury filled tube that stored electronic pulses that represented binary data points - a pulse represented 1; no pulse represented 0), computing hardware saw the inculcation of the Magnetic Core Memory and the creation of the Hard Disk. But an equal if not more diverse progress was also made in the space of software development. From punch cards and simple logic gates, software's ability to access, compute and handle data underwent leaps and bounds of progress. Languages such as COBOL and FORTRAN (FORmula TRANslation), helped in the creation of early operating systems and over the years we have seen the rise software design and programming languages and such as BASIC, LISP, SIMULA, C, C++, UML, Unix, Linux, etc... Ultimately it was these advents that led to the construction of distributed communication networks, the internet and the worldwide web.

The history of computing cannot be summarised in a short blurb and readers are encouraged to have a look at the excellent books cited in the references cited at the beginning of this note for a more detailed understanding. The point of providing this short note is to highlight how technology grows. With every advance in different sectors of the natural sciences, technology borrows from its ancestors and novelty comes from combining cumulative small changes in different technological families. Computers may have started from mathematics, but it is only the evolution in physics, chemistry and, more recently, biology that have allowed us to develop today's technologies. Without this method of scientific enquiry and consilience of science, we would not have today's technologies and definitely would not be talking about the Blockchain. As affective computing gains strides, the role that human emotions will play in the evolution of technology will gain an increasingly important role.

Neuroplasticity

The brain contains approximately 80 billion neurons which wire the brain and each cell is connected chemically and electrically with 10,000 others. At give or take 100 Trillion synapses (connections between neurons), the brain is the most complex network loaded with more dynamic interconnections than there are stars and planets in the milky way.

It is the number of interconnections in the brain that is key to learning. When it comes to thinking and learning, the brain teaches itself things by making new synaptic connections in the brain, based on the exposure to new ideas and existing memories. These connections keep changing as the brain is exposed to new ideas and in response to experience, thought and mental activity. In other words, mental activity (thinking) is not a product of the brain but what shapes it. This is called Neuroplasticity and it is what enables us to learn new ideas. It is how any skill or talent is developed.

Neuroplasticity changes through connectivity (synapses). As new information is received, new synapses form, existing ones are broken off and new ideas emerge. Based on which neurons are stimulated, certain connections become stronger and more efficient. In case an action is repeated, the existing connection is strengthened and the ability to perform the repeated task gets faster. Repetition does not help us learn something better, it makes us faster at doing it.

As more connections are formed, we learn more and are able to connect ideas to existing knowledge. This enables us to form cognitive maps to interpret the world, or a certain belief system based on the information we have at hand. When exposed to new ideas, the brain either attempts to safeguard its ideas by verifying the new information to what it already knows or updates its belief system based on the new information it receives.

This upgrading activity is also governed by social attributes and our position in a community. Psychologists refer to this as the self-image, in which we the adaptation of our belief system is based on how others interpret us. Intelligence is thus a collaborative effort and the primary reason we communicate - to transfer knowledge by reading, listening, watching, and more recently, from brain to brain. It is no wonder that the advance of science is based on consilience, for we are hardwired to be social transmitters of information, experience and knowledge.

Types of Macroeconomic Models

Source: 'The Role of Expectations in the FRB/US Macroeconomic Model', Flint Brayton, Eileen Mauskopf, David Reifschneider, Peter Tinsley, and John Williams (1997).

FRB/US is one of many macroeconomic models that have been developed over the past 30 years. Macroeconomic models are systems of equations that summarize the interactions among such economic variables as gross domestic product (GDP), inflation, and interest rates. These models can be grouped into several types:

Traditional structural models typically follow the Keynesian paradigm featuring sluggish adjustment of prices. These models usually assume that expectations are adaptive but subsume them in the general dynamic structure of specific equations in such a way that the contribution of expectations alone is not identified. The MPS and Multi-Country (MCM) models formerly used at the Federal Reserve Board are examples.

Rational expectations structural models explicitly incorporate expectations that are consistent with the model's structure. Examples include variants of the FRB/US and FRB/MCM models currently used at the Federal Reserve Board, Taylor's multi-country model, and the IMF's Multimod.

Equilibrium business-cycle models assume that labor and goods markets are always in equilibrium and that expectations are rational. All equations are closely based on assumptions that households maximize their own welfare and firms maximize profits. Examples are models developed by Kydland and Prescott and by Christiano and Eichenbaum.

Vector autoregression (VAR) models employ a small number of estimated equations to summarize the dynamic behaviour of the entire macroeconomy, with few restrictions from economic theory beyond the choice of variables to include in the model. Sims is the original proponent of this type of model.

Cellular automata (CA): "Automaton" (plural: "automata") is a technical term used in computer science and mathematics for a hypothetical machine that changes its internal state based on inputs and its previous state. (Sayama, 2015). A cellular automaton consists of a regular grid of cells, each in one of a finite number of states, such as on and off. Each cell is surrounded by a set of cells called it *neighbourhood*. At a particular time (t), the cell and its neighbourhood cells are in a specific state according to some fixed mathematical rules. These rules also determine how the cells will update over time and how they interact with their neighbourhood. As time progresses from (t) to (t + t), a new generation of cells is created by interacting with each other and updating simultaneous.

221

The original idea of CA was invented by John von Neumann and Stanisław Ulam. They invented this modelling framework, which was the very first to model complex systems, in order to describe self-reproductive and evolvable behaviour of living systems. CA is used in computability theory, mathematics, physics, complexity science, theoretical biology and microstructure modelling.

Neural networks: More specifically Artificial Neural Networks (ANN), are processing devices (they can be algorithms or actual hardware) that are loosely modelled after the neuronal structure of the brains' cerebral cortex but on smaller scales (Figure 4-12).

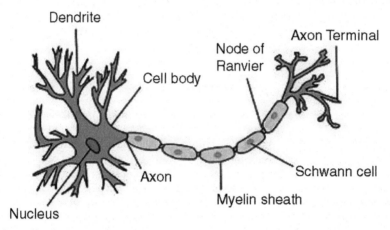

Figure 4-12. *Sketch of a biological neural network*
Source: Boundless Psychology, 2013

The origin of modern ANNs is based on a mathematical model of the neuron called the *perceptron* introduced by Frank Rosenblatt in 1957 (Papay and Hey, 2015). As it can be seen in Figure 4-13, the model closely resembles the structure of the neuron with inputs resembling dendrites.

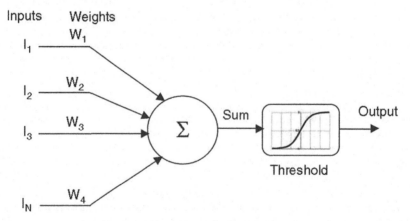

Figure 4-13. *Representation of an artificial neuron with inputs, connection weights, and the output subject to a threshold function*
Source: 'The computing universe,' Gyuri Papay and Tony Hey, 2015

In the original model made by Warren McCulloch and Walter Pitts, the inputs were either 0 or 1. Each dendrite/input also had a weight of +1 and - 1. The input was thus multiplied by its weight and the sum of the inputs was then fed to a model. The perceptron thus takes several binary inputs, I_1, I_2, ...I_N, and produces a single binary output. If the output is greater than a set threshold level, then the model delivers a certain output. This can be mathematically interpreted as:

$$\text{Output} = 0 \text{ if } \sum_j W_j I_j \le \text{Threshold}$$

$$\text{Output} = 1 \text{ if } \sum_j W_j I_j \le \text{Threshold}$$

Based on this initial schema, the perceptron model developed to allow both the inputs to the neurons and the weights to take on any value. ANN is nothing more than interconnected layers of perceptron's as seen in Figure 4-14.

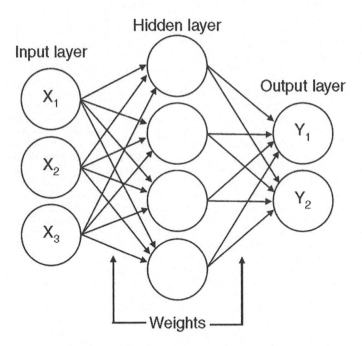

Figure 4-14. *Perceptron's interconnected layers*
Image source: The computing universe, Gyuri Papay and Tony Hey, 2015

By varying the weights and the threshold, we can get different models of decision-making. The outputs from a hidden layer can also be fed into another hidden layer of perceptron's. The first layer of column of perceptron's makes very simple decisions, by weighing the input evidence. These outputs are then fed to a second layer of perceptron's which make a decision by weighing up the results from the first layer of decision-making. By following this method, a perceptron in the second layer can make a decision at a more complex and more abstract level than perceptron's in the first layer. If a third layer is involved, then the decisions can be made by those perceptron's will be even more complex. In this way, a many- layer network of perceptron's can engage in sophisticated decision making. The greater the number of layers of perceptron's, the higher the decision-making ability (Figure 4-14).

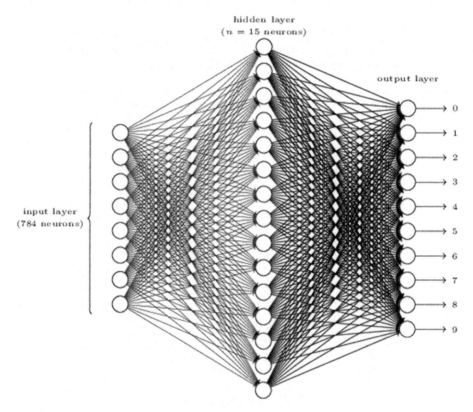

Figure 4-15. *Milti-layer network of perceptrons*
Source: http://neuralnetworksanddeeplearning.com/

Genetic algorithms: A Genetic algorithm (GA) is a heuristic search method used in artificial intelligence and computing inspired by Darwin's theory about evolution. It is used for finding optimized solutions to search problems based on the theories of natural selection and evolutionary biology, i.e.: selection, mutation, inheritance and recombination.

GAs are based on the classic view of a chromosome as a string of genes. R.A. Fisher used this view to found mathematical genetics, providing mathematical formula specifying the rate at which particular genes would spread through a population (Fisher, 1958). They key elements of Fisher's formulation are (Holland, 2012):

1. A specified set of alternatives for each gene, thereby specifying the permissible strings of genes that can evolve.

2. A generation-by-generation view of evolution where, at each stage, a population of individuals produces a set of offspring that constitutes the next generation.

3. A fitness function that assigns to each string of alternatives, the number of offspring the individual carrying that chromosome will contribute to the next generation.

4. A set of genetic operators, particularly *mutation* in Fisher's formulation, that modify the offspring of an individual so that the next generation differs from the current generation.

When solving constrained and unconstrained optimization problems, a classical algorithm generates a single data point at each iteration. The sequence of data points then approaches an optimal solution. A GA on the other hand uses a process similar to natural selection - it repeatedly modifies a population of individual solutions and at each step, randomly selects data points from the current population of points and uses them as 'parents' to produce the children for the next generation. Over successive generations, the population 'evolves' toward an optimal solution (Holland, 2012).

Although randomised, GAs are by no means random, instead they exploit historical information to direct the search into the region of better performance within the search space. GAs simulate the survival of the fittest among individuals over consecutive generations for solving a problem. Each generation consists of a population of character strings that are analogous to the chromosome that we see in our DNA. Each individual represents a point in a search space and a possible solution. The individuals in the population are then made to go through a process of evolution.

GAs are used for searching through large and complex data sets as they are capable of finding reasonable solutions to complex issues by solving unconstrained and constrained optimization issues. They are used to solve problems that are not well suited for standard optimization algorithms, including problems in which the objective function is discontinuous, nondifferentiable, stochastic, or highly nonlinear. GAs also work particularly well on mixed (continuous and discrete) combinatorial problems, as they are less susceptible to getting 'stuck' at local optima than classical gradient search methods. However, they tend to be computationally expensive.

APPENDIX A

■ ■ ■

Bibliography and References

Bibliography
Chapter 1

Basel Committee on Banking Supervision. (2016). *Basel III Monitoring Report.* Basel: Bank for International Settlements.

BIS. (2008). *Credit Risk Transfer - Developments from 2005 to 2007.* Basel Committee on Banking Supervision.

BIS. (2011). *Basel III definition of capital - Frequently asked questions.* Basel: Bank for International Settlements. Retrieved from http://www.bis.org/publ/bcbs198.pdf

BIS. (2015). *OTC derivatives statistics at end-June 2015.* Bank for International Settlements - Monetary and Economic Department.

Braudel, F. (1982). *Civilization and Capitalism, 15th-18th Century: The wheels of commerce.* University of California Press.

Conesa, P. (2015, March 16). *Le coût exorbitant des guerres de la France.* Retrieved from Libération: http://www.liberation.fr/planete/2015/03/16/le-cout-exorbitant-des-guerres-de-la-france_1221844

Das, S. (2016). *The Age of Stagnation.* Prometheus Books.

Dorling, D. (2014). *All That Is Solid: How the Great Housing Disaster Defines Our Times, and What We Can Do About It.* London: Allen Lane - Penguin Random House.

Doug Campbell, F. O. (2010). *Overextended, Underinvested: The Debt Overhang Problem.* Cleveland: Federal Reserve Bank of Cleveland.

Economic Costs. (2015, April). Retrieved from Costs of War: http://watson.brown.edu/costsofwar/costs/economic

European Banking Authority. (2013). *Basel III monitoring exercise-Results based on data as of 31 December 2012.* Brussels: European Banking Authority.

Federal Reserve Bank of Chicago. (2011). *Modern Money Mechanics - A Workbook on Bank Reserves and Deposit Expansion.* Chicago: Federal Reserve Bank of Chicago.

Graeber, D. (2012). *Debt: The First 5,000 Years.* Brooklyn, NY: Melville House.

Hill, M. C. (2012). *Cannibal Capitalism: How Big Business and The Feds Are Ruining America.* Wiley.

Hobley, A. C. (Director). (1999). *The Mayfair Set: Destroy The Technostructure* [Motion Picture].

IMF. (2014). *Global Financial Stability Report - Risk Taking, Liquidity, and Shadow Banking.* International Monetary Fund.

IMF. (2014). *Risk Taking, Liquidity, and Shadow Banking - Curbing Excess while Promoting Growth.* International Monetary Fund.

King, M. (2006). Trusting in Money: From Kirkcaldy to the MPC. *The Adam Smith Lecture.* London: Bank of England.

Kocherlakota, C. A. (2014). Internal debt crises and sovereign defaults. *Journal of Monetary Economics, Elsevier, vol. 68(S)*, S68-S80.

Koo, R. (2014). *The Escape from Balance Sheet Recession and the QE Trap: A Hazardous Road for the World Economy.* Wiley. Retrieved from `http://www.eunews.it/docs/koo.pdf`

Luigi Buttiglione, P. R. (2014). *Deleveraging? What Deleveraging?* Geneva: International Center for Monetary and Banking Studies (ICMB).

Michael McLeay, A. R. (2014). *Money creation in the modern economy.* London: Bank of England's Monetary Analysis Directorate.

Michael McLeay, A. R. (2014). *Money in the modern economy: an introduction.* London: Bank of England's Monetary Analysis Directorate.

Milesi-Ferretti, L. A. (2013). *External Liabilities and Crises.* International Monetary Fund.

Òscar Jordà, M. S. (2015). *Mortgaging the Future?* Federal Reserve Bank of San Francisco.

Richard Dobbs, S. L. (2015). *Debt and (not much) deleveraging.* McKinsey Global Institute.

Stuart Berry, R. H. (2007). *Interpreting movements in broad money.* London: Bank of England's Monetary Analysis Division.

Sufi, A. M. (2014). *House of Debt.* Chicago: University of Chicago Press.

Taylor, Ò. J. (2016). The great mortgaging: housing finance, crises and business cycles. *Economic Policy, CEPR;CES;MSH, vol. 31(85)*, 107-152.

Tett, G. (2013, September 19). *West's debt explosion is real story behind Fed QE dance.* Retrieved from Financial Times: `https://next.ft.com/content/76b6f332-2133-11e3-8aff-00144feab7de`

Thompson, M. (2015, January 01). *The True Cost of the Afghanistan War May Surprise You.* Retrieved from Time: `http://time.com/3651697/afghanistan-war-cost/`

Turner, A. (2010). Market Efficiency and Rationality: Why Financial Markets are Different. *Lionel Robbins Memorial Lectures* (p. 24). London: London School of Economics.

Turner, A. (2015). *Between Debt and the Devil - Money, Credit, and Fixing Global Finance.* Princeton and Oxford: Princeton University Press.

Who owns the Federal Reserve? (2016, April 22). Retrieved from Board of Governors of the Federal Reserve System: `https:// www.federalreserve.gov/faqs/about_14986.htm`

Wildau, G. (2016, February 29). *China injects cash to boost growth and counter capital outflows.* Retrieved from Financial Times: `https://next.ft.com/content/aa8a84fa-deda-11e5-b7fd-0dfe89910bd6`

Wisensale, S. K. (2001). *Family leave policy: The Political Economy of Work and Family in America.* Routledge.

Zoltan Pozsar, T. A. (2012). *Shadow Banking.* New York: Federal Reserve Bank of New York.

Chapter 2

FDIC. (2000, June 05). *History of the 80s.* Retrieved from Federal Deposit Insurance Corporation: https://www.fdic.gov/bank/historical/history/vol1.html

Fintech Innovation . (2016, April 21). *Accenture study says Chinese deals dominate Q1 2016 global Fintech investment.* Retrieved from Fintech Innovation: http://www.enterpriseinnovation.net/article/accenture-study-says-chinese-deals-dominate-q1-2016-global-fintech-investment-1052478246

Accenture. (2016). *Fintech's Golden Age: Competition to Collaboration.* Accenture.

Bernanke, B. S. (2016, May 13). *Ending "too big to fail": What's the right approach?* Retrieved from Brookings: https://www.brookings.edu/2016/05/13/ending-too-big-to-fail-whats-the-right-approach/

Bipartisan Policy Center. (2014). *The Big Bank Theory: Breaking Down the Breakup Arguments.* Bipartisan Policy Center.

Birch, D. (2014). *Identity is the New Money.* London: London Publishing Partnership.

Buterin, V. (2016). A Next Generation Smart Contract & Decentralized Application Platform. *DC Blockchain Summit.* Washington DC: Chamber of Digital Commerce.

Cawrey, D. (2014, July 01). *BitPay Seeks to Decentralize Digital Identification with BitAuth.* Retrieved from Coindesk: http://www.coindesk.com/bitpay-decentralize-digital-identification-bitauth/

Clare Hutchison, J. D. (2015, May 21). *Barclays hit with record fine as six banks settle forex scandal.* Retrieved from Independent: http://www.independent.co.uk/news/business/news/barclays-hit-with-record-fine-as-six-banks-settle-forex-scandal-10265665.html

Claude Lopez, E. S. (2016). *Dodd-Frank: Washington,* We Have a Problem. Milken Institute.

Cooper, C. (2015, July 07). *6 economists who predicted the global financial crisis.* Retrieved from INTHEBLACK - Leadership, Strategy, Business: https://intheblack.com/articles/2015/07/07/6-economists-who-predicted-the-global-financial-crisis-and-why-we-should-listen-to-them-from-now-on

Crosman, P. (2016, June 30). *How Banks Could Regain Ground from Fintechs.* Retrieved from American Banker: http://www.americanbanker.com/news/bank-technology/how-banks-could-regain-ground-from-fintechs-1081785-1.html?utm_medium=email&ET=americanbanker:e7057963:4976612a:&utm_source=newsletter&utm_campaign=daily%20briefing-jul%201%202016&st=email&eid=1c00fac598f

Davison, M. (2015). Financialisation. In N. F. Patrick O'Sullivan, *The Philosophy, Politics and Economics of Finance in the 21st Century: From Hubris to Disgrace* (pp. 47-73). Routledge.

Earthport. (2015, August 18). *Compliant gateway for real-time payments.* Retrieved from earthport: http://www.earthport.com/news/earthport-launches-the-first-fully-compliant-gateway-for-real-time-payments-2/

Edwards, J. (2015, January 26). *That $1 Billion TransferWise Deal Is Exactly Why Mark Carney Worries About "An Uber-Type Situation In Financial Services."* Retrieved from Business Insider UK: http://uk.businessinsider.com/transferwise-mark-carney-and-uber-type-situation-in-banking-2015-1?r=US&IR=T

Forelle, C. (2012, May 11). *What Beached the London Whale? Credit Indices.* Retrieved from The Wall Street Journal: http://blogs.wsj.com/marketbeat/2012/05/11/more-on-what-beached-the-london-whale-credit-indices/

Freeman, J. (2011 , March 19). *Mega-Banks and the Next Financial Crisis.* Retrieved from The Wall Street Journal: http://www.wsj.com/articles/SB10001424052748703899704576204594093772576

Hellwig, A. A. (2013). *The Bankers' New Clothes: What's Wrong with Banking and What to Do about It.* Princeton University Press.

Heltman, J. (2016 , April 7). *Yellen Fires Back on Kashkari's TBTF Assessment.* Retrieved from American Banker: http://www.americanbanker.com/news/law-regulation/yellen-fires-back-on-kashkaris-tbtf-assessment-1080338-1.html

Huckstep, R. (2016, April 03). Dynamis – If Insurance, Then Blockchain. *InsurTech Weekly, Issue Number 46.*

James Schneider, Alexander Blostein, Brian Lee, Steven Kent, Ingrid Groer, Eric Beardsley. (2016). *Profiles in Innovation: Blockchain - Putting Theory into Practice.* Goldman Sachs.

James-Lubin, K. (2015, January 22). *Blockchain scalability.* Retrieved from O'Reilly: https://www.oreilly.com/ideas/blockchain-scalability

Johns, A. (2015, May 8). *[WMD 2015] Wealthfront, Andrew Johns "3 Mandatory Skills Every NextGen CMO Should Know."* Retrieved from https://www.youtube.com/watch?v=p-xxkmvPYck

Kendall, J. (2016, June 22). *Gates Foundation Presents: Crucial Areas of Fintech Innovation for the Bottom of the Pyramid.* Retrieved from Microsoft Research: https://www.youtube.com/watch?v=7R_uFb-X1s8

KPMG. (2016). *The Pulse of Fintech, Q1 2016 - Global Analysis of Fintech Venture Funding.* KPMG.

Kupiec, A. M. (2014, August 11). *Why the "Living Will" Process Sets Banks Up for Failure.* Retrieved from American Banker: http://www.americanbanker.com/bankthink/why-the-living-will-process-sets-banks-up-for-failure-1069285-1.html

Kyle Croman, C. D. (2016). *On Scaling Decentralized Blockchains.*

Maxfield, J. (2013, April 24). *How Banks Became Too Big to Fail.* Retrieved from The Motley Fool: http://www.fool.com/investing/general/2013/04/24/how-banks-became-too-big-to-fail.aspx

Monvoisin, S. A. (2015). The bank as economic agent and democracy. In N. F. Patrick O'Sullivan, *The Philosophy, Politics and Economics of Finance in the 21st Century: From Hubris to Disgrace* (pp. 283-299). Routledge.

Myers-Lipton, S. (2009). *Rebuild America: Solving the Economic Crisis Through Civic Works.* Routledge.

Nadler, D. (2016, May 3). *The Transformation of Finance: Technology's Impact on Wall Street.* Retrieved from Milken Institute Global Conference: http://www.milkeninstitute.org/events/conferences/global-conference/2016/panel-detail/6251

Noonan, L. (2015, May 28). *Banks face pushback over surging compliance and regulatory costs.* Retrieved from Financial Times: https://www.ft.com/content/e1323e18-0478-11e5-95ad-00144feabdc0

Nordrum, A. (2016, February 02). *The Next Financial Crisis Could Be Predicted By A Smarter Economic Model, Experts Say.* Retrieved from International Business Times:

http://www.ibtimes.com/next-financial-crisis-could-be-predicted-smarter-economic-model-experts-say-2313345

Palley, T. I. (2007). *Financialization: What It Is and Why It Matters*. Washington, D.C.: The Levy Economics Institute and Economics for Democratic and Open Societies.

Palmer, D. (2016, Feburary 24). *7 Cool Decentralized Apps Being Built on Ethereum*. Retrieved from CoinDesk: http://www.coindesk.com/7-cool-decentralized-apps-built-ethereum/

Partnoy, F. (2009). *Infectious Greed: How Deceit and Risk Corrupted the Financial Markets*. New York City: PublicAffairs.

Plotkin, A. J. (2016). Small groups and long memories promote cooperation. *Nature*, Scientific Reports 6, Article number: 26889, doi:10.1038/srep26889.

PwC. (2016). *Blurred Lines: How FinTech is shaping Financial Services*. Pricewaterhouse Cooper.

PYMNTS. (2015, August 18). *How Earthport And Ripple Are Teaming Up To Make Cross-Border Payments Instant*. Retrieved from PYMNTS: http://www.pymnts.com/in-depth/2015/how-earthport-and-ripple-are-teaming-up-to-make-cross-border-payments-instant/

Raval, S. (2016). *Decentralized Applications - Harnessing Bitcoin's Blockchain Technology*. California: O'Reilly Media, Inc. .

Rizzo, P. (2015, October 8). *Ripple Releases Interledger to Connect Banks and Blockchains*. Retrieved from Coindesk: http://www.coindesk.com/ripple-interledger-connect-bank-blockchain/

Santos, V. M. (2012). *The Rise of the Originate-to-Distribute Model and the Role of Banks in Financial Intermediation*. New York City: Federal Reserve Bank of New York Economic Policy Review.

Scannell, K. (2016, February 23). *London Whale complains of unfair blame for $6.2bn JPMorgan losses*. Retrieved from Financial Times: https://next.ft.com/content/3f558d16-da51-11e5-a72f-1e7744c66818

Smaghi, L. B. (2010). The paradigm shift after the financial crisis. *Nomura Seminar*. Kyoto: European Central Bank.

Stefano Battiston, J. D. (2016, February 19). Complexity theory and financial regulation - Economic policy needs interdisciplinary network analysis and behavioral modeling. *Science*, pp. 818-819.

Sweney, M. (2008, November 28). *FT rolls out "St. Bernard" poster push*. Retrieved from The Guardian: https://www.theguardian.com/media/2008/nov/28/financial-times-advertising

The Swift Institute. (2015, August). *The Impact and Potential of Blockchain on the Securities Transaction Lifecycle*. Retrieved from The Swift Institute: https://www.swiftinstitute.org/wp-content/uploads/2015/07/Call-for-Proposal-Blockchain-in-Securities-Transactions_v7.pdf

Treanor, J. (2016, April 26). *UK's big four banks face £19bn in compensation, fines and legal costs*. Retrieved from The Guardian: https://www.theguardian.com/business/2016/apr/26/uk-big-four-banks-face-19bn-compensation-fines-legal-costs-libor-ppi

Ülgen, F. (2015). The 2007-08 financial crisis as a (de)regulatory deadlock. In N. F. Patrick O'Sullivan, *The Philosophy, Politics and Economics of Finance in the 21st Century: From Hubris to Disgrace* (pp. 370-391). Routledge.

WEF. (2015). *Deep Shift Technology Tipping Points and Societal Impact*. Davos: World Economic Forum - Global Agenda Council on the Future of Software & Society.

WEF. (2015). *The Future of Financial Services- How disruptive innovations are reshaping the way financial services are structured, provisioned and consumed*. Davos: World Economic Forum.

World Bank. (2015). *Remittance Prices WorldWide - Issue Number 15*. World Bank.

Yurcan, B. (2016, May 23). *What Banks and Fintech Need to Ponder Before They Partner*. Retrieved from American Banker: http://www.americanbanker.com/news/bank-technology/what-anks-and-fintech-need-to-ponder-before-they-partner-1081139-1.html?utm_medium=email&ET=americanbanker:e6785466:4976612a:&utm_source=newslett er&utm_campaign=daily%20briefing-may%2024%20 2016&st=email&

Zimmerman, E. (2016, April 6). *The Evolution of Fintech*. Retrieved from The New York Times: http://www.nytimes.com/2016/04/07/business/dealbook/the-evolution-of-fintech.html?_r=0

Zorn, D. M. (2000). *Here a Chief, There a Chief: The Rise of the CFO in the American Firm*. Princeton University.

Chapter 3

Accenture. (2016). *Trade finance: The landscape is changing — are you?*

Andolfatto, D. (2016, May 01). *MacroMania*. Retrieved from Monetary policy implications of blockchain technology: http://andolfatto.blogspot.fr/2016/05/monetary-policy-implications-of.html

Autor, D. (2014). *Polanyi's Paradox and the Shape of Employment Growth*. Cambridge, MA: National Bureau of Economic Research (NBER).

Autor, D. A. (2010). *Skills, Tasks and Technologies: Implications for Employment and Earnings*. National Bureau of Economic Research.

BIEN. (2016, September). *About Basic Income*. Retrieved from Basic Income Earth Network: http://basicincome.org/

Bregman, R. (2016). *Utopia for Realists: The Case for a Universal Basic Income, Open Borders, and a 15- hour Workweek* . Amazon Digital Services LLC.

Brown, R. G. (2016, April 05). *Introducing R3 Corda™: A distributed ledger designed for financial services*. Retrieved from Thoughts on the future of finance: https://gendal.me/2016/04/05/introducing-r3-corda-a-distributed-ledger-designed-for-financial-services/

Busby, M. J. (2016, August 6). *Chatbots will not replace 5 million jobs, as the data suggests*. Retrieved from Venture Beat: http://venturebeat.com/2016/08/03/chatbots-will-not-replace-5-million-jobs-as-the-data-suggests/

CB Insights. (2016, September 7). *51 Corporate Chatbots Across Industries Including Travel, Media, Retail, And Insurance*. Retrieved from CB Insights: https://www.cbinsights.com/blog/corporate-chatbots-innovation/

David Autor, F. L. (2003). The Skill Content of Recent Technological Change: An Empirical Exploration. *Quarterly Journal of Economics, 118*(4).

Desai, M. (2015). *August of Money: Quest for Cashless Society*. Charlotte, NC: Let's Talk Payments.

ECB. (2015). *Virtual currency schemes – a further analysis*. European Central Bank.

Euro Banking Association. (2016). *Applying cryptotechnologies to Trade Finance*. EBA Working Group on Electronic Alternative Payments.

Finkle, J. (2016, September 01). *Exclusive: SWIFT discloses more cyber thefts, pressures banks on security*. Retrieved from Reuters: http://www.reuters.com/article/us-cyber-heist-swift-idUSKCN11600C

Florence Jaumotte, S. L. (2008). *Rising Income Inequality: Technology, or Trade and Financial*. Journal of Economic Literature (IMF Working Paper).

Giles, C. (2015, September 23). *In cash we trust — abolish it and you invite tyranny*. Retrieved from Financial Times: https://www.ft.com/content/ffdb3034-610e-11e5-9846-de406ccb37f2#axzz49l23qjEv

Giles, C. (2015, September 18). *Scrap cash altogether, says Bank of England's chief economist*. Retrieved from Financial Times: https://www.ft.com/content/7967908e-5ded-11e5-9846-de406ccb37f2

Graeber, D. (2012). *Debt: The First 5,000 Years*. New York: Melville House.

Guy Michaels, A. N. (2010). *Has ICT polarized skill demand? Evidence from eleven countries over 25 years*. Cambridge, MA: National Bureau of Economic Research (NBER) Working Paper Series.

Guy Michaels, A. N. (2010). *Has ICT Polarized Skill Demand? Evidence from Eleven Countries over 25 years*. Cambridge, MA: National Bureau of Economic Research (NBER).

Harris, P. (2016, May 25). *How Blockchain Technology Is Reinventing Global Trade Efficiency*. Retrieved from Bitcoin Magazine: https://bitcoinmagazine.com/articles/how-blockchain-technology-is-reinventing-global-trade-efficiency-1464206286

Hayek, F. A. (1999). *Denationalisation of Money: The Argument Refined (An Analysis of the Theory and Practice of Concurrent Currencies Series)*. Coronet Books Inc; 3rd edition (June 1990).

Helbing, K.-K. K. (2016). *A "Social Bitcoin" could sustain a democratic digital world*. arXiv:1604.08168.

Hodgson, B. D. (2014). *Increasing Competition in Payment Services*. London: Positive Money.

Hodgson, B. D. (2016). *Digital Cash - Why Central Banks Should Start Issuing Electronic Money*. London: Positive Money.

Jacobs, M. M. (2016). *Rethinking Capitalism*. Wiley.

Jesús Fernández-Villaverde, D. S. (2016). *Can currency competition work?* NBER Working Paper No. 22157.

Katua, N. T. (2014). The Role of SMEs in Employment Creation and Economic Growth in Selected Countries. *International Journal of Education and Research Vol. 2 No. 12*.

Koren, J. R. (2015, November 30). *After subprime collapse, nonbank lenders again dominate riskier mortgages*. Retrieved from Los Angeles Times: http://www.latimes.com/business/la-fi-nonbank-lenders-20151130-story.html

Kumhof, J. B. (2012). *The Chicago Plan Revisited*. IMF.

Kumhof, J. B. (2016). *The macroeconomics of central bank issued digital currencies - Staff Working Paper No. 605*. London: Bank of England.

Lawrence F. Katz, D. H. (1999). Changes in the Wage Structure and Earnings Inequality. In O. C. Card, *Handbook of Labor Economics* (pp. 1463-1555). North Holland.

Maarten Goos, A. M. (2014). Explaining Job Polarization: Routine-Biased Technological Change and Offshoring. *American Economic Review, Vol 104, No.8*, 2509-26.

Marinoni, A. C. (2015). Regulation and Fraud - A critical assessment of accounting information, corporate governance and complex systems of business control. In N. F. Patrick O'Sullivan, *The Philosophy, Politics and Economics of Finance in the 21st Century: From Hubris to Disgrace (Economics as Social Theory)* (pp. 332 - 343). Routledge.

Meiklejohn, G. D. (2015). *Centrally Banked Cryptocurrencies.* arXiv.org - arXiv:1505.06895v2.

Meiklejohn, G. D. (2016). *Centrally Banked Cryptocurrencies.* arXiv:1505.06895.

Michael Jacobs, M. M. (2016). *Rethinking Capitalism: Economics and Policy for Sustainable and Inclusive Growth.* Wiley.

Murphy, E. V. (2015). *Who Regulates Whom and How? An Overview of U.S. Financial Regulatory Policy for Banking and Securities Markets.* Congressional Research Service .

Nesisyan, L. R. (2016). Understanding Money and Macroeconomic Policy. In M. J. Mazzucato, *Rethinking Capitalism: Economics and Policy for Sustainable and Inclusive Growth* (pp. 47-65). Wiley.

Nir Jaimovich, H. E. (2012). *The Trend is the Cycle: Job Polarization and Jobless Recoveries.* Cambridge, MA: National Bureau of Economic Research (NBER).

OECD. (2010). *SMEs, Entrepreneurship and Innovation.* OECD.

Osborne, C. B. (2013). *The Future of Employment: How susceptible are jobs to computerisation?* Oxford: Oxford Martin School.

Paine, T. (1795). *Agrarian Justice.* Retrieved from Geolibertarian: `http://geolib.com/essays/paine.tom/agjst.html`

Paul Beaudry, D. A. (2013). *The Great Reversal in the Demand for Skill and Cognitive Tasks.* Cambridge, MA: National Bureau of Economic Research (NBER) Working Paper 18901.

Raj Chetty, N. H. (2015). *The Effects of Exposure to Better Neighborhoods on Children: New Evidence from the Moving to Opportunity Experiment.* Harvard University and NBER.

Ravikanth, N. (2015, August 18). *The Tim Ferriss Podcast Episode #97: The Evolutionary Angel, Naval Ravikant.* Retrieved from The Tim Ferris Podcast: `http://fourhourworkweek.com/2015/08/18/the-evolutionary-angel-naval-ravikant/`

Rogoff, K. (1998). Blessing or curse? Foreign and underground demand for Euro notes. *Economic Policy, 26*, 263-303.

Rogoff, K. (2014). *Costs and benefits to phasing out paper currency.* NBER Working Paper No. 20126.

Rogoff, K. (2016). *The Curse of Cash.* Princeton University Press.

Sandeep Davé, A. S. (2016). *Releasing the flow of digital money - hitting the tipping point of adoption.* Citigroup.

Schwartz, M. F. (1987). Has Government Any Role in Money? In A. J. Schwartz, *Money in Historical Perspective* (pp. 289 - 314). University of Chicago Press.

Shafik, M. (2016). *A new heart for a changing payments system.* Bank of England.

Sims, E. (2012). *Intermediate Macroeconomics: New Keynesian Model.* University of Notre Dame.

Slater-Robins, M. (2016, February 5). *Microsoft is carrying out a massive social experiment in China —and almost no one outside the country knows about it.* Retrieved from Business Insider: `http://uk.businessinsider.com/microsoft-xiaoice-turing-test-in-china-2016-2`

Slayton, J. (2014, November 14). *The Angelist Way.* Retrieved from Slideshare: `http://www.slideshare.net/abstartups/dia01-02-keynotejoshuaslaytonangellistdoing-the-wrong-things-the-right-way`

Stavins, S. S. (2015). *The 2013 Survey of Consumer Payment Choice: Summary Results*. Federal Reserve Bank of Boston.

Stefan Avdjiev, A. K. (2013). *CoCos: a primer*. Bank of International Settlements (BIS) Quarterly Review.

Stern, A. (2016). *Raising the Floor: How a Universal Basic Income Can Renew Our Economy and Rebuild the American Dream*. Public Affairs.

Sufi, A. M. (2014). *House of Debt: How They (and You) Caused the Great Recession, and How We Can Prevent It from Happening Again*. Chicago: University of Chicago Press.

Swanson, T. (2015). *Consensus-as-a-service: a brief report on the emergence of permissioned, distributed ledger systems*. R3CEV.

Tett, G. (2016, February 4). *The benefits of scrapping cash*. Retrieved from Financial Times: https://www.ft.com/content/8ef4dcb0-ca6f-11e5-be0b-b7ece4e953a0

Thibaut Desjonqueres, S. M. (1999). Another Nail in the Coffin? Or Can the Trade Based Explanation of Changing Skill Structures Be Resurrected? *The Scandinavian Journal of Economics*, 533-554.

Tracxn. (2016, July). *Top Funded Startups, Business Models, And The Most Active Investors In Chatbots*. Retrieved from Tracxn: http://blog.tracxn.com/2016/06/16/top-funded-startups-business-models-and-the-most-active-investors-in-chatbots/

Turner, A. (2015). *Between Debt and the Devil: Money, Credit, and Fixing Global Finance* . Princeton University Press.

Uematsu, P. O. (2013). *The State of the Poor: Where are the Poor and where are they Poorest?* World Bank.

UK Government Chief Scientific Adviser. (2016). *Distributed Ledger Technology: beyond block chain*. UK Government Office for Science.

Varoufakis, Y. (2016, August 13). *Universal Basic Income Will Be Required Because of Automation*. Retrieved from https://www.youtube.com/watch?v=SMAkhDZqx9k

WTO. (2016). *Trade finance and SMEs - Bridging the gaps in provision*. World Trade Organization.

Yermack, M. R. (2016). *Digital Currencies, Decentralized Ledgers, and the Future of Central Banking*. NBER Working Paper No. 22238.

Zarlenga, S. A. (2002). *The Lost Science of Money: The Mythology of Money, The Story of Power*. American Monetary Institute.

Zucman, G. (2015). *The Hidden Wealth of Nations: The Scourge of Tax Havens*. University of Chicago Press.

Chapter 4

Argia M. Sbordone, A. T. (2010). *Policy Analysis Using DSGE Models: An Introduction*. Federal Reserve Bank of New York.

Arthur, W. B. (1994). Inductive Reasoning and Bounded Rationality: The El Farol Problem. *The American Economic Review, Vol. 84, No. 2, Papers and Proceedings of the Hundred and Sixth Annual Meeting of the American Economic Association*, 406-411.

Arthur, W. B. (2013). *Complexity Economics: A Different Framework for Economic Thought*. Santa Fe Institute.

Arthur, W. B. (2014). *Complexity and the Economy*. Oxford: Oxford University Press.

Beinhocker, E. (2007). *The Origin of Wealth*. Harvard Business School Press.

Béla Nagy, J. D. (2013). *Statistical Basis for Predicting Technological Progress*. PLoS ONE 8(2): e52669. doi: 10.1371/journal.pone.0052669: PLoS.

Bernanke, B. S. (2015, April 28). *The Taylor Rule: A benchmark for monetary policy?* Retrieved from Brookings Institute: https://www.brookings.edu/blog/ben-bernanke/2015/04/28/the-taylor-rule-a-benchmark-for-monetary-policy/

Bruna Bruno, M. F. (2016). Complexity Modelling in Economics: the State of the Art. *Economic Thought, Vol 5, Number 2*, 29-43.

Buchanan, M. (2014 , January 21). *Wall Street Shorts Economists*. Retrieved from Bloomberg View: https://www.bloomberg.com/view/articles/2014-01-21/wall-street-shorts-economists

Buiter, W. (2009, March 06). *The unfortunate uselessness of most "state of the art" academic monetary economics*. Retrieved from Centre for Economic Policy Research: http://voxeu.org/article/macroeconomics-crisis-irrelevance

Carriero, D. G. (1992). Coordination languages and their significance. *Communications of the ACM , Volume 35 Issue 2*, 97-107.

Cohen, P. D. (2003). *Information Inequality and Network Externalities: A Comparative Study of the Diffusion of Television and the Internet*. Princeton University.

D. Hartmann, M. G.-F. (2015). *Linking Economic Complexity, Institutions and Income Inequality*. MIT Media Lab.

E. Samanidou, E. Z. (2007). Agent-based models of financial markets. *Reports on Progress in Physics, Volume 70, Number 3*, 409-450.

Farmer, R. A. (2015, December 10). *Old economic models couldn't predict the recession. Time for new ones*. Retrieved from The Christian Science Monitor: http://www.csmonitor.com/Science/Complexity/2015/1210/Old-economic-models-couldn-t-predict-the-recession.-Time-for-new-ones

Flint Brayton, E. M. (April 1997). The Role of Expectations in the FRB/US Macroeconomic Model. *Federal Reserve Bulletin Volume 83, Number 4*, 227 - 245.

FRB/US Model. (2014, November 21). Retrieved from Board of Governors of the Federal Reserve: https://www.federalreserve.gov/econresdata/frbus/us-models-about.htm

Garcia, N. E. (2011). *DSGE Macroeconomic Models: A Critique*. Institut des Sciences Mathématiques et Économiques Appliquées, Economie Appliquée, N°1.

Goldstein, J. (1999). Emergence as a Construct: History and Issues. *Emergence, Volume 1, Issue 1*, 49-72.

Grigg, M. A. (2013). A Framework for an Agent-Based Model to Manage Water Resources Conflicts. *Water Resour Manage, Volume 27, Issue 11, doi:10.1007/s11269-013-0394-0, 4039-4052* .

Hidalgo, C. A. (2015). *Why Information Grows: The Evolution of Order, from Atoms to Economies*. Basic Books.

Holland, J. H. (2012). *Genetic algorithms*. Retrieved from Scholarpedia: http://www.scholarpedia.org/article/Genetic_algorithms

Hyejin Youn, D. S. (2015). *Invention as a combinatorial process: evidence from US patents. Royal Society* Publishing.

Jaromír Beneš, A. B. (2009). *K.I.T.T.: Kiwi Inflation Targeting Technology*. Reserve Bank of New Zealand.

Kauffman, S. (1996). *At Home in the Universe: The Search for the Laws of Self-Organization and Complexity Reprint Edition*. Oxford University Press.

King, M. G. (1997). The New Neoclassical Synthesis and the Role of Monetary Policy. In B. S. Rotemberg, *NBER Macroeconomics Annual 1997, Volume 12* (pp. 231 - 296). MIT Press.

Kirman, A. P. (1992). Whom or What Does the Representative Individual Represent? *Journal of Economic Perspectives - Volume 6, Number 2,* 117-136.

Kirman, D. H. (2014). *Rethinking Economics Using Complexity Theory.* Iowa State University.

Kirman, M. G. (2013). *Reconstructing economics: Agent based models and complexity.* Baltzer Science Publishers, DOI :10.7564/12-COEC2.

Lawrence J. Christiano, M. E. (1998). *Monetary Policy Shocks: What Have We Learned and to What End?*

LeBaron, B. (2002). *Building the Santa Fe Artificial Stock Market.* Brandeis University.

Levy, D. L. (2000). Applications and Limitations of Complexity Theory in Organization Theory and Strategy. In G. J. Jack Rabin, *Handbook of Strategic Management* (pp. 67-87). Routledge.

Levy, M. (2012). Agent Based Computational Economics. In R. A. Meyers, *Computational Complexity: Theory, Techniques, and Applications* (pp. 18-39). Springer.

Manson, S. M. (2001). Simplifying complexity: a review of complexity theory. *Geoforum, Volume 32, Issue 3,* 405-414.

Morçöl, G. (2008). A Complexity Theory for Policy Analysis. In K. A. Richardson and Linda F. Dennard (Editors), *Complexity and Policy Analysis* (pp. 23 - 35). ISCE Publishing.

Pfleiderer, P. (2014). *Chameleons: The Misuse of Theoretical Models in in Finance and Economics.* Stanford Graduate School of Business.

Pierce, A. (2008, November 05). *The Queen asks why no one saw the credit crunch coming.* Retrieved from The Telegraph: http://www.telegraph.co.uk/news/uknews/theroyalfamily/3386353/The-Queen-asks-why-no-one-saw-the-credit-crunch-coming.html

Rand, U. W. (2015). *An Introduction to Agent-Based Modeling: Modeling Natural, Social, and Engineered Complex Systems with NetLogo.* MIT Press.

Romer, P. M. (May 2015). Mathiness in the Theory of Economic Growth. *American Economic Review: Papers & Proceedings, Vol. 105 No. 5,* 89-93.

Rosen, A. W. (2014). *Spaces of the possible: universal Darwinism and the wall between technological and biological innovation.* The Royal Society Publishing.

Salzano, M. (2008). Economic Policy Hints from Heterogeneous Agent-Based Simulation. In K. A. Richardson and Linda F. Dennard (Editors), *Complexity and Policy Analysis* (pp. 167-194). ISCE Publishing.

Sayama, H. (2015). *Introduction to the Modeling and Analysis of Complex Systems.* Open SUNY Textbooks.

Sinclair Davidson, P. D. (2016). *Economics of Blockchain.* Social Science Research Network.

Sinha, S. (2012, August 11). Econophysics An Emerging Discipline. *Economic & Political Weekly, Vol. 47, Issue No. 32,* pp. 44 - 65.

Sitabhra Sinha, A. C. (2010). *Econophysics: An Introduction.* Wiley-VCH.

Slanicay, M. (2014). Some Notes on Historical, Theoretical, and Empirical Background of DSGE Models. *Review of economic perspectives - Národohospodářský Obzor, Vol. 14, Issue 2, doi: 10.2478/revecp-2014-0008 ,* pp. 145-164,.

Stefania Bandini, S. M. (2012). Chapter 7: Agent Based Modeling and Simulation. In R. A. Meyers, *Computational Complexity: Theory, Techniques, and Applications* (pp. 105 - 121). Springer.

Stuart Russell, P. N. (2009). *Artificial Intelligence: A Modern Approach.* Pearson.

Syll, L. P. (2016, April 7). Deductivism - the fundamental flaw of mainstream economics. *Real-world economics review, Issue no. 74,* pp. 20 - 41.

Tovar, C. E. (2008). *DSGE models and central banks.* Bank for International Settlements.

Walker, D. A. (1996). *Walras's market models. .* Cambridge: Cambridge University. doi: `http://dx.doi.org/10.1017/CB09780511664502`.

Wilson, E. (1998). *Consilience: The Unity of Knowledge.* Vintage.

Wouters, S. S. (2012). Learning in a Medium-Scale DSGE Model with Expectations Based on Small Forecasting Models. *American Economic Journal: Macroeconomics Vol.4, No.2, April 2012,* pp. 65-101.

Zhang, C. H.-C. (2008). *Minority Games.*

References

Chapter 2

Table A-1 provides a list of books that offer technical and/or business application insights. All books have been referred to in the writing of this book

Table A-1. *Technical and business reference list*

Name	Author	Area of focus
Mastering Bitcoin: Unlocking Digital Cryptocurrencies	*Andreas Antonopoulos*	Technical book that gives readers an understanding of how bitcoin works. Useful for computer scientists and advanced readers.
Understanding Bitcoin: Cryptography, Engineering and Economics	*Pedro Franco*	Technical book that gives readers an understanding of how bitcoin works and the economic implications of the technology. Useful for students, business persons, and advanced readers.
Value Web	*Chris Skinner*	General book that offers a holistic view of how FinTech and Blockchain firms are using technology to create a new internet of value. Useful for business persons and students.

(continued)

Table A-1. (*continued*)

Name	Author	Area of focus
Blockchain: Blueprint for a New Economy	*Melanie Swan*	General book that looks at usability and potential impact of Blockchain from a number of sectors. The author also discusses theoretical, philosophical, and societal impacts of cryptocurrencies and Blockchain. Useful for general readers, novices included.
The Business Blockchain: Promise, Practice, and Application of the Next Internet Technology	*William Mougayar*	Ideal for business persons with a proclivity for business models. The author amalgamates his experience in the business consulting field with his knowledge of Blockchain. The book is useful for business persons and business students, especially those looking to implement this technology in the near future.
Blockchain Revolution: How the Technology Behind Bitcoin Is Changing Money, Business, and the World	*Don Tapscott and Alex Tapscott*	This recent success is filled with insights and interviews with a number of key persons in the financial field. The book is a general read but offers readers a look into how key persons are thinking about the Blockchain, while offering a dictionary of whom to follow in this space.

Chapter 3

Following is a list of literature resources for learning about Universal Basic Income (UBI):

- *"The Simple Analytics of Helicopter Money: Why It Works – Always" (2014), Willem H. Buiter*

- *The Precariat: The New Dangerous Class (2011), Guy Standing*

- *Inventing the Future: Postcapitalism and a World Without Work (2015), Nick Srnicek and Alex Williams*

- *Raising the Floor: How a Universal Basic Income Can Renew Our Economy and Rebuild the American Dream* (2016), Andy Stern

Index

© Kariappa Bheemaiah 2017
K. Bheemaiah, *The Blockchain Alternative*, DOI 10.1007/978-1-4842-2674-2

■ F

■ U

■ V

■ W, X, Y, Z

Get the eBook for only $4.99!

Why limit yourself?

Now you can take the weightless companion with you wherever you go and access your content on your PC, phone, tablet, or reader.

Since you've purchased this print book, we are happy to offer you the eBook for just $4.99.

Convenient and fully searchable, the PDF version enables you to easily find and copy code—or perform examples by quickly toggling between instructions and applications.

To learn more, go to http://www.apress.com/us/shop/companion or contact support@apress.com.

CPSIA information can be obtained
at www.ICGtesting.com
Printed in the USA
LVOW01s1824030417
529447LV00007B/28/P

9 781484 226735